Pushing the
Pause Button
on Your Life

Janet,
Hope you find
the contents helpful.
Bruce

Pushing the Pause Button on Your Life

ISBN: 978-1-60920-004-6
Printed in the United States of America

Front cover design, photography, and interior graphics by Mark Penner-Howell
Interior design by Isaac Publishing, Inc.

Library of Congress Cataloging-in-Publication Data

IPI
Isaac Publishing, Inc.
P.O. 342
Three Rivers, MI 49093
www.isaacpublishing.com

Please direct your inquiries to admin@isaacpublishing.com

Pushing the Pause Button on Your Life

by

Bruce E. Howell

Isaac Publishing, Inc.
PO Box 342
Three Rivers, MI 49093
1.888.273.4JOY
www.isaacpublishing.com

ACKNOWLEDGEMENTS

Words cannot fully express the high level of gratitude and regard that I have for Jeanine as she supported and encouraged me while I traveled this graphic road for the first time.

Thanks also to Marilyn Hendricks for the superb work she did in editing the manuscript. And to Mark for his willingness to share his artistic gift to make this project a family affair.

CONTENTS

INTRODUCTION

IT HAPPENED ON A DARK NOVEMBER MORNING. I still cannot quite believe I did it. I swung into McDonald's for a cup of coffee before hurrying on to a meeting. As I approached the drive-through I noticed that there were about five cars ahead of me, just sitting there. I sat there thinking it might be quicker just to park and go on into the restaurant. But then the cars in front of me began to move slowly. I stayed with it. I ordered my usual: "Senior's decaf, please." I proceeded to the first window, paid the 54 cent fee and drove right past the next window without getting my coffee. As I started to leave the parking lot, it dawned on me—they have my 54 cents, but I do not have anything to show for it. I was able to back all the way to the proper window and get my coffee. The young lady was holding my cup, waiting for me, with a big smile on her face. I could tell that she had seen this before. She said, "Here you are, have a nice day!" Flushed as I was, I managed to blurt out, "Life gets a little hectic at times; sorry about that!" I knew at that very instant that I had contracted that dreaded social disease, "scurry." That is right, not scurvy, but scurry. My body was in drive, but my mind was in neutral.

That incident is, in part, the reason for this book. I do not think I am terribly different from the average twenty-first century American. We are all running to and fro and need to pause now and then, to catch our breath—especially our spiritual breath.

"Time Out!" "Take Five!" "Recess!" "Break Time!" These are terms that we are all familiar with. They scream for the need to rest, relax, and recuperate. And it really does not matter whether one is using them in reference to work, athletics, or education. It is a fact of life that we all need periods away from the routine of our lives—time to regroup and refresh our bodies, psyches, and emotions.

But what about our spirits? Do we value our relationship with God enough to "push the pause button on our life" in order to be refreshed inwardly? Jesus set the example for us by taking time away from His ministry to be alone with His Father. Dare we do any less?

Let us face it, we are living in a hectic world. The pace at which most of us operate is frightening. We have deadlines to meet, places to go, meetings to attend, schedules to keep, and multi tasks to accomplish. More than ever before we need to budget our time so that we can achieve our desired goals. Each of us must decide what our priorities must be. We do not want to be enslaved by the "tyranny of time," yet often we find ourselves kneeling at its feet. In our quest for a balanced life, we need to hear again the voice of the past saying, "Beware of the barrenness of an over-busy life."

Sad to say, many believers do not schedule into their lives a time to get alone with the One who can refresh their souls and thereby bring a sense of normalcy to an otherwise frantic agenda. According to a recent poll by George Barna, *quiet times* do not rank very high on the believer's list of priorities. That which should be most important is often pushed aside and neglected, resulting in lives that are spiritually anemic.

Quiet times are like spiritual baths. They cleanse, they refresh, they restore. When we take time to listen to God and meditate upon His Word, something miraculous transpires. We are inwardly equipped to face the day's challenges, to make a difference, to share His love.

This is the age of distractions. We are bombarded by them. Noise pollution takes its toll on every one of us. Radio and television sets blare all day long. Telephones ring constantly. The intruding sounds of cars and jet planes drown out the beauty of solitude. Oh, how our souls long for a place of retreat—a pause that will refresh. That is partly what this book is all about—an attempt to assist the weary traveler to stop by the roadway of life, rest under the shade of one of God's great oaks, and drink deeply from His many wells.

We need to quench our spiritual thirst, often. There is little hope of living victoriously unless we spend time regularly with our Father. In the pages that follow the reader will discover pools from which to drink—the Scriptures, prayer, and memories, just to name a few. The writer's attempt is not to supplant the Word of God, but to supplement it. So sit a spell, relax in God's presence and allow Him to rejuvenate you on your journey to His eternal home.

PREFACE

Thus the heavens and the earth were completed in all their vast array. By the seventh day God had finished the work he had been doing; so on the seventh day he rested from all his work. And God blessed the seventh day and made it holy, because on it he rested from all the work of creating that he had done (Genesis 2:1–3). [1]

ACCORDING TO A GREEK LEGEND, in ancient Athens a man noticed the great storyteller, Aesop, playing childish games with some little boys. He laughed and jeered at Aesop, asking him why he wasted his time in such frivolous activity.

Aesop responded by picking up a bow, loosening its string, and placing it on the ground. Then he said to the critical Athenian, "Now, answer the riddle, if you can. Tell us what the unstrung bow implies."

The man looked at it for several minutes but had no idea what point Aesop was trying to make. Aesop explained, "If you keep a bow always bent, it will break eventually; but if you let it go slack, it will be more fit for use when you want it."

---

1 Verses are from the NIV unless otherwise noted.

People are also like that. That is why we all need to take time to rest, to go slack occasionally. Jesus prescribed time off for His wearied disciples after they had returned from a prolonged period of ministry. And in the Old Testament, God set a pattern for us when He "rested from all His work" (Genesis 2:3).

Should we not take His example seriously? If God felt the need to rest, who are we to ignore it? We could start by setting aside a special time to relax physically and renew ourselves emotionally and spiritually. We will be at our best for the Lord if we have taken time to loosen the bow.

"Every now and then go away, have a little relaxation, for when you come back to your work your judgment will be surer, since to remain constantly at work will cause you to loose power of judgment. Go some distance away because then the work appears smaller, and more of it can be taken in at a glance, and lack of harmony or proportion is more readily seen."

These are the words of Leonardo da Vinci, and no idler he; he excelled as a painter, sculptor, poet, architect, engineer, city planner, scientist, inventor, anatomist, military genius, and philosopher. We would do well to heed his words of wisdom.

Human beings need rest (the Hebrew word *Shabbat* means literally, "cessation") from their toil, and no society can be healthy which does not recognize that need.

But we also need rest from our cares—from this life of getting and spending and laying waste our powers, which only faith in God can give us. In this faith we can find here the rest for our souls that Jesus promised in Matthew 11:28-30. And beyond that we can look forward to that Sabbath rest which remains for the people of God (Hebrews 4:9).

Because of her arrival at a railroad station, a lady had but five minutes to make connection with an outgoing train. As she ran toward the train, a Pullman car porter waved her to slow down and said, "Lady, you better take it easy or you're going to come down with "*Americanitis.*" "What's that?" gasped the lady, to which the porter replied, "I can't tell you what it is, but I can tell you how it acts. *Americanitis* is running up an escalator. It is walking rapidly on a people-mover at the airport terminal."

Have you ever seen anyone running up an escalator? Sure you have. Perhaps you have been guilty of it yourself—trying to catch that plane or get to that interview.

So many of us are getting nowhere fast! Like ants disturbed on an anthill, we scurry hither, thither, and yon. Taut nerves are snapping and over-wrought minds are cracking with the result that there are more mental patients in hospitals than any other kind.

Centuries ago the Lord addressed this issue. He saw it coming, so He spoke to us through the prophet Isaiah. And if ever a scripture was contemporary, this one surely is: "Be still and know that I am God. In returning and rest shall you be saved. In quietness and in confidence shall be your strength."

"But Lord, it's so hard to be still with all that is happening in our world. The information highway beckons to me; she lures me to her side with promises of news, current events, politics, entertainment, sports, weather, and a whole host of other facts. It is important that I stay up-to-date and improve my scope of knowledge, isn't it?" And then I hear within my soul, this refrain, "BE STILL AND KNOW THAT I AM GOD."

"But Lord, this is a fast-paced culture. We have to keep up or we will be left behind. There are projects to complete, assignments to finish, goals to meet. The prize is always to the swift. Everyone wants it ASAP. In fact, they want it yesterday. The pressure is on to produce in record time. You understand, don't you, Lord?" "BE STILL AND KNOW THAT I AM GOD."

"But Lord, how can one be still when the world is so filled with constant racket? Highway noise, sirens, car stereos, television, crying babies, telephones, factory whistles, clocks, beepers, cell phones, lawn mowers, chain saws, barking dogs. There is no end of clamor. Even nature offers no help for there is always the distant sound of the call of the wild." "BE STILL AND KNOW THAT I AM GOD."

"I wish I had more time for you, Lord, but the demands are great. There is so much to do. The church needs my gifts of service. My boss expects me to finish that project. My wife wants me to devote more time to our relationship. My children want me to help them with their school work. And beside all of this, I need to take time to care for my body. Exercise is important. Right? "BE STILL AND KNOW THAT I AM GOD."

"I am so tired, dear God. My strength is sapped, my energy depleted. The demands upon my time have left me weak and numb. I can't think straight. A quiet time is the last thing I am interested in, even though I know it is the very thing I most need. After I have rested, I promise to get alone with You. You do understand, don't you, Lord?" "BE STILL AND KNOW THAT I AM GOD."

"My mind is more preoccupied than ever, Lord. It is so difficult to concentrate for even a few moments. I find myself thinking of the day's events—appointments, chores, etc. I know I must focus and learn to listen to You. If only I could somehow push out of my mind these annoying distractions." "BE STILL AND KNOW THAT I AM GOD."

"But sometimes I feel as did the Psalmist when he penned these words from his anguished heart: 'Fear and trembling have beset me; horror has overwhelmed me. I said, O, that I had the wings of a dove! I would fly away and be at rest. I would flee far away and stay in the desert' (Psalm 55:5-7). These are troublesome times. Fear is running rampant. Fear of the economy. Fear of terrorists. Fear of disease. Fear of growing old. My mind is fidgeting. My nerves are frayed." And then, again, I hear these words ringing in my mind: "BE STILL AND KNOW THAT I AM GOD."

In the midst of teaching, healing, traveling, and preaching, Jesus never allowed the pace of life to deter Him from spending time with His heavenly Father. Mark wrote, "In the morning, having risen a long while before daylight, He went out and departed to a solitary place; and there He prayed" (Mark 1:35).

"BE STILL AND KNOW THAT I AM GOD." Know that I AM. Know that I am in control. Be assured that I am with you. Be confident of My presence. Rest in Me. Let me soothe your troubled mind and calm your anxious fears. Be still and know.

I have a treasure which I prize,
It's like I cannot find;
There's nothing like it on the earth,
'Tis this—*a quiet mind.*

But 'tis not that I am stupefied,
Or senseless, dull, or blind;
'Tis God's own peace within my heart
That forms my *quiet mind.*

I found this treasure at the Cross,
And there to every kind
Of weary, heavy-ladened soul,
Christ gives a *quiet mind.*

My Savior's death and risen life
To give them were designed;
His love's the never failing spring
Of this, my *quiet mind.*

The love of God within my breast,
My heart to Him doth bind;
This is the peace of heaven on earth—
This is my *quiet mind.*

—Anonymous

If ever there was "a word from the Lord" that relates to the subject at hand, it would be that found in John 10:27. Jesus is speaking, or rather teaching, and He says, "My sheep listen to my voice; I know them, and they follow me."

Beepers and pagers are everywhere! From physicians to police, to clergy, there they are, clipped to belts and protruding from pockets—fiendish reminders of the mastery of electronics.

Getting one's attention in this way has its comical moments. One doctor claims he got so ruffled when his beeper sounded as he drove down the highway that he threw it out the window and tried to shut off his cigarette. Another person though, emphasized the positive value of being able to stay in touch with his office. He had a certain amount of peace of mind, not only in knowing he can be reached if needed, but also in being assured that if he does not get beeped, he is not needed.

This development in communications is a good reminder of the kind of open line that we should be maintaining with Heaven. Let us check the ears of our hearts. Are they dull because of sin? Do we have the confidence of a clean conscience? Can we be reached if are we not within calling distance? It may be that God is trying to get our attention. He has something to say that we need to hear. He sends a signal, but we are often not in a position to hear. "He that hath an ear, let him hear what the Spirit says unto the church" (Revelation 2:7, KJV).

In our day the air is filled with voices that clamor to be heard. In order to avert confusion we must learn to be discriminate listeners. The voice which matters most is God's. In I Samuel chapter three, we read about how young Samuel had to learn to detect the voice of God in the sanctuary. We must discipline our ears and hearts to hear God's voice as well and respond to it. The question is, How can we hear the voice of God so that we, like Samuel, might know His will for our lives? Let me suggest four avenues.

First, there is the voice from WITHIN. Here I speak of the conscience—the eye of the soul which looks out either toward God or toward what it regards as the highest. We have to make an effort to keep our consciences so sensitive that we walk without offense. Paul testified to the importance of a clear conscience in II Corinthians 1:2: "For our rejoicing is this, the testimony of our conscience, that in simplicity and Godly sincerity, not with fleshly wisdom, but by the grace of God, we have had our conversation in the world, and more abundantly to you-ward."

Again, Paul warned Timothy that next to his faith, a clear conscience was his most essential weapon: "I...sent you out to battle for the right armed only with your faith and a clear conscience. Some, alas, have laid these simple weapons aside, and as far as their faith is concerned, have run their ships on the rocks" (I Timothy 1:18,19, Phillips).

Do not lay aside this wonderful weapon that God has given you. Grieve not the Holy Spirit. He does not usually come with a voice like thunder; His voice is so gentle that it is easy to ignore or miss altogether. How glad I am that even as calloused and insensitive as we are at times, the conscience is still there. It is a mechanism that God has built into our human framework.

But someone may ask, "What is the difference between the conscience and the Spirit of God?" Very simple—one is a Person, while the other is a psychological function of the mind. The conscience is an educated thing. In the life of an unbeliever, it can be very dangerous. But as the child of God allows the Holy Spirit to re-educate the conscience, it becomes that for which God originally intended—a vehicle for implementing and sustaining righteousness. As Paul put it, "I am speaking the truth in Christ, I am not lying; my conscience bears witness in the Holy Spirit" (Romans 9:1).

Yes, God is especially present in the conscience of all persons by way of testimony and judgment; that is, He is there to call our actions to mind, a witness to bring them to judgment, and a judge to acquit or condemn. The voice from within: the conscience.

Secondly, there is the voice from BEHIND—experience. Accumulated knowledge is one of the best teachers. An ancient proverb puts it this way: "A prudent man profits from his own experience; a wise one from the experience of others." We should carry our experiences around like coins in our pockets—ready to use them when needed.

Just before the children of Israel entered the Promise Land, Moses delivered a series of farewell addresses, the first of which looked backward. He reviewed their wilderness wanderings and the reasons for them. An eleven day journey from Mount Horeb to Kadesh took over forty years! How slow they covered the ground. And how often we have to go over the same ground again and again. We marvel at Israel's slowness to learn, while ignoring our own. We, like they, are often kept back by unbelief because we are tuned into God's frequency. We do not have our ears on and we ignore the prompting from above.

Paul tells the Corinthian believers that the history of Israel's wilderness wanderings was written for our admonition, upon whom the end of the ages is to come. Thank God for the voice of the past.

Thirdly, there is the voice AHEAD—vision, that is, our goals, dreams, and ideals. We long to accomplish in life what God intends for us to accomplish. Every day we pray, "Thy kingdom come, Thy will be done in earth as it is in heaven" (Matthew 6:10 KJV). That glorious day is just ahead.

To reach our full potential in Christ—this is what we aim for. And hope for the future keeps us pressing on. When hope is alive, the night is less dark; the solitude less deep, fear less acute. It is like the sun, which as we journey toward it, casts a shadow of our burden behind us. And thus our motto becomes: "Life with Christ is an endless hope; life without Him a hopeless end."

There is a second sense in which the voice ahead calls to us. Beyond this life there is the hope of heaven. Its sound beckons us, calling, "Come up hither." Listen often and it will sustain you amidst the negative, depressing noise of the world.

Evangelist Merv Rosell relates a story from his childhood when he and his brother contracted diphtheria. They were wrapped in white sheets and taken to the contagious ward of the hospital. He could still see his mother's face pressed against the glass of the ward, peering lovingly at her two boys during those days and nights of suffering. Little Robert wept day and night. Although the nurses tried to comfort him as best they could, it was almost impossible to give him relief in his complicated condition.

The nurses tried to comfort Merv as he explained that it was his brother who kept crying. After two weeks they explained how they had moved Robert to a sunny room on the other side of the hospital. A week later their mother came to take Merv home. On the way home,

Merv asked his mother, "Is Robert home yet?" His mother answered that he had been at home for several days.

As they pulled up to their house, Merv jumped out of the car and ran up the steps shouting, "Robert! Hey Robert!" But there was only silence. He persisted in calling his brother's name. Finally, his mother drew him aside, and sitting him on her lap, she tried to explain that Robert wasn't "home" to this house, but to his "heavenly" home.

Merv said, "You mean he's dead!" But even as carefully as his mother talked about the resurrection and temporary loss and reunion and the joys of heaven, all little Merv could do was shout over and over, "But he's dead!"

They backed away, stumbling through the lilac bushes and out to the street wondering what had happened to Merv. He walked back into the dining room. It was now the loneliest, emptiest house he had ever known.

But that is not the end of the story. For since those days there came to Merv an ever-deepening faith in the reality of eternal life through the teaching of that godly mother, the quiet assurance that what she said in those days and lived out in the subsequent years is actually the truth, a fact, not just a fantasy.

Standing by the front door was a crowd of boys calling for Merv to come out and play ball—welcoming him back to the neighborhood again. He marched from the dining room to the front door and shouted, "Kids, get out of here! Beat it! Don't come back again. Don't you know my brother's dead? I'll never play ball again. He's dead, I tell you. Get out of here and leave me alone!"

Paul put it well when he wrote, "If only for this life we have hope in Christ, we are to be pitied more than all men" (I Corinthians 15:19). We shall live again. This blessed hope is the substance of every human heart that stands beside the little white crosses; the brown mounds of earth; the small coffins—every lonely heart that stands alone, save for the assurance in Jesus Christ, the Son of God.

Lastly, there is the voice from ABOVE—God's voice. Many ask, "Does God speak to man audibly?" And to that there is a divergence of opinion. However, on one thing we can all agree: God communicates through His written Word. "All scripture is given by inspiration and is profitable for doctrine and for reproof, and for correction, and for instruction in godliness."

The study of God's Word for the purpose of discovering His will is the secret discipline which has formed the greatest characters. The healthiest Christian, the one who is best fitted for godly living and godly labors, is he who feeds most on Christ. Here lies the benefit of Bible reading.

The Bible is the mirror of its Author, meant first of all to reveal, unveil, magnify and glorify Him from whom it originally went forth. Holy Scripture should be thought of as "God preaching"—God preaching to me every time I read or hear any part of it—God the Father preaching God the Son in the power of God the Holy Spirit. God the Father is the Giver; God the Son is its Theme; God the Spirit, its Interpreter.

God has spoken, says the Bible, and godliness means hearing His Word with the hearing heart—giving attention, assent, and application to its truth.

Yes, God is still speaking, but the question is, are we listening? Centuries ago John the Apostle penned these words, convinced that they were from God: "Look at me. I stand at the door. I knock. If you hear me call and open the door, I'll come right in and sit down to supper with you…Are your ears awake? Listen. Listen to the Wind Words, the Spirit blowing through the churches" (Revelation 3:20,22, The Message).

•

Just suppose in our hurried state of mind, we took the time to re-interpret Psalm 23 in order to make it fit our twenty first century lifestyle. It might come out something like this…

The clock is my dictator, I shall not rest.
It makes me lie down only when exhausted.
It leads me into deep depression.
It hounds my soul.

It leads me in circles of frenzy, for activities sake.
Even though I run frantically from task to task,
I will never get it all done.
For my ideal is with me.
Deadlines and my need for approval, they drive me.
They demand performance from me,
beyond the limits of my schedule.
They anoint my head with migraines,
My in-basket overflows.

Surely fatigue and time pressures shall follow me
All the days of my life.
And I will dwell in the bonds of frustration forever.

–Source unknown

Now would it not be sad if we looked at our lives in that manner? How much better to leave the ancient Shepherd-King's thoughts alone. After all, was he not inspired by God to pen the words of Psalm 23? The inspiration must have come from those moments in his youth when, during the heat of the mid-day, he rested by a quiet stream. He took time to meditate on the father-like qualities of his God—protection, provision, presence. How much better to have a Shepherd than a clock as our leader? After all, the best shepherds were those who truly cared for their flock—knew each by name. David had but one Master and it was not the clock! He had no reason to read, *The Tyranny of Time*. The truth is, his sense of complete serenity and security captured in this great Psalm is the direct result of his relationship with his Lord. I suppose you could have a relationship with a clock, albeit a stunted, cold one. But can time bring one a feeling of love and tender care. I think not! David viewed himself as one of God's sheep. He knew that rest was a necessary part of restoration.

Shepherds will often reach into a rushing stream and, using rocks and muck, form quiet little pools for the sheep to drink from. Is it not true that there is something restful about quiet ponds and rivers and lakes?

Did you ever stop to consider that the Lord provides little pools of spiritual refreshment for us, even in the midst of our busy schedules? For example, consider the following: retreats, worships services, private devotional times, long walks with God as your only Companion, Christian concerts, and Christian literature, to name a few.

It is a fact that if sheep are not led to the good water supplies of clean, pure water, they will end up drinking from polluted pot holes (false teaching). Jesus made it clear that the thirsty souls of men can be fully satisfied from drinking from His well because His water is pure, endless in its supply, life-giving, and extremely rewarding.

Most people are not aware that sheep can go for months without drinking if there is a heavy dew each morning. By habit, they rise just before dawn and start to feed. There is no more beautiful picture of still waters than the silver droplets of dew on the grass. Since we are compared to sheep in the Bible, how beautiful it must be for our heavenly Father to watch one of His sheep rise early in the morning and drink from the dew of His Word. This Word is fresh every morning. Jesus said, "If anyone thirst, let him come to me and drink. He who believes in me, as the Scriptures has said, out of his heart will flow rivers of living water."

Nancy Spiegelberg, in a November issue of Decision magazine, wrote these words: L*ord, I crawled across the barrenness to You with my empty cup, uncertain but asking any small drop of refreshment. If only I had known You better I would have come running with a bucket.*

There are those who seek to quench their thirst by drinking from the wells of the world only to turn away with parched spirits. Jeremiah wrote of this centuries ago: "My people have committed two sins: they have forsaken me, the spring of living water, and have dug their own cisterns, broken cisterns that cannot hold water."

What are these wells of the world? Could they not include fame, fortune, career, and pleasure? J. Samuel Hoffman, a missionary to Mexico was asked to give his impressions of the United States after returning on a furlough. He states that in his view, Americans are spiritually impoverished because they are drinking from "worldly wells" which he characterized as three in scope: (1) Schizophrenic Wells—some organizations urged their drivers not to drink alcohol when behind the wheel, while at the same time beer and wine companies fill TV screens with ads which glorify and glamorize booze. We spend millions fighting drugs and yet the rich and famous use them openly. (2) Polytheistic Wells—We worship two gods in America—sports and recreation. One TV ad says that weekends were made for fun. (3) Materialistic Wells—Get rich quick! That is the goal of life. Be set by the time you reach age forty. Use the lottery. Ignore your family if that is what it takes.

Now contrast these wells with the "Living Water" offered by Christ. There is no comparison. Our Shepherd knows what our spirits really long for. He waits patiently in line until we have exhausted all of our resources. Then, when we are tired and in need of refreshment, He extends His hand, which contains a large cup of life-giving water. We are wise if we drink often and deeply.

THE REJUVENATING POWER OF THE WORD OF GOD

You will find yourself breathed upon by divine will, affected, seized, transfigured, in an ineffable manner, if you approach Scripture religiously with veneration, humbly.

—DESIDERIUS ERASMUS
Enchriridion, 1501

THE INDISPENSABLE COMMODITY

How can a young man keep his way pure? By living according to your word. I seek you with all my heart; do not let me stray from your commands. I have hidden your word in my heart that I might not sin against you (Psalm 119:1-11).

AS THE GREAT SCOTTISH POET AND NOVELIST, Sir Walter Scott, lay on his deathbed, he called for the "Book." There was a vast library in his home and so he was asked, "Which book?" His reply: "There is only one Book. Bring me the Book!" It was then that those attending him realized that he was referring to the Bible. To Scott, there was really only one Book that really mattered—only one Book that had all the answers to life's perplexing questions—one Book that brings comfort and hope to the dying and purpose to the living.

John Wesley was a man of one Book as well. He wrote, "I am a creature of the day, passing through life, as an arrow through the air. I am a spirit come from God, and returning to God; just hovering over the great gulf; till a few moments hence, I am no more seen! I drop into an unchangeable eternity! I want to know one thing, the way to heaven: how to land safe on that happy shore. God himself has condescended to teach the way; for this very end he came from heaven. He has written it down in a book! Oh, give me that book! At any price, give me that book! I have it: here is knowledge enough for me. Let me be *homo unis libri:* a man of one book. Here then I am fat from the busy ways of men. I sit down alone; only God is here. In his presence I open, I read this book; for this end, to find the way to heaven."

The Pony Express was a thrilling part of American history. It ran from St. Joseph, Missouri, to Sacramento, California—a distance of some 1,900 miles. The trip was made in ten days. Forty men, each riding fifty miles a day, dashed along the trail on 500 of the best and fastest horses money could buy. To conserve weight, clothing was very light, saddles were extremely small and thin, and no weapons were carried. The horses wore small shoes or none at all. The mail pouches were flat and very conservative in size. Letters had to be written on thin paper, and postage was $5.00 an ounce. Yet, with all these restrictions, each rider carried a full sized Bible! It was presented to him when he joined the Pony Express and he took it with him despite all the scrupulous weight precautions. This book became the "indispensable commodity."

"There's just one Book," cried the dying sage,
"Read me the old, old story."
And the winged words that can never age
Wafted him home to Glory.
There's just one Book.

There's just one Book for the tender years,
One Book alone for guiding
The little feet through the joys and fears,
The unknown days are hiding.
There's just one Book.

There's just one Book for the bridal hour,
One Book for loves own coining;
Its truths alone lend beauty and power,
To vows that lives are joining.
There's just one Book.

There's just one Book for life's gladness,
One Book for the toilsome days,
One Book that can cure life's madness,
One Book that can voice life's praise.
There's just one Book.

There's just one Book for the dying,
One Book for the starting tears.
And one for the soul that is going home,
For the measureless years.
There's just one Book.

—Anonymous

We can do without most books—books that instruct, educate, advise, inspire—the "how to" books. These enlighten us as we make our way through this journey. But there is only one Book that we really need—the Book that explains where we came from, why we are here, and where we are going. It contains the mind of God, the doom of sinners, the plan of redemption, and the hope of the ages. To begin the day with it is delightful. To build one's life upon it is wise. After all, there's just one Book!

SWEETER THAN HONEY

How sweet are your words to my taste, sweeter than honey to my mouth! (Psalm 119:103)

I CAN VISUALIZE DAVID, the writer of Psalm 119, preparing to lead his sheep into the hills for greener pastures. He is just a teenager, a hungry teenager at that. In his knapsack his mother has carefully placed some figs, fruit, barley loaves, and honey. Since there were no candy bars in those days (and what teenager would want to carry a lunch without one), this young shepherd boy is fully prepared for an energy-boost.

About mid-way in the morning, he rests from his labor. The sheep seem quite content, so David sits down under the shade of a mighty oak. From out of knapsack he pulls some honey. In ancient times honey was called "the nectar of the gods" and was mankind's principle sweetener. David knows that he is about to experience a special treat. Right at that very moment, he thinks that nothing in all the world could be more satisfying or delightful than the taste of this honey.

Could it be that some years later, when King David sat writing Psalm 119, he recalled this moment? As good as this honey tasted, the Word of the Lord was even more pleasant to his hungry heart.

The Bible, like honey, is sourced in God alone. Try as we may, we cannot find a way to synthetically fabricate anything that even remotely resembles the properties of honey. Like honey, the Scriptures are pure spiritual food containing every spiritual vitamin and nutrient we need.

Like honey, the Word of God comes to us via others. When God created the earth He gave bees the exclusive contract for honey. They alone are licensed to make and market it. Not birds. Not buffaloes. Not even other bugs. In a similar manner, human authors were simply conduits of God's revelation. Like bees, they were His agents for writing, collecting, and preserving His truth.

The parallel to God's mystery of honey is striking. Agricultural scientists have tested honey produced from plants heavily sprayed with pesticides and found that it never contains even a trace of any foreign chemical. There is a certain mystery also to the Word of God. Like honey, we do not know exactly how it is produced or preserved.

Again, the Bible, like honey, has a healing quality about it. Among many respected old home remedies is a mixture of lemon and honey for the relief of colds and sore throats. No one knows just how this works, only that it does. When the Word of the Lord is applied to a hurting soul, renewal takes place.

God's Word, like honey, is selectively derived. Bees do not reap every flower they see. They are very particular. Twenty five thousand round trips are required by one bee to produce just one pound of honey! Then it is stored in one central place—the honeycomb. It is always fresh and ready to eat. Oh, how like the Scriptures! Fresh and ready to devour. As the Psalmist wrote, "Taste and see that the Lord is good" (Psalm 34:8).

Like honey, the Bible must be applied personally and individually. It would be of no use for David to simply admire the honey provided for him. It might look appetizing; it might smell delicious. But until he sampled it, he would never know its amazing benefits. How like the Word. To put it on display is commendable. To carry it to worship is admirable. To read it is beneficial. But unless and until one ingests and digests its contents, the greatest benefits are not apprehended.

Lastly, the Bible, like honey, is long-lasting. In fact, it is eternal. When one of the pyramids of Egypt was opened, they found honey that was preserved. We carry the Word of the Lord in our minds and hearts as we journey through life and on into the heavenlies. "The ordinances of the Lord are more precious than gold; they are sweeter than honey" (Psalm 19:10).

THE TALKING BIBLE

IF THE BIBLE COULD SPEAK, I wonder what it would say? Actually, in a sense, it does speak. It informs, testifies, proclaims, and inspires. Sometimes, in the right environment, the Scriptures seem to whisper words of comfort. At other times, when the need arises, they scream words of warning. And wise is that person who pushes the pause button and listens.

Suppose a Bible miraculously was given the power to communicate its thoughts through a diary. Let us peek into the pages and see what one year in its life reveals.

February 16	*The day of my birth—seems like only yesterday that I came forth from the printing press at Acme Publishing Company.*
May 12	*A woman in her forties picked me off the shelf at a local bookstore. So glad to be out of that place! Can't wait for my new home.*
May 13	*Seems like a nice family, these new owners of mine, but I'm back on the shelf once again, feeling rather useless.*
May 22	*The man of the house grabbed me and shoved me into an overnight bag. Heard him say something about a camp meeting. Perhaps at last I will be used!*
June 2	*I have been resting quietly for about a week. The first few nights after camp meeting my owner read me regularly, but now it seems as though I have been forgotten.*
July 10	*Clean-up day! I was dusted off, along with some other things, but was placed back on the shelf. I long for human hands to touch me…for this I was created.*

July 17	*Owner bought me a new leather cover with a zipper; makes me feel secure and important, but haven't been unzipped lately.*
July 24	*Owner used me for a short time today, after dinner. He looked up a few verses; went to Sunday school today.*
August 8	*Dusted off today and put on the center table in the sitting room. The minister came for a visit. After he left I quickly found myself back on the shelf again.*
September 3	*Busy day. My owner had to lead a devotional lesson and had to look up some references…had quite a time finding me and then hunted and hunted to find the references.*
October 12	*I'm in Grandma's lap now. I love it here. It's so warm and comfortable. I feel needed. She's here on a visit. Hope she stays a long time. She let a tear drop on Colossians 2:5-7: "For though I am absent from you in body, I am present with you in spirit and delight to see how orderly you are and how firm your faith in Christ is. So then, just as you received Christ Jesus as Lord, continue to live in him, rooted and built up in him, strengthened in the faith as you were taught, and overflowing with thankfulness." I love it when she handles me—with such gentleness. She turns my pages as though they were made of the finest silk.*
October 13	*In Grandma's lap again. She has spent most of her time reading I Corinthians 13.*
October 14-16	*I have been in Grandma's lap each afternoon. It's such a comfort to be loved and appreciated. She reads me as though I was a personal love letter to her.*
October 17	*Grandma is gone and I am back in the same old place. She kissed me before she left.*

November 9	*Had a couple of four-leaf clovers stuck in me today. What's that about?*
December 1	*Packed in a suitcase today with some clothes. Off on a vacation, I guess.*
December 8	*Still in suitcase.*
December 11	*Still in suitcase, although everything else has been in and out several times. Wish they would take the dirty socks off me.*
December 13	*Home again and on the shelf. Quite a journey…don't know why I went along.*
December 24	*Was carried to church this evening for the candle-lighting service.*
January 10	*Owner read me every day for the first seven days of the new year—something about a resolution.*
February 9	*Stuffy and hot. Two magazines, a novel and an old hat are on top of me. I am suffocating for lack of use!*
March 16	*Carried to church today and held up to be counted. Something about a contest.*
April 7	*Dusted again. Sure do get lonely. Wish Grandma would visit again. I love to feel her warm embrace.*
May 18	*Thought about my cousins today—they are so blessed. One is in a prison library—gets lots of use. Another is in a courtroom and is the object of much respect. Still another lies in a motel room and is referenced often. I do envy them.*

May 22 — *Annual Spring revival at church—owner took me every night this week. Made a commitment to read me daily, just as he did last year.*

June 10 — *Owner's father died yesterday. The whole family is taking turns reading me, especially the Psalms. Sure does feel good to be used.*

June 15 — *Owner loaned me to his teenaged boy for summer camp. He is so rough with me—throws me around like I was a sack of potatoes. Spent a lot of time stuffed in his knapsack, but he reads me every night by the light of a flashlight and I can tell that he is changing for the good.*

June 22 — *Back home again. Owner has given me to his son for good.*

August 27 — *Son took me to first day of school today and placed me on top of his other books on his desk for all to see. He is a courageous young man. Things are really beginning to look up now!*

UNSHACKLED!

So is my word that goes out from my mouth: It will not return to me empty, but will accomplish what I desire and achieve the purpose for which I sent it (Isaiah 55:11).

JOHN WYCLIFF TRANSLATED THE BIBLE into the language of the common people. He wanted to make it possible for all to know the Word of God. Before the Inquisition could slay him, he died and was buried. But the inquisitors exhumed his remains and publicly burned them. They then cast his ashes upon the River Swift. If any man in England was found with a Bible, it was hung around his neck and he was publicly hanged and burned.

What the English inquisitors did not realize was that when they burned the body of Wycliffe and scattered his ashes on the River Swift, they were metaphorically contributing to the spread of the Word of God. For you see, the River Swift flowed into the Avon and the Avon flowed into the Severn. The Severn flowed into the sea, and the sea lathed the shores of the world, including the new land called America.

Wherever the sea carried the ashes of John Wycliffe, there also God scattered the truth of the living Lord. Those of us who have been born again into God's forever family are the recipients of this living Word. That is the way it is with God's truth. When it goes out from His mouth, in whatever form, it eventually lodges within the heart of man.

We have heard about those in other lands who have experienced the truth of His Word for the first time. Even today, someone, somewhere, is hearing the liberating truth contained in the Book. This unchained, unbound, Word is indeed accomplishing God's purpose. And what is that purpose?—to set men and women free!

In the city of Grand Rapids, Michigan, a man entered a church, walked up to the pastor and asked to be baptized. When asked to explain further, he told the pastor that he had recently been lodged in the county jail, serving time for a drug-related charge. Feeling lonely and without much hope, he was about to give in to despair when a Gideon New

Testament was handed to him. At first he ignored it. Then one day he picked it up only to discover that the cover had been printed upside down. "How appropriate," he thought. "That's exactly what my life is like." He began to believe it was a trick. The Gideons had purposely given these Testaments with the imperfect covers just to gain the prisoners attention. He asked the chaplain to verify his assertion, but was amazed when the chaplain replied, "I have checked the other 299 Testaments and not one of them was like the one you were given."

It was a "Eureka" moment! This convict realized that God had meant it just for him. He read the Testament for the next three days, then prayed to receive the Christ revealed therein. Needless to say, there was a baptism that day!

Oh, the power of the Book! It abides forever as unchangeable and unalterable truth. It continues to flow like a mighty river to reach all the parched peoples of the world. Following is just one example of its ability to influence.

When John Wanamaker was a boy of 11, he worked in his father's brickyard. He had earned enough to purchase his first Bible. It cost $2.75, and he paid for it in installments. He read this Book all his life and applied it literally to his own problems. He accepted without question its claim that faith would remove mountains.

When, at 22, he started his first store with his savings of $1,900, everyone said he would fail. But he had faith, and he succeeded. Three times, during three successive panics, his business almost went on the rocks. But he found that the miracle of faith always pulled him through.

The Bible not only shaped his character, he got all his most important business ideas from it. Through these ideas, which revolutionized the whole theory of retail buying and selling, and created our modern principle of "service," John Wanamaker became, as President Taft once said, "The greatest merchant in America."

"That little red Bible," he wrote, "was the greatest and most important and far-reaching purchase I have ever made; and every other investment in my life seems to me only secondary."

IMPERISHABLE POSSESSION

Forever, O Lord, thy word is settled in heaven (Psalm 119:89, KJV)

ALEXANDER DUFF, THE GREAT MISSIONARY, sailed for India on the Lady Holland. His clothes, his prize possessions, his library of 800 volumes, were all on board. And within a few miles of India a shipwreck occurred. The passengers were all saved, but the possessions of all the passengers were lost. On the beach Alexander Duff looked out to sea, hoping against hope that some part of his possessions might have drifted onto the shore.

Then he saw something—something small, floating on top of the water. Nearer and nearer it came while anxious eyes watched it. What would it be? Duff waded into the water, got hold of the floating object and brought it to shore. What was it? A Bible, and not just any Bible. It was Duff's! Of all his books, of all his possessions, that single Book survived. The missionary took it as a sign from the Lord. He took it to mean that this one single Book was worth all his books and all his possessions.

Thus heartened, he began his career as a missionary. The very next day, reading from that Bible, he began his first class—a group of five boys meeting under the shade of a banyan tree. A week later the class had swelled to over three hundred listeners!

The power of the Word of God to survive is awesome indeed. Whether by nature's assault or man's design, this living Sword remains. Attempts to destroy and discredit it come to naught, testifying to its divine origin.

After writing some fine pamphlets on freedom, including *The Right of Man,* Tom Paine penned, *The Age of Reason*. He said, "This will destroy the Bible. Within one hundred years the Bible will be found only in museums or in musty corners of second-hand bookstores." Paine's book became the scourge that tormented him until his death. Later, he deeply regretted having written that slanderous attack against the Bible and Christianity. Year after year the Bible continues to be among the best sellers in our land, while *The Age of Reason* is limited to required reading for those studying American history.

In Isaiah 40:8, the prophet, under the inspiration of the Holy Spirit, wrote these remarkable words: "The grass withers, the flowers fall, but the word of our God stands forever." The Hebrew word for "stand" is *yagum* and literally means "rises to stand." It describes something that is beaten and battered, yet rises to stand. For centuries enemies of God have tried to destroy the Bible, but have failed. They have been on an impossible mission. The Scriptures contain the mind of God. They are as imperishable as their Author.

Did you know that every American military plane that flies over water now carries a collapsible boat which contains food rations and a copy of the Bible in a waterproof package? Someone at the decision-making level in the Armed Forces realizes that spiritual equipment can be as important as food and drink in saving lives. It is the key Book of our faith. Its truths are indestructible. May we learn to cherish it and appropriate its promises.

WORD POWER

For the word of God is living and active. Sharper than any double-edged sword. It penetrates even to dividing soul and spirit, joints and marrow; it judges the thoughts and attitudes of the heart (Hebrews 4:12).

IT HAS BEEN SAID THAT THERE ARE THREE GREAT POWERS IN LIFE: the power of love, the power of prayer, and the power of God. While it is difficult to argue with this assertion, I would hasten to add a fourth: the power of words.

Very few people realize the power of words. We toss them about carelessly, day after day, without any consideration for their tremendous impact. Words, both spoken and written, are considered to be by many the single greatest force in the world. We would know nothing about God, or love, or prayer apart from them. Words may be used to comfort a crying child or order an execution. They may be used to express love or to incite hatred.

Think of the influence of the media on our generation. They shape our way of thinking—our values, goals, and ideals. Think of the power that one possesses through the careful, discriminating use of words. The parent, the teacher, the preacher, the politician—they are all aware of the power of words. We read, we listen, and then we form opinions, then we decide. We simply dare not underestimate the power of words.

God knew long before He created humanity about the strength of communication. As a result He devised a plan whereby a Book would be written that would contain the thoughts and intents of His great heart. It took over 1,500 years to compile it. More than 30 authors were involved, coming from various cultures and social classes. It was written in four languages and in many countries. But the unity of the Bible was maintained. The Spirit of God "breathed upon holy men of old." Through the unique personalities of the prophets and apostles, the Word was delivered to us. And what a wonderful Book it is—powerful and unique among all the holy books. It contains the mind of God, the state of man, the way of salvation, the doom of sinners, and the happiness of believers.

Its doctrines are holy, its precepts are binding, its histories are true, and its decisions are unchangeable. Read it to be wise, believe it to be safe, and practice it to be holy.

The Bible itself attests to the power of words when describing its impact on those who dare to read it with an open, searching mind. For example, it is said to be like a *mirror*, showing us ourselves, a *hammer*, breaking our stubborn wills, a *lamp*, guiding us through the pathway of life, *water*, cleansing the soul, and *seed*, sown in the human heart to produce much fruit.

Scientists have discovered a variety of uses for the laser beam. We once thought that it was a design of science fiction. Now lasers are used for many industrial, medical, navigational, and communicative purposes. The difference between lasers and an ordinary light bulb is direction. God's Word is like a laser. It can pierce into the very heart and soul of everyone on earth. It can separate the soul from the spirit. It can discern the highest and lowest thoughts. It can speak to our attitudes and intentions. But without doubt the greatest testimony to the power of the Word lies in its ability to transform the lives of men and women, boys and girls of all races, classes and backgrounds.

An American missionary was sent to Burma to investigate the various languages with the intent to eventually begin translation work among the people groups. One night he encamped near a small village. He heard prayer going on in a Burmese dialect that he was familiar with. He listened and to his utter astonishment heard, not the name of Buddha, or that of any idol, but the name of Jesus. He was puzzled because he knew that no missionary or white man had ever been to that part of the world, and so he went into the village and began to make inquiries.

He found that the head man of the village some years previously had been down to another village some distance away and had brought an article of food wrapped in a Burmese printed paper, which happened to be one single chapter of the Word of God with a piece torn out of the corner. He read it, and realized that Jesus Christ, the Son of God, had died to take away his sin. He embraced the message and called his friends together and read that same piece of Scripture to them. He encouraged them to put away their idols and serve the Living God. So when this missionary found them, they had been praying to Christ as the Savior for six years! Who can fathom the power of this Word?

The Bible, a very dangerous book, indeed—dangerous in that when read by a seeking heart will result in dramatic change because it is God-breathed, eternal, and immutable. Something mysterious, supernatural, takes place when a seeker after truth encounters the written Word. The Spirit of God breathes upon the mind of the reader and "revelation" takes place.

ARMED AND READY!

Therefore put on the full armor of God, so that when the day of evil comes, you may be able to stand your ground, and after you have done everything, to stand. Stand firm then, with the belt of truth buckled around your waist, with the breastplate of righteousness in place, and with your feet fitted with the readiness that comes from the gospel of peace. In addition to all this, take up the shield of faith, with which you can extinguish all the flaming arrows of the evil one. Take the helmet of salvation and the sword of the Spirit, which is the Word of God. (Ephesians 6:13-17).

SEVERAL YEARS AGO I had the privilege of visiting the Holy Land in conjunction with a college study program. I will never forget the sight awaiting our group at the Tel Aviv airport. There were military personnel everywhere. Each soldier had a machine-gun strapped over his shoulder, a sight I would become accustomed to as we traveled throughout Israel. These soldiers were prepared for war! They were not going to be caught off guard. Their enemies are determined to this day to eliminate them. The threat is real and the danger is constant. It is a strange sight to behold and the irony cannot be overlooked.

At the Western (Wailing) Wall in Old Jerusalem, men and women are praying, while just a few yards away soldiers stand guard with their weapons at the ready, watching, alert to those who would end their time of worship with violence if given the chance.

Of course there have been other times in Israel's history when a similar scene was played out. Nehemiah instructed the builders of the wall surrounding Jerusalem to work with a tool in one hand and a sword in the other (Nehemiah (4:17). As Paul reminds us in Ephesians 6, the believer has his struggles against the forces of darkness. He would do well to be properly armed. How absurd it would be for a soldier to go out into the field minus his weapon. He would be courting disaster. The same may be said for the Christian. We dare not venture into Satan's territory without the "Sword of the Spirit." Properly armed, we are more than a match for the enemy. We are now ready for spiritual warfare.

When faced with temptation, trial, or persecution, we draw upon our knowledge of His blessed Word. The promises of God are brought forth to hold us steady in the fight.

Back to the Israeli soldier for a moment. The weapon he carries is sometimes used for offense as well as defense. So it is with those who wage spiritual warfare. I am reminded about the time when John Wesley was traveling to his next appointment when suddenly a robber accosted him and demanded his money or his life. After giving him the money, Wesley said, "Let me speak one word to you: The time may come when you will regret the course of life in which you are now engaged. Remember this: The blood of Jesus Christ cleanses from all sin" (I John 1:9). No more was said, and they parted company. Many years later, as Wesley was leaving a church where he had just finished preaching, a stranger approached him and asked him if he remembered being robbed at a certain time and place. Wesley remembered. "I was that man," said the stranger. "And that single verse you quoted was the means of a total change in my life and habits. I have long since been attending the house of God and giving attention to His Word."

The Word of God spoken. It has the ring of victory to it. It engages the enemy in the realm of the mind. Very wise indeed is the one who has committed portions of it to memory, for out of the storehouse of knowledge battles are won. "Let the word of Christ dwell in you richly, in all wisdom…" (Colossians 3:16). That was exactly the strategy employed by our Lord during His temptation experience in the wilderness of Judea. Each time He was enticed, He said, "It is written…" This is the secret to victory: letting the Word become our spokesman. While the Scriptures cannot be broken, they certainly do break the enemy's strongholds.

When Peter used his own sword in the Garden of Gethsemane he succeeded only in cutting off one man's ear. But when he used the Sword of the Spirit following Pentecost, about three thousand souls were brought under conviction. Christ, who healed Malchus' ear, healed these three thousand heart-wounds as well.

At the coronation of King Edward VI of England, three swords were brought and laid before him, emblems of his power. "Bring another," he said. "I need most of all the Sword of the Spirit." The Bible was delivered and has retained its place in subsequent coronations.

When GI's are enduring basic training, they learn all there is to know about a rifle. They learn how to disassemble and reassemble it. They clean it several times daily. They drill with it day after day. It is their constant companion—never out of their sight. It becomes a part of them—an extension of themselves. All of this is necessary and the soldier knows why. It will be his means of survival in the field.

Listen, my Christian brother-at-arms! Keep your sword sharpened and always at your side. It is much more than an emblem. It is alive and powerful. Do not let it out of your sight. Be armed and ready!

BIBLE ARITHMETIC

MATHEMATICS NEVER CAME EASY TO ME while in school. Can you identify with me? I mean I really had to work hard at it. And would you not know that a few years after graduating from high school I found myself working in a testing laboratory which meant working with mathematical formulas constantly. The various tests required accurate calculations, and I had a weakness when it came to simple arithmetic. At first I thought God was playing a cruel joke on me, but eventually this actually worked to my benefit because it forced me to depend more on Christ in everything, which enhanced my witness.

Now I know that the Bible is not a textbook on mathematics, but I also know that it has a lot to say about arithmetic. If you follow its amazing formula, it will enhance your Christian witness. Let me explain.

Addition: 2 Peter 1:5-7: "For this very reason, make every effort to *add* to your faith goodness; and to goodness, knowledge; and to knowledge, self-control; and to self-control, perseverance; and to perseverance, godliness; and to godliness, brotherly kindness; and to brotherly kindness, love."

Spiritual growth is a never-ending process and an important dynamic for all believers. It is absolutely crucial for many reasons. First, it *tones our spiritual muscles* for the stresses we find in the world. The person without a deep well of spiritual resources is apt to cave in to our culture's pressures. The Christian with a firm and growing faith will still have problems, but will also have the inner strength to handle them.

Second, spiritual growth *puts a wall around us* to protect us from sin so that we can fend off the attacks of Satan. As we grow in knowledge of God's Word, we can repel those fiery darts hurled at us.

Third, spiritual growth will help us *model Christ to others*. People today are searching for examples of godliness and our lives can become shining reflections of what God can do as He continually transforms us.

I read about a woman who grew backward. She lived in Virginia some years ago. The *Virginia Medical Monthly* carried her story: She had grown normally and had three children. Life was great until her husband died when the children were in high school. The mother doubled her devotion to the children. But at that point, something happened within her. She snapped. Whether it was the result of trauma or stress, we do not know. She changed her clothes to those of a twenty-year-old and joined in her children's parties and fun.

In a few years the children noticed that as they grew older their mother was growing younger. Psychiatrists call it "personality regression," which means a person is walking backward. Usually such people stop going backward at a certain age. But not this woman.

She slipped backward at the rate of one year for every three or four months that went forward. When she was 61 she acted like a 6-year old. Eventually she was institutionalized, where she insisted on wearing the clothes appropriate to that age. She played with toys and babbled like a child.

Then she became like a 3-year-old.; she spilled her food, crawled on the floor, and cried "Mama." Finally she went back over the line and died.

While this may be an extreme example, I do believe that if we do not fill our minds with God's Word, we too will shrink spiritually, or at best we will remain spiritual "babes."

God has willed our growth and devised a plan. This plan includes the earnest study of His Word. He wants to ADD to our lives perpetually as we expose ourselves to His truth.

Subtraction: 1 Peter 2:1-2: "Therefore, *rid* yourselves of all malice and all deceit, hypocrisy, envy, and slander of every kind. Like newborn babies, crave pure spiritual milk, so that by it you may grow up in your salvation,"

When a person becomes a Christian he often undergoes some radical life changes. This is especially true if he has had an immoral background. Through the first steps of spiritual growth and self-denial he gets rid of the large, obvious sins. But, sad to say, many believers stop there. They do not go on to eliminate the little sins that clutter the landscape of their lives. Gordon MacDonald, in his book, *Ordering Your Private World,* told of an experience in his own life that illustrates this truth. He and his wife bought the old abandoned New Hampshire farm that they named "Peace Lodge." Before they could build their country home, they had to remove the countryside of rocks and huge boulders. The spot where they envisioned their home was strewn with them. They knew it would take a lot of hard work to clear it all out. Removing the boulders went quickly, but the little rocks, that was another thing. But they got at it and when they had removed the boulders and rocks, lo and behold, there were stones and pebbles everywhere. The rocks had hidden them. This was much harder, more tedious work. But they stuck to it and there came a day when the soil was ready for planting grass.

How often have patients heard these words from their physician: "If you would just lose some weight, your condition would improve greatly." Excellent advice! Carrying excess fat contributes to a whole host of health problems. The same is true in the spiritual realm. If we want to be healthy, productive Christians, we must rid ourselves of those things that endanger and restrict us. God will not do it for us, however. His part is to bring it to our attention. Our part is to act upon His counsel. Perhaps the writer to the Hebrews had this is mind when he wrote Hebrews 12:1: "Therefore, since we are surrounded by such a great cloud of witnesses, let us throw off everything that hinders and the sin that so easily entangles, and let us run with perseverance the race marked out for us.

Multiplication: 2 Peter 1:2: "Grace and peace be yours in *abundance* through the knowledge of God and of Jesus our Lord." II Corinthian 9:10: "Now he who supplies seed to the sower and bread for food will also supply and *increase* your store of seed and will *enlarge* the harvest of your righteousness."

The Living Bible's rendering of II Peter 1:2 is worth considering at this point: *"Do you want more and more of God's kindness and peace? Then learn to know him better and better."* The more we know of God's great love, the more we will experience it personally. It will manifest itself in waves and waves of peace—a sense of security, of belonging, of care and protection. He has an abundant supply. It is His intention to supply more than enough virtue that, in turn, would spill out to enrich others. Who can measure the influence of a godly life? Only heaven will reveal how many hearts were touched as the Spirit of God flowed through His people.

Here is a young boy who, under the influence of a godly minister, became burdened for the lost. He heard about a lady who was preparing packages for the mission field. All he had was a dime. He presented it to her and breathed out a prayer that his small gift of "seed" would be planted in someone's heart and thus, bear fruit. With this single dime this kind lady purchased a gospel tract and inserted it into one of the packages. It eventually found its way into the hands of a pagan tribal chief in Burma and led to his conversion to Christ. His transformation was so real and life-changing that he felt the need to share his new found faith with as many as possible. Being a tribal chief, he had opportunity and influence, so he called together the other tribal chiefs in the area. As he shared his testimony with them, many gave their hearts to the Lord and threw away their idols. And they, in turn, began to sow the seed with their people and a great harvest of souls was swept into the kingdom of God—all because one small boy invested a dime and covered it with prayer.

Division: Acts 4:32: "All the believers were one in heart and mind. No one claimed that any of his possessions was his own, but they *shared* everything they had."

Let me share a scene with you from the life of General Gordon. He had just returned from China after a military campaign. He went as a poor man, and he came back as poor—lots of honor, but nothing more substantial. When leaving China, the emperor, out of gratitude for the services Gordon had rendered the empire, presented him with a large gold medal. When the general reached Plymouth, and saw the first copies of the English papers, he read of the famine among the silk weavers in and around Coventry. The people were starving, some were even dying, and public funds were being collected for the relief of the distress. Gordon had nothing but his gold medal, which was his most highly cherished possession; and yet he took the medal, erased the inscription, and then sent it anonymously to the treasurer of the Coventry relief fund. And so it is with all who have been truly filled with God's gracious Spirit. Generosity gushes forth, especially in the light of need. It is said there are three levels of giving: (1) because we have to (law); (2) because we ought to (obligation); (3) because we want to (grace). Spirit-filled believers are those who have moved to level three.

God's arithmetic—addition (growth), which includes subtraction (getting rid of anything which hinders), which results in multiplication (a harvest of spiritual blessings), and division (a spirit of generosity). This is the formula for abundant living. Sign up for His class today!

REFRESHING CONVERSATIONS

To pray means to relieve one's heart, to bid care begone, to breathe out misery and distress, to breathe in the pure mountain air and the energy of another world.

—PAUL WILHELMVON KEPPLER
More Joy, 1911

CLOSING THE DOOR

On the evening of that first day of the week, when the disciples were together, with the doors locked for fear of the Jews, Jesus came and stood among them and said, "Peace be with you." (John 20:19)

WHEN THE DISCIPLES LOCKED THE DOORS, Jesus knew He was sure of a welcome. He could not get their ear because of the noise and confusion that came through the open doors. CLOSING THE DOOR TO THE WORLD IS OPENING THE DOOR TO THE MASTER. We must not be afraid of shutting the door, either to the world or to fear. Both will keep us from hearing from heaven. The shut door is the best invitation for the Lord to enter.

But how difficult it is to "shut ourselves in" with Him. There are so many voices beckoning to us, so many demands made on us. Our minds are filled with concerns, uncertainties, and desires that we often cannot hear the "still small voice." Listening to God demands a quieting of the soul. We must learn to hush our bodies and minds and put ourselves in a receptive mood—one of waiting, of openness.

The story is told about a steamship company that was seeking a wireless operator. Numerous applications arrived at the stated time, awaiting their interviews. Soon the waiting room was alive with conversation. The men were so involved in idle talk that no one heard a soft series of dots and dashes coming over a loud speaker in the corner of the room. No one, that is, except for one man. Suddenly he jumped to his feet and bounded through an office door. A few minutes later he came out of the office door with a huge grin of fortune. He had received the position.

When the news reached the other applicants, cries of "unfair" rose from among them. They had not been given a chance, or had they? The message that came over the loud speaker in Morse Code stated that the first man who reported to a particular office would be given first consideration. The moral is obvious. Those who learn the art of listening receive the most.

Listening in prayer are those who really tap God's power. In all areas of life it is the quiet forces that affect most.

A moment in the morning,
Before the cares of day begin,
Before the heart's wide door is open,
For the world to enter in.
Oh, then alone with Jesus,
In the silence of the morn,
In heavenly, sweet communion,
Let your joyful day be born.

OPENING THE DOOR

Come, all you who are thirsty, come to the waters; and you who have no money, come buy and eat! Come buy wine and milk without money and without cost (Isaiah 55:1).

PRAYER IS THE BREATH OF THE SOUL, the organ by which we receive Christ into our parched and withered hearts. To pray is to let Jesus INTO our needs—to give Him permission to employ His powers to alleviate our distress—to let Him glorify His name in the midst of our anxieties.

He who gave us the privilege of prayer knows us well. He knows our frame; He remembers that we are dust. That is why He designed prayer in such a way that the most impotent can make use of it. When we pray, we open the door to Jesus. And that requires no special knowledge or skill. It is only a question of our wills. Will we give Jesus access to our needs? That is the great and fundamental question in connection with prayer.

To pray is to expose ourselves to His thoughts, goals, and purposes. God's Word is vital to our prayer life because it is the parent to all faith. The Apostle Paul believed this as attested to in his statement to the believers at Rome: "Faith comes by hearing and hearing by the word of Christ" (Romans 10:17). To live in the Word of God is to live in the faith of God. Faith comes by familiarity with the Word. How can the pray-er engage in faith-praying apart from the promises of God? Let me suggest a prayer before you begin your Bible reading: *"Dear Father, as I open your Book, I also open my heart and mind. Teach me your holy ways, O Lord, and help me to walk in your truth. In Jesus name, Amen."*

Dr. Tomas N. Carter, an ex-convict, told a thrilling story of his mother's faith. He had been wayward for many years and finally was sent to prison. On one occasion while he was there, his mother received a telegram stating that her son was dead and asking what she wanted done with the body. Carter's mother had prayed for years that he would one day be saved and become a preacher of the Gospel. Stunned at the receipt of the telegram, she immediately went to prayer, instructing other members of the family not to disturb her.

Opening the Bible, she placed the telegram beside it and began to pray, "O God, I have believed the promise you gave me in Your Word, that I would live to see Tom saved and preaching the Gospel. And now a telegram has come saying he is dead. Lord, which is true, this telegram or Your Word?"

When she rose from her knees, having definite assurance of God's answer, she wired the prison as follows: "There must be some mistake. My boy is not dead!"

And do you know what? There was a mistake. Tom Carter was alive and when he had finished his time in prison, he became a preacher, just as his mother believed. God had honored the trusting prayer of this faithful woman because she had opened the door to God's presence.

To pray is to open the door to the miraculous. "Call unto me," said the Lord through the prophet Jeremiah, "and I will answer thee, and show thee great and mighty things which thou knowest not" (Jeremiah 33:3, KJV). Again and again, in answer to believing prayer, eyes have been opened, ears unstopped, the lame made to walk again, souls set free, marriages restored, and prodigals reclaimed. Oh, who can fathom the power of willingness of Almighty God who delights to act on behalf of His dear children?

To pray is to open the door to personal change, for prayer changes the pray-er. As Habakkuk stated, "When I heard...my lips quivered at the voice...and I trembled in myself" (3:16). The answer to prayer often takes place within the seeker. Habbakuk was deeply distressed by the injustice he saw all around him and could not understand why God permitted it. He longed to see it come to an end and his enemies punished. So he took his burden to the Lord and the answer came. No, the circumstances were not altered, but he was! As he gained a new perspective of God's plan, he also gained a new confidence for the future.

If you are perplexed or frustrated, bring your difficulties to the Lord God. But as you do, be sure to search your own heart. Be open to hear from the Holy Spirit. Remember, you who pray for a change in circumstances, God may instead change your character, for He specializes in working from the inside out.

THREE WAYS TO PRAY

In the same way, the Spirit helps us in our weakness. We do not know what we ought to pray for, but the Spirit himself intercedes for us with groans that words cannot express (Romans 8:26).

THE KEY WORD in the above verse is "groan." Actually, there are three groans found in Romans 8. Creation groans, waiting for her deliverance from the curse set upon her since the Fall of mankind. Everything in creation is being more or less held back. God reigns it in until both creation and all the creatures are ready and can be released at the same moment on that grand and glorious day.

The second groan has to do with the child of God as he awaits his full deliverance as well. But we wait in eager expectation. We know that on that day we shall receive our new bodies.

The third groan has to do with the work of the Holy Spirit in our lives—our lives of faith and prayer.

Those who make a study of the art of communication tell us that we convey our feelings through the use of nonverbal skills as well as verbal. Body language, such as posture, gestures, and facial expressions, are used daily by those who wish to communicate ideas and opinions. In fact, the impact of words upon the listener ranks about 7%. The tone in which a thing is said has a 38% impact. But by far, it is body language that has the greatest effect upon the observer, accounting for the remaining 55%.

All communication has three essential components: (1) thought, (2) feelings, and (3) actions. These features are also found in prayer because, after all, prayer is essentially communication—both verbal and non-verbal. If we can convey our thoughts verbally to the Lord, it stands to reason that at times we can make use of "soul language."

Our prayers at times are deplorably cheap because we do not take the trouble to study the nature of prayer. The supreme textbook on the topic, of course, is the Bible. And in its pages we can distinguish three major types of prayer.

First, there is praying without words, as is exemplified in Psalm 109:4: "I am a man of prayer." It is almost as if the writer was telling us that his very life was synonymous with prayer. It is far better to have wordless prayer than prayerless words. Brother Lawrence wrote, "Hold yourself in prayer before God like a dumb or paralytic beggar at a rich man's gate." John Bunyan put it this way: "When you pray, rather let your heart be without words, than your words without heart."

To pray you must not simply say a prayer; you must be a prayer. Hannah is an excellent example of wordless prayer. In I Samuel 1:13, we read, "She spake in her heart; only her lips moved, but her voice was not heard" (KJV).

Second, there is prayer with words—giving verbal expressions to our praises and supplications. Once we are convinced that we are in the presence of the Holy One and that He delights in our dependence upon Him, then it is that words flow from lips and heart. Hannah Whitehall Smith wrote of this: "Every aspect of our soul is done before Him, and that a word spoken in prayer is as really spoken to Him as if our eyes could see Him and our hands could touch Him."

Third, there is prayer beyond words. It is often difficult for us to concentrate on prayer or spiritual thoughts when our bodies are wracked with pain, or when our minds are numb with grief. How comforting it is to know that the Spirit gives us aid in our praying. It is He that presents our petitions before the throne of God. Knowing the Father's will, He can articulate our request clearly and in an acceptable form, so that we can be certain that it will be heard and answered. When we do not know how to pray we must remember that the indwelling Spirit of God will take our deep inexpressible longings and present them before the Father.

A historian, in narrating the surrender of General Robert E Lee to General Ulysses Grant at Appomattox Court House, said, "Few words were spoken by General Lee and his officers. Their lips quivered with a sorrow too deep for words."

Have you not had a time when you were completely speechless? The trauma was too great; the grief too overwhelming. Perhaps it was at the side of a hospital bed or casket. You tried to talk to God about your feelings, but words just would not come. He understands. He cares. And that is why he sent the Comforter to us—to speak on our behalf and make known to the Father the aches of a broken heart. How wonderful are His compassions. How awesome His concern.

Prayer is the soul's sincere desire,
Unuttered or expressed,
The motion of a hidden fire
That trembles in the breast

Prayer is the burden of a sigh
The falling of a tear,
The upward glancing of an eye,
When none but God is near.

—J. Montgomery

PRAYING IN THE SPIRIT

And pray in the Spirit on all occasions with all kinds of prayers and requests. With this is mind, be alert and always keep on praying for all the saints (Ephesians 6:18).

But you dear friends, build yourselves up in your most holy faith and pray in the Holy Spirit (Jude 20).

WHAT IN THE WORLD does it mean to "pray in the Spirit?" This has always perplexed me. I am not sure I have the complete answer because it is such a unique and mystifying phrase, but I am going to take a stab at it. One thing is certain, it should not go unnoticed that in both of the above verses the context is spiritual warfare. "Pray in the Spirit"—as opposed to praying in the flesh, that is, with self-serving or impure motives. Realize that in this unseen warfare you will need supernatural assistance. The enemy is too strong for us to battle alone.

To pray in the Spirit has everything to do with the *attitude* that we carry with us as we approach God. To pray in the Spirit is to pray with His impulse and direction, His wisdom, His power.

What we are comes largely out of our surroundings. A swan cannot do his best in the air or an eagle in the water. Just so, the power of prayer depends largely on the element in which it works. If occasionally we deliberately push the pause button, we will help create an atmosphere that will be conducive to the Spirit's enduement. As I see it, there are five things that take place and, thereby, help define this blending of human and divine spirits.

The Spirit *creates* a prayerful heart. It is He that calls us to prayer in the first place. He beckons and we act. Why? Because we have a deep longing to reach out beyond ourselves. This desire is not innate. It comes from above.

In the second place, the Spirit *reveals* the love and helpfulness of God and encourages us to present our needs to Him. It is as if He whispers in our ear, reminding us of a passage of Scripture, such as

Zechariah 13:9: "They will call on My name, and I will answer them. I will say, 'This is my people'; And each one will say, 'The Lord is my God'" (NKJV).

Thirdly, the Spirit *suggests* the substance of our prayer. He brings to our minds the general and specific needs of others. How often has a child of God knelt in prayer with an agenda in mind, only to have a name or ministry suddenly pop into his mind? And He says, "Where did that come from?" Is it not the work of the Holy Spirit, urging us to engage in intercessory prayer?

He brings freshness, vitality, and spontaneity to our praying. Without His prompting our dialogue with God would be sterile. Whether it is spontaneous or well-thought out beforehand, the true author is the Holy Spirit.

And do not forget about how the Spirit *energizes* us. Prayer is hard work. It taxes our minds, emotions and wills. We wrestle in prayer. We engage in prayer burdens. It requires power to tear down Satan's strongholds. Somehow, when we are near exhaustion, a renewed vigor is present as the Spirit fills our being with His strength, enabling us to continue the struggle. He sustains us, giving us both the desire and the ability to persevere so that we never stop praying. We never give up because our prayers seem to go unanswered. Sometimes we are tempted to give up too quickly and easily. We are like the shy salesman who knocks once on the front door and, if no one answers right away, walks off quickly instead of waiting on the doorstep and knocking several times in the hope of rousing the householder. Jesus told us to knock tirelessly on the door of heaven. He told us to bother God, pester Him, and make a nuisance of ourselves. And it is the Spirit who will remind us of our need to persist.

Lastly, the Spirit *guides* us as we pray by calling us to prayer at crisis moments, by helping us to pray in the Father's will, and by reminding us of the promises of God.

It is impossible to overestimate the Spirit's role in prayer. We simply must have His presence. To pray in the power of the Spirit is to let the God within us speak to God above us; it is to pray with a mind filled with the thoughts of God—a voice that can utter the words of God. Prayer is hollow without Him. It is certainly devoid of power. Oh, may His divine might rest upon every believer who calls upon heaven.

GO AHEAD AND ASK!

This is the confidence we have in approaching God: that if we ask anything according to his will, he hears us. And if we know that he hears us—whatever we ask—we know that we have what we asked of him (I John 5:14,15).

ONE DAY DURING THE CIVIL WAR, an elderly gentleman sat outside the main gate to the White House in Washington, D.C. His threadbare clothes were covered with dust, and his eyes were filled with tears. A young boy saw him and stopped to ask him why he was weeping. The man answered that his son was in the Union Army and been sentenced to death for desertion. He told the boy, "I want to see the President to appeal for a pardon, but the guards won't let me in. Somehow I know if I could just see Mr. Lincoln he would understand. I have heard that he is a kind and compassionate man. I just know that if he heard the full details of my son's desertion that he would pardon him." The boy was very moved by the man's story and said, "I can take you to the President." "You?" asked the man with surprise. "Yes, he's my father and he lets me go in and out and talk with him any time I feel like it." So the little fellow took the man by the hand and marched him past the guards straight into the oval office. And, just as the boy had said, after Lincoln had heard the man's story, he did indeed pardon his son.

The believer has the same kind of access to God. He can go in and out and talk with his heavenly Father at any time. He simply takes the hand of Jesus and walks right into the presence of a kind and generous Benefactor. Believers are not beggars; they are children with certain rights, coming to the One who delights to give them what they need.

Ask for whatever you want! Some say that we should only ask for needs, not wants. Do you suppose God cannot afford more than the bare necessities? Do you think He never gives without pouring abundance like an earthly father gives to a cherished and well-pleasing child? Oh, but of course He does. Listen to what Jesus said in Matthew 7:11: "If you then, who are evil, know how to give good gifts to your children, how much more will your Father who is in heaven give good things to those who ask him."

Of course prayer must meet certain conditions. Our attitude toward others must be right (Matthew 5:23-25). We must abide in Christ (John 15:7). There must be no unconfessed sin in our lives (I John 3:21,22). We must pray in God's will and our motives must be in accord with His Word.

If these conditions are met, we can believe God for big things! He wants us to. He is a mighty God and He invites us to ask for those things that a mighty God would be honored to do. One of the most popular worship choruses of our day is, *What A Mighty God We Serve.* But to hear some pray, one would think that they do not really believe it. Someone has said, "Blessed is the man who expects nothing, for he shall never be disappointed." Whoever invented that gloomy beatitude certainly did not know the Bible. The main reason we are so impoverished is because we expect so little from God.

D. L. Moody used to relate the following true story of an experience that happened to him in 1893. At the time, he was holding his World's Fair Campaign and needed a large sum of money very badly. He knelt by his desk in his room and prayed, "Lord, You know I need $3,000 today. I must have it and I am too busy with Your work to go out and get it. Please send it to me. And I thank You that You will do just that. Amen." He then arose and went back to his work.

At the meeting that night, a young woman went to an usher and asked to see Mr. Moody. She was told that the service was about to begin and that it was an inappropriate time. Undaunted, she went to a second usher with the same result. Finally she went directly to the platform and handed Moody an envelope. He hastily pushed it into his pocket and went on with the meeting. After the service he remembered the incident and opened the envelope. He found a check for $3,000! Later he learned it had first been written for $1,000 and then changed to $2,000. Then, just before the woman left for the meeting, the Holy Spirit prompted her to tear up the check and make another one out for $3,000. That is a big answer to a big prayer to a big God!

When we ask for much it does not leave God poorer. Listen to the testimony of the Word of God: "Call unto me and I will answer thee, and show thee great and mighty things, which thou knowest not (Jeremiah 33:3, KJV). Psalm 81:10: "I am the Lord thy God, which brought thee out of the land of Egypt; open thy mouth and I will fill it" (KJV). In the New Testament, Paul expresses his belief in a God who is ready to do more for us than we sometimes dare to believe. "Now unto him that is able to do exceeding abundantly above all we ask or think, according to the power that worketh in us…" (Ephesians 3:20,KJV).

In this matter of believing prayer, our faith must always rest on the promises of God. We can bring a Bible promise and say to the Lord reverently, "Father, You said You would." If the request is scripturally the will of God, then we have every right to ask. It is not a case of twisting God's arm. We are learning to pray in the will of God and for the things that honor Him.

Abraham negotiated with God about Lot down in Sodom. God was pleased and spared Lot's family. He honored Abraham's bold prayer of faith. Abraham reminded God of His essential nature by appealing to His justice and mercy.

Moses appealed to God when he found the Israelites drunken and dancing before a golden calf, worshiping it. He said, in effect, "What will the heathen think, Lord? They'll say You couldn't keep Your promises. If You're going to blot these Israelite's name out, blot my name out as well!" So the Lord spared Israel (see Exodus 32). What audacious praying!

Moving over into the New Testament, there is the case of the Syrophonician woman who was begging for her devil-possessed daughter. Jesus said, "It would not be right to take the children's bread and give it to you Gentile dogs." The woman replied that if she was a dog, she was His dog! She would stay under the table and get the crumbs. Jesus was pleased with her persistence, so her daughter was healed, as He intended it all along.

The Lord is pleased when we have this kind of faith—bringing strong reasons why He should answer our prayers. Search the Scriptures and your heart to learn what will please God. Ask for big things. Ask in faith.

SWIFT AND CERTAIN COMMUNICATION

Call upon me in the day of trouble: I will deliver thee (Psalm 50:15, KJV)

ONE OF MY DREAMS was to have the opportunity to travel around the world visiting various mission fields. Recently that dream came true—and at little cost to me personally! In the last month I have visited over 30 countries, in Europe, Asia, Africa, Australia, and Latin America. Oh, I did not actually travel to these places bodily, but through prayer. Each day I visited a different nation, raising my heart to the throne of God on behalf of missionaries, national leaders, medical workers, and especially the lost of these lands.

Think for a moment of the marvel of modern, space-age communications. The use of satellites in space has made it possible to transmit information over great distances almost instantly. Earth-based dishes beam signals into outer space. A satellite receives the signals, amplifies them, and transmits them back to the earth. All of this is done in a matter of milliseconds.

In a similar fashion, when a believer is prompted by the Spirit to pray for someone in another land, he or she has simply to transmit that request to the Father in the name of Jesus. And out of the abundance of His riches, our great God ministers to that person's need. Distance and time mean nothing to Him. He operates outside of time and space. He is sovereign and all of natural law is subject to His divine power! As marvelous as is the working of modern communications, the simple prayer of one of God's dear children is more powerful. Hundreds of years before such communication was thought of, the Psalmist said, "The righteous cry, and the Lord heareth, and delivereth them out of all their troubles" (KJV).

Have you not read reports or heard testimonies from missionaries who have sensed during times of difficulty and stress, that someone, somewhere, was lifting their name to the Father? One such incident happened in a little hut in Africa. A missionary awoke suddenly. She had a feeling of imminent danger. Fear held her in a vise-like grip. The moon's rays shone through the window, but she could see nothing wrong. She continued to have a feeling of great danger so she woke her husband up. They talked in a whisper. Looking beside the bed, they saw a fearsome creature—a giant cobra whose head was raised, ready to strike and inject poisonous venom into their flesh. Quickly, but carefully the husband reached for his rifle and shot the cobra through its head.

But the story does not end there. One day while a friend of this missionary couple was sweeping the floor in her Canadian town, she had an irresistible urge to pray for these missionaries. She felt that they were at that very moment in great danger of some sort. So she began to lift them to the Lord for protection. And after a few moments she felt a peace sweep across her soul, as if everything was now all right. She knew that God had worked on behalf of her faraway friends.

Later, when the missionaries told her of their frightful experience, she compared the date and time of the two experiences. The peril of the missionaries and the sudden call to prayer corresponded to the minute!

What an awesome privilege it is to travel to other lands through prayer—to dare to trust God to do the impossible—to spread a map of the world before one's eyes and begin to focus in upon the nations and see them as God sees them—people with common physical and spiritual needs, people for whom His Son died, then to begin to visualize God at work, answering prayer, healing the sick, giving new courage to the downtrodden, anointing the preached Word, rescuing those in danger.

Charles H. Spurgeon is reported to have said about prayer: "Prayer pulls the rope down below and the great bell rings above in the ears of God. Some scarcely stir the bell, for they pray so languidly; others give only an occasional jerk at the rope. But he who communicates with heaven is the man who grasps the rope boldly and pulls continuously with all his might."

Our prayer ought to be, "Dear Lord, help me to yank hard and often on the rope, regardless of how distant or impossible the need may seem to be."

Today I am going to *push the pause button* on my schedule and visit India on the wings of prayer. Won't you join me on this fantastic journey?

PIT-STOP PRAYING

For thus says the Lord God, the Holy One of Israel; In returning and rest you shall be saved; in quietness and confidence shall be your strength (Isaiah 30:15, KJV)

HAVE YOU VISITED A NATIONAL PARK RECENTLY? If so, you are one of 250 million Americans who do so each year. Most people are in and out rather quickly. They are called "day-trippers." They spend an average of four and one-half hours during their visit. Think about it! Do not these amazing natural wonders deserve a little more? The Glaciers, the mighty Redwoods, the stunning waterfalls. To rush in and out of these temples of granite is a shame. How much better to linger, taking time to listen, see, and even smell the landscape—letting the beauty and grandeur sink in and reflect afresh God's majesty as revealed in mountains and rivers. Who knows? One may never venture that way again. What a pity to hurry through and miss so much.

If we are not careful, we can adopt a similar attitude toward our prayer life. We rush into the presence of God and after a few hastily said petitions, we are quickly on our way to other things. I have heard it referred to as "fast-food conversations with the Almighty." What an insult to the One who waits and longs for us to come to Him. We miss His majesty in our haste to go nowhere fast. We need time for reflection on the nature of our Father. We are in such a hurry that we do not have time to hear from Him. Consequently, our prayer times often look more like a "pit-stop" at the Daytona 500 instead of a thoughtful conversation with the lover of our souls.

Jesus did His best to teach us differently. And His example of a life of prayer was anything but a hurried endeavor. He spent long periods with His Father, pouring out His soul. He emphasized again and again the good nature of God. How can one whose knowledge of God is ever expanding treat Him so casually? May God deliver us from "drive through" spirituality.

Hebrews 5:7 tells us that during His earthly ministry, Jesus offered up both requests and supplications with "loud cries and tears" to the One who was able to save Him from death; and He was heard because of His reverent submission.

This is serious praying—the kind that demands time, energy, and effort. Our Lord prayed seriously and without ceasing. He loved His Father deeply and longed for His fellowship and strength.

So how do we pray? Constantly? Occasionally? With great effort or casually? In times of crisis only, or habitually? And what of the depth of our praying? Is it intense and heartfelt or hurried? The Apostle Paul seems to echo our Lord's approach to prayer. No short cuts for him. Listen to what he wrote to the Ephesian believers: "…praying always with all prayer and supplication in the Spirit, being watchful to this end with all perseverance and supplication for all the saints" (6:18, NKJV).

No pit-stop praying for Paul. Remember, this scripture is set within the context of spiritual warfare. The enemy is too powerful for us to handle by ourselves. The darkness is too great. No sentence praying here. This calls for wrestling, and wrestling takes time and supreme effort.

Again, in I Thessalonians 5 Paul deals with the subject of the Lord's coming. His final exhortation includes, "…pray without ceasing" (5:17). He wants their souls to be *preserved blameless* at the coming of Christ. This calls for a LIFE of prayer—which implies a commitment of time and effort.

The hymn writer, William D. Longstaff, captured the essence of the matter in stanza one and two of his hymn, Take Time to Be Holy.

Take time to be holy, Speak oft with thy Lord;
Abide in Him always and feed on His Word.
Make friends with God's children, Help those who are weak;
Forgetting in nothing His blessings to seek.

Take time to be holy, The world rushes on;
Spend much time in secret with Jesus alone,
By looking to Jesus, like Him thou shalt be;
Thy friends in thy conduct, His likeness shall see.

Those who abandon "pit-stop praying" in favor of "perpetual praying" will discover a new strength that will enable them to face each day with renewed confidence and boldness.

For some years, Rev. Andrew Murray, Sr. longed and prayed for revival in South Africa. Every Friday evening he spent several hours in prayer. The revivals of 1858 in the United States and 1859 in Northern Ireland were reported in the Dutch Reformed journals. A little book on "The Power of Prayer" was published. Prayer groups sprang up all across South Africa and revival was the main petition. Then in April 1860, a conference attended by 374 was convened at Worcester, South Africa. Representatives of 20 congregations from three denominations gathered. The main topic was revival. Andrew Murray, Sr. was moved to tears and was unable to continue his speaking assignment. He knew that God was about to do something wonderful—something that would assure him that his prayers were about to be answered.

His son, Andrew Murray, Jr., prayed with such power that some say the conference marked the beginning of a national spiritual awakening. Fifty days after the Worcester conference, revival fires began to burn. In Montague, near Worcester, a prayer revival began in the Methodist Church. Prayer meetings were held every night, and on Monday, Wednesday, and Friday mornings, sometimes as early as 3 a.m., people who had never prayed before began to cry out to God for mercy and continued until midnight. As Dutch Reformed people left their prayer meetings, they crowded into the Methodist Church.

For weeks, the village of Montague experienced great conviction of sin. Strong, self reliant men cried out to God in anguish. Six prayer meetings were going on throughout the village. The report reached Worcester, and prayer meetings began there as well. Whole families, both European and native African, were humbled before God.

One Sunday evening during the youth fellowship meeting, an African servant girl arose and asked permission to sing a verse and pray. The Holy Spirit fell upon the group as she prayed. In the distance there came a sound like approaching thunder. It surrounded the hall and the building began to shake. Instantly everyone burst into prayer. The assistant minister knelt at the table. Andrew Murray had been speaking in the main sanctuary to those assembled there. He was notified and came running. Murray called in a loud voice, "I am your minister, sent from God. Silence!" No one noticed as all continued calling out loudly to God for forgiveness. Murray asked his assistant to sing a hymn, but the praying continued undiminished.

All week long the prayer meetings were held. Each service began with profound silence. But as soon as several prayers had arisen the place was shaken as before and the whole company of people engaged in petition to the throne of grace. The meetings often continued until 3 a.m., and as the people reluctantly dispersed, they went singing their way down the streets.

Services were moved to a larger building because of the crowds. On Saturday, Andrew Murray led the prayer meeting. As he prayed, once again the mysterious sound of thunder approached from a distance, coming nearer until it enveloped the building. And again, everyone broke out in simultaneous prayer.

Murray walked up and down the aisle trying to quiet the people, but a stranger in the service tiptoed up to him and whispered, "Be careful what you do, for it is the Spirit of God that is at work here." Murray learned to accept the revival praying. As many as 20 found the Lord in one service. Mrs. Murray wrote, "We do feel and realize the power and presence of God so mightily. His Spirit is indeed poured out on us."

The South African revival then scattered like buckshot and spread to other areas. One pastor reported something of "the glory of the church in the first century." Prayer meetings multiplied. Many Christians met each week in prayer groups of three to four. Some churches could not hold all who came to worship. Spiritual awakening came to places up to 200 miles away.

It all began because one man took the time to call upon God unceasingly for revival. A movement of God like unto this can spring up anywhere and, in fact, has from time to time, if and when godly people seek the Lord with all their hearts.

THE FAITH OF A CHILD

AN INCIDENT TOOK PLACE SEVERAL YEARS AGO that left an indelible impression on my mind. I had performed a monologue during the Advent season, portraying a shepherd who had come forward through time to share his experiences on that holy night. Following the service I stood in the narthex, dressed in my shepherd garb, with staff in hand, greeting folks as they exited the sanctuary. I felt someone tugging on my robe and looked down to see a little boy of about four years old. I said, "Yes, young man, may I help you?" He looked up at me with huge black eyes and answered, "Excuse me, sir. Are you God?" I assured him that I was only a lowly shepherd and he responded, "Oh." And off he went. I pondered that moment for some time. I wonder what he would have said if I had answered in the affirmative.

I have always admired the simple faith of children. They are so trusting, so open, and so quick to believe. They stand in front of us with wide-open eyes; they let us look freely into their little souls. As long as we let them be children, they will tell us right away what they feel. They always reveal what is in their hearts. Certainly Jesus had these qualities in mind when he told his disciples that unless they had the faith of a child, they would not be able to enter the kingdom of God. The disciples were often un-child-like. They wanted to learn from Jesus, but they were still not of a child-like spirit. They were all about wanting to know who would be the greatest in the kingdom of God. The only spirit Jesus acknowledges is the child-like spirit.

Who has not marveled as a child expressed his wonder at the love of God? A mother in New England was helping pack a box to be sent to India. Her son, aged four, insisted on putting in something all his own, a little leaflet entitled "Come to Jesus." His name was written on it with a little prayer, "May the one who gets this soon learn to love Jesus." When the child's leaflet reached India, it was given to a Hindu priest who was teaching some missionaries the language. He took it without looking at it, but on his way back to his home he thought of the leaflet, took it out, and read the writing on the outside.

The child's prayer so touched him that he was then eager to read further. He soon gave up his idols and became a devoted missionary to his own people. Fifteen years after that, American missionaries visited his village, and there found this converted Hindu priest with a congregation of 1,500 people who had learned to love Jesus as their Savior—all because of the influence of a simple child's prayer and the leaflet that it was written on.

Ann Landers relates some humorous incidents concerning her children and prayer. When her twin daughters were young, she taught them to say the Lord's Prayer before going to sleep. As she listened outside their door, she could hear them say, "Give us this steak and daily bread, and forgive us our mattresses." She and her husband had a good laugh over this. It was over fifty years ago, but the memory still remained in their hearts.

When Ann was a child, she learned this same prayer and in her little mind she prayed this way: "Our Father, who art in heaven, Howard be thy name." And for a little while she actually thought that was God's name. And her mother spent her early childhood saying, "Hail Mary, full of grapes..." Chuckle as we may, not all childhood prayers are this shallow. Let me illustrate.

One November day in England, a minister was telling his two boys, one five and the other eight, about a lady who had been their governess and how the Lord had called her to the mission field. She had gone to Ceylon to take the gospel to a people who had never heard it before. He told of some of the hardships which she had to undergo, of the roof which let the rain through during the long wet season, of the spiders and insects that invaded the house, and of the poisonous snakes which sometimes made it unsafe to venture out of doors.

To the oldest boy the adventurous nature of this calling appealed most. But to little Fred, the thought of all she had to endure troubled him. That night as he knelt down beside his bed to pray, his father heard him say, "God bless my dear father and mother and make me good, for Jesus' sake" Then in a voice which quivered with emotion, little Fred added, "And, oh, please dear God, take care of my Miss Price and keep her safe from the snakes. Amen." Then the little five-year-old went to bed and the minister, with moist eyes, went to his evening service and preached on "The Power of Prayer" with more conviction than ever before.

And now for the rest of the story. Far away in Ceylon, the missionary was returning to her home when suddenly, right across her path, was a small but extremely dangerous snake—the neck and head raised and arched, its eyes gleaming with a malignant fire, ready to strike. To escape seemed impossible and for one terrible moment she stood as still as a statue, in fear for her life. Then to her astonishment, the snake, for no apparent reason, turned around in the opposite direction and slithered off into the brush. With a prayer of thanksgiving, the tired missionary reached her home as fast as her trembling legs would take her.

When the mail came, among her piles of letters was one from her English pastor. As she read it, her eyes quickly fell down to the postscript..."Little Fred never forgets to pray for you. And he is very specific in regard to your safety. For example, two Sundays ago I overheard him lifting your name to God in simple faith, asking Him to keep the snakes from causing you harm."

Miss Price read that postscript over and over again and her eyes were dim as she laid the letter down. Yes, the encounter with the snake was the very same time as Fred's prayer. Now she understood, and with new meaning she read the text hanging over her couch: "Before they call, I will answer; and while they are yet speaking, I will hear" (Isaiah 65:24).

If a lesson is to be gained from this story, it is simply this: Never underestimate the power of a prayer that is offered by a child in simple faith. Perhaps our Father bends a little lower to carefully listen to a child's request. Perhaps He will even listen in this manner to an adult whose attitude is child-like.

THE ART OF LISTENING

Very early in the morning, while it was still dark, Jesus got up, left the house and went off to a solitary place, where he prayed (Mark 1:35)

PARTICIPATION IN ATHLETICS HAS ITS BENEFITS. I learned many valuable lessons from my high school basketball coach. Among those was one I cherish greatly, namely, the art of listening. In one of our first practice sessions, Coach made several things very clear in relationship to a "time out." He said there would be four times when a time out would be called. First, when the opponent called for it, second, when he signaled it, third, when an official decided it was necessary, and fourth, when a player asked for it due to an injury or tiredness. The correlation between these respites and personal devotional life is intriguing. Let us examine them.

Coach went on to say that when we heard the referee's whistle blow signaling a time out, we were to hustle to the sideline where he stood. Then he said we were to focus in on him and what he had to say—no talking, no looking around. We were to fix our gaze intently on him, for what he was about to say might well determine the outcome of the game—whether we would win or lose. When a comparison is made between the "time out" and a time alone with God, several truths emerge.

First and foremost, there is the issue of rest—physical rest. Catching one's breath rejuvenates the body—to get our second wind. The world seems rushed. Are you? Do you speed to work or appointments? Do you get less than eight hours of sleep a night? Do you skip breakfast? And when the stoplight turns yellow, do you want to scream? A "Yes" to these questions means you may have "Hurry Sickness." What is "Hurry Sickness?" It is a term that was created over 40 years ago by a cardiologist who noticed that all his heart disease patients rushed through life. What we are talking about here is stress overload. Advances in technology have made life move quickly. The long term effects of Hurry Sickness can lead to heart attacks, depression, a depleted immune system, digestive problems, migraines and insomnia. Physicians recommend that we slow down our day, schedule periodic down times where we are not in constant motion.

When we take time to pause from life's hurried pace and get alone with God, it is like a rest of the soul. We breathe in the oxygen of His Word and our spiritual stamina is restored. If we fail to discipline ourselves in this area we are going to suffer a different kind of heart problem.

Second, time outs provide a time of teaching and correction. Coach told us where we were failing or succeeding. It was a reminder of what we went over in practice. Sometimes it was his way of praising and encouraging us. Is this not exactly what the Lord does in our private times with Him? He speaks to our soul and invites us to make a course correction. Or perhaps we receive a "boost" from His Word.

Third, on occasion Coach would make a substitute. To be yanked from the starting lineup was never pleasant, but he was in charge and we all understood that. I believe that there are times when God sees to it that we get the rest we need. It is part of the disciplining hand of God that the writer to Hebrews mentions. It is always motivated by love. Sometimes Coach would call us to sit by him so that he could remind us of our strategy or to thank us for our effort. Can you relate? Do you understand how valuable these moments with God are? Personal attention, investment of time and energy—all on our behalf.

Fourth, communication was paramount. After we received Coach's instructions, he would always ask, "Any questions?" If anything was unclear, he would try his best to make sure we understood.

Listening was the key. I can remember specific "time outs" when Coach would say, "Didn't you hear what I said?" Sometimes we heard it all right, but decided to do it our way. And even if we won the game, the coach was not happy because he felt that the next time we would likely flounder. When the Lord speaks to us, we need to listen carefully and carry out His Word to us. As the hymn writer put it, *Trust and obey, for there's no other way, to be happy in Jesus, but to trust and obey.*

In the game of life "time outs" are essential. Our Lord Jesus put a premium on His time with His heavenly Father. He would get up very early in the morning and find some spot where He could commune with Him. If this was a priority in His life, should it be any less in ours? His defeat of the Foe and succeeding victory at Calvary were in large part due to the times He spent in earnest prayer.

> O the pure delight of a single hour
> That before Thy throne I spend,
> When I kneel in prayer and with Thee, my God
> I commune as friend with friend.
>
> Draw me nearer, nearer, blessed Lord,
> To the cross where Thou has died;
> Draw me nearer, nearer, nearer, blessed Lord,
> To Thy precious bleeding side.
>
> —Fanny Crosby

THE INVIGORATING SENSE OF HIS PRESENCE

The knowledge that God is present is blessed, but to feel His presence is nothing less than sheer happiness.

—Dr. Allen Fleece

THE WHEREVER GOD

Where can I go from your Spirit? Where can I flee from your presence? If I go up to the heavens, you are there; if I make my bed in the depths, you are there. If I rise on the wings of the dawn, if I settle on the far side of the sea, even there your hand will guide me, your right hand will hold me fast (Psalm 139:7-10).

THEY SAT IN A DAYROOM—patient and pastor—in a local hospital for emotionally disturbed people, trying to enjoy as much privacy as you can in a place like that. The young lady kept glancing around the room until finally the minister asked her why she was doing this. She said even though she knew the videotape cameras were in special, smaller rooms, wherever she was she felt the cold stare of those cameras. "Just like God—always looking at you," she said.

It makes one think of the psalmist, who in a place far away and a time long ago, felt the presence of God. Not the presence of a cold camera's stare, but the warm presence of a Person with an arm outstretched, pointing the way, and a right hand to steady.

It was not that he wanted to flee from God's presence that he wrote, "Where can I go from your Spirit?" or, "where can I flee from your presence?" It was a rhetorical question. Or was it? Was there some urge deep within him, a thought that gave birth to the words that produced a flight away from the God he wrote the song to praise? We know because we flee from this presence with regularity.

To us the flight from God's presence may really be our avoidance of a God who is trying to say something to us. Neither this psalmist nor any other biblical writer has prepared a list of God's channels of communication. The natural variety of the psalmist's experiences with God produces the beginning of the list and nudges our memories with stories from Eden to Patmos where God has sought—and sometimes found—a way to communicate himself. He got through to Elijah not in the wind of fire or earthquake, but in the still, small voice. A cross was God's way once. At Pentecost He did come in the wind, and on the road to Damascus He came in a blinding light and a fall to earth.

One thing is certain—whatever else we know of God, we know that He is everywhere trying to communicate with us. But we are often to busy or too engrossed in the affairs of life to notice. Surely there can be no greater moment in one's life than to pause long enough to sense His real presence, than to bask in the light of His countenance.

But take heart, my fellow traveler. God makes Himself known as He will—sometimes through a musically inferior gospel chorus badly sung on the radio on a lonely drive. I have heard Him in a provocative lecture by a skilled scholar and in a half-sentence of penetrating insight in another lecture from whose dullness I had yearned only a few moments before to be delivered.

It has to be God who speaks through the embrace of an eleven-year-old girl after I have preached what I believed to be a horrible sermon that fell on deaf ears. The words spoken by her were surely from the Lord: "I love you pastor and I will never forget you."

And who else is it but God in the spouse who listens patiently about the impossible demands of the ministry—who lovingly lets you cry or withdraw? Is it not God who reveals himself in the cool, spring air and in the stark beauty of the monochrome painting on the wall behind the branch manager at the bank? And what of that time when in a lonely motel room you pick up a Gideon Bible and your eyes fell on a passage that made your heart race with excitement and delight?

He speaks...wherever...whenever...however. And, as C. Austin Miles put it, *He speaks and the sound of His voice is so sweet the birds hush their singing; and the melody that He gave to me within my heart is ringing.* Even in the winter of life, you can hear some birds if you pause long enough to listen.

EMBRACED BY GOD

The eternal God is thy refuge, and underneath are the everlasting arms (Deuteronomy 33:27, KJV)

DO YOU REMEMBER GRIMM'S FAIRY TALES? One of them, called *The Princess and the Frog*, can be summarized thusly: A prince, having fallen under the curse of a witch, was changed into a frog. He could not become a prince again until a certain princess took him home and shared her home with him. Each day the frog sat by a spring in the forest until one day the princess came near, tossed a golden ball into the air and it fell into the depths of the pool. She found it impossible to retrieve it so the frog made a deal with her. He would get the ball if she would take him home with her. She hastily agreed. So the frog fetched the ball for her and in her excitement she dashed happily home, forgetting her promise to the frog. As the story turns out, she finally kept faith with the frog after her father and the frog persisted in their efforts to persuade her.

Most of us, I think, are inclined to criticize the princess for lapsing in her promise to the frog. But we know something that she does not—that the slimy, green croaker, is in fact, a handsome prince! To her the frog was merely a frog. The thought of the little beast eating at the same table with her caused each bite of food to stick in her throat.

Who of us would have reacted differently? It is hard to embrace the unlovely: not simply a frog, but perhaps a spouse in an ugly mood, or a defiant child, or a fellow employee with a bad attitude—let alone the sick and dying of our world. One cannot help but be impressed when reading the Gospels to see how Jesus responded to the unlovely. Rather than avoiding them, He *embraced* them. And this is not a fairy tale! Such acts of love spoke dramatically with the people of His day, and they also contributed, in a large extent, to His death.

In the Gospels I see three such embraces of our Lord that are particularly worthy of note. The first embrace has to do with the Master and His relationship with children. In Mark 10:13-16, Jesus became indignant when He saw how children were treated. He wanted to make a statement so He took some children in His arms and blessed them—in the presence of not only His disciples, but Jewish religious leaders as well! This act of embracing children represented His concern for those who had not yet arrived. Children were not viewed with much affection in His day. Politicians did not seek votes by kissing babies. In fact, the rabbis considered children to be in the same category as women—members of the people of God by virtue of their association with adult males. A male child was not even granted full status in the synagogue until he was thirteen. A female child never achieved this status. One would have to search long and hard in Jesus' time to find any benevolence toward the young comparable to Jesus' embracing and blessing

But, lest we become too critical of the Jews, we would do well to consider the modern view of children. W.C. Fields is said to have once remarked sarcastically, "Anyone who hates children and dogs can't be that bad." Just look at our treatment of the little ones in twenty-first century America: child pornography, child abandonment, child physical and sexual abuse, latch-key kids, drugs available in elementary schools, permissive parents, divorce's impact, and on and on it goes.

Notice how Jesus took their side. More than that, He declared them models of the kingdom of God because they had nothing to show for themselves and were most likely to receive God's kingdom as a gift of grace.

The second embrace of Jesus is found in Mark 1:40-42. This incident has to do with outcasts. Jesus' willingness to touch the leper made Him a marked man. Josephus and some of the rabbis referred to a leper as a "living corpse."

They were considered unclean, untouchable. The Jews despised them, feared them, and said that if they were cured it would be as great a miracle as raising the dead.

It is hard for us to fully appreciate what the lepers experienced. We live in a society that, for the most part, institutionalizes the outcast, i.e., the insane, defamed, and impaired. When Jesus reached out and put His hands on the leper, the Jews found it very offensive. The normal reaction when approached by a leper was to spit on him, stone him, and curse him. But Jesus went further than a touch. He said, "Be clean." That act did more than heal a physical ailment. It made it possible for one who had to abandon his clothes, home, hygiene, family, and friends—in short, one who had been banished to non-existence—to return to himself, to society, and to God.

Our Lord is still reaching out to the outcasts of this world—through the hands of those who bear His name and His compassion, embracing them. Mary Slessor, a missionary to West Africa, was the first female vice consul of the British Empire. She was born and raised in the Scottish slums, one of nine children. Her life was difficult to say the least. Her father was an abusive alcoholic; poverty and pain were her constant companion as a child. But her mother prayed daily that one of her children would become a missionary. She would read missionary stories to her children, filling their minds with accounts of faith, victory, and God's power to change the human heart.

When Mary Slessor finally reached the shores of West Africa, her eyes beheld suffering as she had never seen. She went to work immediately, ministering to the natives—teaching them to read and work with their hands, all the while preaching the gospel and nursing in a place filled with pain and disease. She personally rescued hundreds of women and children thrown half-dead into the jungle. Rarely did she have fewer than a dozen children at a time living with her—truly a remarkable woman who had been embraced by God, and now allowed her hands and arms to be used by God to enfold others.

The third embrace of Jesus is plainly seen at Calvary. It is His strongest because He embraced the whole world. Peter writes, "He bore our sins in his body on the cross, that we might die to sin and live to righteousness; for by his wounds you were healed" (I Peter 2:24). There is no record in all of history of a nobleman suffering the penalty of crucifixion. This was reserved for the vilest of criminals. And yet the King of kings and Lord of lords submitted to it for our benefit. Oh, how great the embrace of the cross!

He endured the cross for the same reason that He embraced the outcast and the downcast—love compelled Him. And it was because of the cross that God is enabled to embrace sinners. Those of us who were once afar off were brought near to God by the blood of the Lamb. It is His righteousness that makes us acceptable to God. Have you not felt His embrace—the embrace of Calvary? Have you felt His powerful, and yet tender arms about you? That is where it all begins. All other embraces are a reflection of this one divine and glorious clasp.

Not long ago a newspaper carried an unusual headline. It read, "TEST TAKES RISK OUT OF DYEING." Of course it was speaking of dyeing hair. The expert on feminine beauty said that a woman should make a strand test of her hair before dyeing all of it. That makes sense, but it was the headline that attracted all of the attention. Is not it wonderful to realize that the risk was taken out of DYING long ago at Calvary? When we embrace the cross the fear of death vanishes. We have His promise on it! 1 Corinthians 15:55-57: "Where, O death, is your victory? Where, O death, is your sting?" The sting of death is sin, and the power of sin is the law. But thanks be to God! He gives us the victory through our Lord Jesus Christ.

The strong embraces of Jesus reach out for the needy, the forgotten, and the forsaken of each generation. They extend to those whose problems surpass human abilities to solve. They remind us that God is real, that He cares, that He is present. Once we are held by God we can begin to fulfill His purposes for our lives: to be His arms reaching out to enfold the lost, the lonely, and the least. He longs to hold us that He might impart to us His grace and love—that in turn we would enfold our hurting world with His amazing compassion.

SURROUNDED!

As the mountains surround Jerusalem, so the Lord surrounds his people both now and forevermore (Psalm 125:2).

CAN YOU IMAGINE A MORE BEAUTIFUL PROMISE? It is a wonderful concept. Around the chosen city the mountains stand like sentinels, guarding, watching over its inhabitants. It is a beautiful picture of the loving concern and protection of our heavenly Father. He surrounds us—protecting, providing, even performing on our behalf, if you will.

Some years ago a poem was sent to a publisher by a GI, with a note attached which read, "My buddy wrote the enclosed lines just before he was reported missing in action."

I'm standing guard at sunset,
But I know I'm not alone;
There's another One who's watching
From His place upon a throne.
He's my Lord, my great Protector,
Who once died to make men free.
He is watching, He is guarding,
He is taking care of me.

I'm standing guard at midnight
On an island in the sea,
Far from home and all my loved ones,
But my Lord is still with me;
And the Southern Cross is gleaming
In the starry sky above,
And it serves as a reminder
Of my Lord's undying love.

I'm standing guard at sunrise,
With the dawn's bright sky above,

And I know the Lord will keep me,
Watching over me in love.
Now my watch is almost over,
But His watch shall never cease–
He has given me assurance
And an everlasting peace.

Surrounded by God! Just the thought of it is worth whatever price we might have to pay to "pause"—to take time to meditate on this astounding declaration. Although we do not know all that the psalmist had in mind when he penned these words, we can offer some assertions with a degree of certainty.

First and foremost, God is with us in our problems, our temptations, our sorrow, our loneliness. Isaiah believed it: "So, do not fear, for I am with you; do not be dismayed, for I am your God" (41:10). Years ago, a young missionary had to flee from western China. Enemies of the Gospel hotly pursued him. When he came to the bank of a river, he noticed a boat moored nearby and, without hesitation, jumped aboard. The mob, too, jumped on the boat. Then the missionary jumped into the river. The mob began to throw spears at him, but miraculously he escaped unharmed. Sometime later he was relating his story to a friend who asked him, "What Bible verse came to you as you were darting in the water, trying to escape the wrath of the mob?" "Bible verse!?" he asked in astonishment. "Why the Lord Himself was with me!"

I wonder how many visitors to Westminster Abbey must be touched by reading the three sayings of John Wesley that are carved on the memorial located there?

I look on all the world as my parish.

God buries His workmen but continues His work.

The best of all, God is with us.

The last statement from above is Wesley's triumphant assertion that proceeded from his dying lips. He carried that conviction with him all of his life and right on into glory.

Secondly, God is *above* us, that is to say, over us in position as sovereign Lord, and over us in power as we deal with our enemies. Ephesians 1:20-22: "...which he exerted in Christ when he raised him from the dead and seated him at his right hand in the heavenly realms, far above all rule and authority, power and dominion, and every title that can be given, not only in the present age, but also in the one to come. And God has placed all things under his feet and appointed him to be head over everything for the church."

We rest in His authority. Comfort and peace are our constant companions when we dwell upon His majesty. We look to Him—it is the upward glance to the One seated on the throne. He is above us and that knowledge brings solace to our souls.

Thirdly, we can boldly assert that when the bottom seems to be falling out, He is *beneath* us—ready to catch us lest we perish. He is our safety net. Moses wrote about it out of his personal experience: "The eternal God is our refuge and underneath are the everlasting arms" (Deuteronomy 33:27).

When we sin, His atonement reaches us. When we are in despair, He lifts our spirits to new heights. When we have lost our song, He puts a new melody in our hearts.

Fourthly, our God is *behind* us. He is our rear guard, much the same as He was when the children of Israel were being pursued by Pharaoh's armies. They seemed to be hemmed in—the Red Sea before them and the Egyptians behind. But we are told in Exodus 14:19 that the angel of the Lord withdrew from the front and appeared in a pillar of cloud behind the fleeing Israelites. Here is the precious truth that applies to our lives: If Satan and his hordes try a sneak attack from the rear, they will encounter Almighty God! He watches our back. Do not forget that Jesus came to destroy the works of the devil (I John 3:8). Repose in His presence. Rest in His power.

And who can doubt that our God goes *before* us? I wonder how many times a child of God in the midst of uncertainty has turned to John 10:4 and read these comforting words? "When he has brought out all his own, he goes on ahead of them, and his sheep follow him because they know his voice." Wherever we are headed in life, we can be sure of this one thing: GOD IS ALREADY THERE! Nothing catches Him by surprise—no problem, assignment or failure. He goes before us.

Psalm 34:7 tells us that every believer is a God enclosed person. Hence, we can affirm the fact that He is also *around* us. "The angel of the Lord encamps around those who fear him and he delivers them." Do not pass over the word, *encamp*, quickly. Pause and consider its meaning. It is just another way of stating that God sends His angels to live among us—unseen, yet real. Oh, how wonderful to be surrounded by God! He often uses others to encircle us—friends, loved ones who support us and pray for us. Like Elisha's servant, we need to have our spiritual eyes opened that we might see the armies of heaven and the saints of earth who participate in this divine enclosure.

With us, above us, beneath us, behind us, before us, and around us. What a marvelous display of divine love! Yet the last is the best. He is *within* us—within our spirits, transforming us, making us into His image, providing the strength of character that we need to be at our best. Feast your eyes on the magnificent words of Paul in his letter to the Colossians: "That God would make known what are the riches of the glory of this mystery among the Gentiles; which is *Christ in you* (my italics), the hope of glory" (1:27)

JEHOVAH-SHAMMAH

But Moses said to God, "Who am, that I should go to Pharaoh and bring the Israelites out of Egypt?" And God said, "I will be with you." (Exodus 3:11)

IN THE OLD TESTAMENT God is revealed to us through the meaning of His names. He has seven compound names ascribed to Him which, if carefully examined, tell us a great deal about His nature and His dealings with mankind. They reveal God as meeting every need of man from his lost estate through sin to the end of his pilgrim's progress and the coming of the Lord.

First, there is *Jehovah-Jireh,* which means "the Lord will provide." Then there is *Jehovah-Rapha,* which means, "the Lord that healeth." The third compound name is *Jehovah-Nissi,* "the Lord is our banner," i.e., He is our standard, our motto, the flag under which victory is certain. The fourth alias is *Jehovah-Shalom* which means "the Lord our peace." This brings us to the fifth name, a.k.a. *Jehovah-Ra-ah,* or "the Lord my shepherd." And the sixth name for God is *Jehovah-Tsidkenu,* or "the Lord our righteousness."

Taking these first six names we learn a great deal about the character and purposes of God. He provides, heals, defeats our enemies, grants us His peace, guides us, and fills us with His righteousness. Praise be unto His glorious names!

But it is His seventh and final name that deserves special attention: *Jehovah-Shammah,* or, "the Lord is present." As wonderful as the preceding six names reveal to us, no one likes to have an absent father. Think of it this way: a dad, who provides, protects, guides, etc., but is never around leaves a child with a parental vacuum. This name, *Jehovah-Shammah,* speaks of His abiding presence with His redeemed people. One of the names given to Christ is *Emmanuel,* "God with us." It is a precious name because it brings hope to those who are hopeless. God has always wanted to live with men. He linked arms with our first parents in the Garden of Eden. He talked with Enoch and made known His righteous and holy will to Noah. He visited with Abraham under the tree. He wrestled with Jacob, conquered him and then changed his name to Israel, "a prince with God." He talked with Moses on the mountain face-to-face. He came down and dwelt with His people in the Tabernacle. He filled the Temple with His glory. He made known to Manoah and his wife that a son would be born. He, at last, came down and was born in a stable and cradled in a manger—capping it all off by revealing Himself as *Immanuel* (Matthew 1:23). The angel in his announcement to Joseph is quoting Isaiah 7:14 and 8:8.

The miracle and marvel of *Immanuel* defies description. The hands of God that had tossed solar systems into space became the hands of an infant. Later those same hands would bless and bleed for us. His promise is that He would abide with us all through life. We are enriched by His fellowship, strengthened by His presence, and led by His guidance.

Before He ascended on high, Jesus gave us the great commission and assured us in His own words of His presence, "Lo, I am with you always, even unto the end of the world."

The reality of His presence brings great comfort to the people of God. It inspires us, encourages us, and gives us the strength to carry on. In the pilgrimage of life we hear Him say, "I am with you and will watch over you wherever you go" (Genesis 28:15).

When we are weary of the journey He says, "My presence will go with you and I will give you rest" (Exodus 33:14).

He gives courage in life's many battles. "When you go to war against your enemies and see horses and chariots and an army greater than yours, do not be afraid of them, because the Lord your God, who brought you up out of Egypt, will be with you" (Deuteronomy 20:1).

And when we are face-to-face with life's trials, we hear Him say, "When you pass through the waters, I will be with you; and when you pass through the rivers, they will not sweep over you. When you walk through the fire, you will not be burned; the flames will not set you ablaze" (Isaiah 43:2).

In Kyoto, Japan, tourists can visit one of the nation's most outstanding religious sites—"The Temple of a Thousand and One Gods."

The images of the goddess worshiped there have many arms, depicting her helpfulness. A thousand is considered to be a perfect number. The reference to a thousand and one denotes infinity. It is not an uncommon sight to behold a pilgrim clapping his hands three times as he approaches the several altars. He is letting the goddess know that he is coming to worship her.

In Bangkok, Thailand, one can visit the "Sleeping Buddha." Gazing upon this vast image with its eyes closed, as if in sleep, one cannot help but think of the emptiness of paganism.

In Jaipur, the pink city of India, visitors are told that they cannot enter the temple after 9 p.m. because the god is sleeping.

Those of us who worship the God revealed in the Bible rejoice in His constant presence and availability. As Isaiah reminds us, "He neither slumbers or sleeps" (5:27). He is infinite, always present, and able to help us to the uttermost. We raise our voices in praise to *Jehovah-Shammah*."

All the way my Savior leads me;
What have I to ask beside?
Can I doubt His tender mercy,
Who through life has been my guide?
Heavenly peace, divinest comfort,
Here by faith in Him to dwell!
For I know what e'er befall me,
Jesus doeth all things well
For I know what e'er befall me,
Jesus doeth all things well

All the way my Savior leads me;
Cheers each winding path I tread,
Gives me grace for every trial,
Feeds me with the living bread:
Tho my weary steps may falter,
And my soul athirst may be,

Gushing from the Rock before me,
Lo! A spring of joy I see;
Gushing from the Rock before me,
Lo! A spring of joy I see;

All the way my Savior leads me;
Oh, the fullness of His love!
Perfect rest to me is promised
In my Father's house above:
When my spirit clothed immortal,
Wings its flight to realms of day,
This my song through endless ages:
Jesus led me all the way
This my song through endless ages:
Jesus led me all the way

—Fanny Crosby

WHEN GOD HIDES HIS FACE

How long, O LORD? Will you forget me forever? How long will you hide your face from me? How long must I wrestle with my thoughts and every day have sorrow in my heart? How long will my enemy triumph over me? Look on me and answer, O LORD my God. Give light to my eyes, or I will sleep in death; my enemies will say, "I have overcome him," and my foes will rejoice when I fall. But I trust in your unfailing love; my heart rejoices in your salvation. I will sing to the LORD, for he has been good to me (Psalm 13:1-5).

HAVE YOU EVER FELT AS THOUGH GOD HAD FORSAKEN YOU? Have you sought the will of God and found it evasive? Have you ever prayed and it seemed as though God was not listening or did not care? Have you ever come to the place in your life when you examined your heart and you honestly knew there was no unconfessed sin in your life—you knew you were sincere and willing to do God's will, yet when you turned to God for some answers it was as if He had turned His back on you and hid His face from you? If so, let me point out that David felt the same way—alone, deserted, forsaken. He cries out from the depths of his soul, "How long, O Lord? Will you forget me forever? How long will you hide your face from me?"

This is not an isolated incident. Often in the Bible God seems to hide His presence from His children. Job asked the same question in 13:24: "Why do you hide your face from me?" And, in Deuteronomy 32:20, God said concerning Israel, "I will hide my face from them." God said to Israel through the prophet Isaiah, "For a small moment I have forsaken you; but with great mercies I will gather you. In a little wrath I hid my face from you for a moment; but with everlasting kindness I will have mercy on you, says the Lord your Redeemer" 54:7,8).

It has been said that the worst thing about hell is that God has turned His face from those who are there. While it is true that hell is a horrible place due to its environment and inhabitants, by far the most painful thing about hell is the absence of God. He has eternally hidden

His face from those who dwell there. This is attested to in Psalm 34:16: "The Lord turns his face against those who do evil."

Do you recall what happened in the Garden of Eden? When Adam and Eve sinned they ran and hid themselves from the presence of God. Sin had separated them from God. That is the most horrific thing about the cross. Jesus prayed in Gethsemane, "Father, if you are willing, remove this cup of suffering from me: nevertheless not my will, but yours be done." The worst part of this cup of suffering was when the Father hid His face from His One and only beloved Son because Jesus was bearing our sins—they caused this separation.

It is easy to understand why God would hide His face from someone like Cain. He had sinned against God and killed his brother. It is understandable that God would hide His face from David because he committed adultery and murder. It also makes sense that God would hide His face from Israel because she had forsaken Him and committed spiritual adultery with strange gods.

But why does God sometimes hide His presence from His people when they are not walking in disobedience? This is the common lot of us all, is it not? We pray, we seek God through the diligent study of His Word; we follow His commands, we worship and witness; we seek to love God and our fellows. Yet for some unknown reason there are times when God seems so distant, so absent. And we cry out, "Where is God?"

If we are perfectly honest, there are times when we just do not sense the presence of God because our sensors have been short-circuited. Emotions can do that—sorrow, rejection, disappointment, failure. Pain can hide His face as well. It is not that God is absent so much as our ability to see Him is blurred. The tears of the moment keep us from recognizing His nearness, much like those of Mary Magdalene when she saw the resurrected Christ in the Garden Tomb, but did not realize who He was (John 20).

Fatigue can also contribute to the unawareness of His existence. That is when we must remember Paul's words to the Corinthian believers: "For we walk by faith and not by sight" (I Corinthians 5:7). When all is said and done we must learn to live at times without the sense of His presence for there will undoubtedly be times when God will seem to be unconcerned about our plight. The truth is, He does sometimes deliberately hide His face from us. Why? No one has all the answers when it comes to the mystery of God's dealings with men, but we can offer some reasonable suggestions.

It may be that God wants to get our attention—to restore the depth of fellowship that we once had with Him. We have gotten too busy building careers, establishing homes, chasing success, doing good deeds, pursuing an education. And the Lord says, "I wish you would spend more time with Me. I wish you would get closer to Me. Won't you push the pause button on your life? When you first joined yourself to Me, I had more of your time. Now so many things have crowded Me out of your life. I'm going to turn my face from you for a while. Perhaps you will long for My personal presence again."

Often we forget the whole purpose of the Christian life—that God might redeem to Himself a special people who will fellowship with Him. Christianity is all about relationship, not religion, ritual, or even rigor. It is about a Person, not programs or performance. When we get too busy with the cares and pursuits of life to the degree that we lose that depth of relationship with God, He may hide His face from us in order to draw us back.

Let me suggest a second reason why God would hide His reality from us. It may be that He wants us to depend on Him more. After all, what is faith if it is not dependence upon God's power and ability to meet our every need? As we journey on the Christian pathway our faith should deepen, our wisdom increase. Our talents, our personal charisma, our money, and whatever else we are leaning on, should not be seen as sufficient. They may feed and strengthen our bodies, minds, and souls, but it is the spirit within a man that only the Spirit of God can fully and adequately fill. Sometimes God withdraws so that we might understand afresh just how weak we are and how very strong He is. We are like the fellow who was sliding off the roof of a two-story house. He said, "Help me, Lord! Save me!" All of a sudden his britches caught on a nail on the roof and he said, "Never mind, Lord, I can make it on my own now."

Did you hear about the two men out in a life raft on the ocean? Their boat had sprung a leak and there they were, all by themselves, just two specks afloat on a vast sea. A storm was approaching and they were very weak from the rigors of just trying to stay afloat on the waves. They thought this was the end. One said to the other, "Do you talk to God?" The other replied, "Not since I was a little boy." "Well, one of us had better talk to God now!" said the first man. So the second man prayed, "Dear Lord, I haven't prayed in fifteen years, but if you can get us out of this mess, I promise You that I won't bother You for another fifteen."

But the truth is, God is there for us. He wants us to lean on Him every moment of every day, not just when we are in a pinch. He wants us to avail ourselves of His grace and strength. And if it means that He must appear to be absent, then so be it.

One more thought. Absence can make the heart grow fonder—not just in human relationships, but also in our kinship with God. On occasion perhaps God hides His face from us so that we might appreciate Him more. We take His blessed presence for granted. He is not obligated to be near us and yet He is closer than breath itself. A few days of hurried activity minus that time alone with God leaves us with an empty feeling, the sort of thing one experiences when separated from a beloved spouse for a few days. Oh, how we appreciate being in the company of one we dearly love again—not unlike the little fellow I observed aboard an airplane. He was flying with his father to rejoin his mother. The minor turbulence upset him and he began to cry for his "mommy." Nothing dad tried to do would comfort this little lad. At that moment only the presence of his mother would calm his troubled spirit. I am sure the reunion took care of everything.

And so it is with our heavenly Father. Sensing His nearness once again, we treasure it more with each passing day and Psalm 16:11 comes alive within us: "Thou wilt show me the path of life: in thy presence is fullness of joy; at thy right hand there are pleasures for evermore" (KJV).

SENSING THROUGH THE SENSES

In the year that King Uzziah died, I saw the Lord seated on a throne, high and exalted, and the train of his robe filled the temple. Above him were seraphs, each with six wings: With two wings they covered their faces, with two they covered their feet, and with two they were flying. And they were calling to one another: "Holy, holy, holy is the LORD Almighty; the whole earth is full of his glory." At the sound of their voices the doorposts and thresholds shook and the temple was filled with smoke. "Woe to me!" I cried. "I am ruined! For I am a man of unclean lips, and I live among a people of unclean lips, and my eyes have seen the King, the LORD Almighty." Then one of the seraphs flew to me with a live coal in his hand, which he had taken with tongs from the altar. With it he touched my mouth and said, "See, this has touched your lips; your guilt is taken away and your sin atoned for." Then I heard the voice of the Lord saying, "Whom shall I send? And who will go for us?" And I said, "Here am I. Send me!" (Isaiah 6:1-8, ASV)

THE SENSE ORGANS THAT WE HUMANS POSSESS allow us to receive outside information for evaluation and response. Aristotle classified five senses: hearing, sight, smell, taste, and touch, the last of which has a multiplicity of subdivisions, including the senses of pressure, heat, cold, contact and pain. Using these God-given organs our perception of reality, to a large extent, is perceived.

And if ever there was an experience recorded in holy writ that illustrates one person's encounter with the living God using the five sense organs, the above passage is it! Here the prophet apprehends the presence of Jehovah physically as well as spiritually, through the use of four of the five.

In verse one, Isaiah *sees* the Lord. Of course he sees with his spiritual eyes as well as his physical. He understands he is in the presence of the Holy One, the Majestic Lord of Glory. Is this a vision or reality? What does it matter? In either case, Isaiah is absorbed with the divine. He sees Him as *"the King, the Lord of hosts"* (verse 5).

In verse three, the prophet *hears* the cries of the seraphim as they shout their praises to One seated upon the throne. The words of these angelic beings only add to Isaiah's conviction that he is in the presence of the Ancient of Days. He also hears the Lord speak in verse 8 and the words are obviously directed at the prophet. God has an assignment for him. Isaiah is listening with his heart. After all, is not that the purpose of divine self-disclosure? We are saved to serve, redeemed to represent His cause, forgiven to fulfill His purposes.

In verse four, Isaiah *feels* the foundations of the Temple shake. This is an awesome environment, somewhat akin to the experience of Moses on Mount Sinai when the holy mountain quaked with the presence of God. Three of the five senses are employed and the result is humility, unworthiness, and a sense even, of unholiness on his part.

In verse seven, the prophet's mouth is *touched* with a live coal. The touch of God is the touch of purity! In that moment our Lord touched more than Isaiah's mouth. That live coal reached all the way into his soul! He is cleansed and now fit for service—to be God's spokesperson in a grander sense. He is to be God's ambassador...purity before power, godliness before gospel-preaching.

Smoke fills the Temple in verse four. This is none other than a visible concomitant of the presence of Almighty God in divine self-manifestation. When Moses met with the Lord on Mount Sinai, the mountain was "wrapped in smoke" (Exodus 19:18). In the Book of Revelation, John's vision of the temple included "smoke from the glory of God and from his power" (15:8). Though not specifically stated, one can assume that there was an *aroma* (sensor number five) present. Perhaps the seraphim hold giant censers in their hands, waving them back and forth before the Lord as they fly, shouting "Holy, holy, holy, is the Lord of hosts: the whole earth is full of his glory." It is a sweet-smelling savor, pleasing to the nostrils of the prophet, verifying the fact that this is no ordinary worship experience. God wants us to know Him in the fullness of our being—know that He is real, not abstract; personal, not indefinite; near, not distant; caring, not passive.

But this still leaves the sensation of *taste*. Although we do not have it referred to in this passage, I believe it is implied. Gaze once more at

Isaiah. Do you see that he can almost taste the aroma of God's presence? After all, the sense of smell and taste are inextricably connected. Isaiah "partakes" of the presence of God. In fact, in one sense the entire happening (sight, sound, touch, and smell) is one of taste, that is, of experience. He "absorbs" the Presence. To buttress this assertion, consider Psalm 34:8: "Taste and see that the Lord is good; blessed is the man who takes refuge in him."

Actually, there are numerous passages in the Bible that speak of the use of the senses in experiencing the real presence of God. John's introduction in his first epistle bears witness to the reality of Christ: "That which was from the beginning, which we have *heard,* which we have *seen* with our eyes, which we have looked at and our hands have *touched*—this we proclaim concerning the Word of life" (I John 1:1).

Sensing Him with our senses—using our total selves to apprehend the reality of God. He has designed us in such a way that it is possible. Praise His holy name! Oh that we would take time to open ourselves up to experience the fullness of God and then bear witness to His nearness. He dwells within our temples that he might show us His glory and that we in turn might say to Him, "Here am I, send me."

In Psalm 115:4-7, the writer compares lifeless idols with the one, true, living God. These idols "possess mouths, but cannot speak; eyes, but they cannot see; they have ears, but they cannot hear; noses, but they cannot smell; hands, but they cannot feel." In other words, they are devoid of the five senses.

And then in verse eight we read that those who made the idols and those who put their trust in these images will, in effect, be as lifeless as they are. But the child of God, who has experienced His presence, knows what an important role the senses play, psychologically and metaphorically speaking. After all, we were made in God's image and we are aware that the pages of the Bible are satiated with pictures of the Lord's use of senses. He *sees* our need, *hears* our cries, *speaks* comfort to our souls, and *touches* us where we hurt.

There are those yet today who choose to put their trust in the temporal gods of our age—the gods of science, materialism, money, and fame. But of what use are they for those whose hearts are heavy and lives are broken? Can they feel? Can they reach out and touch? Can they whisper words of reassurance and hope? O how blessed is the sure knowledge that the God of heaven comes alongside of us and His presence brings strength to our soul.

Every day the Lord Himself is near me
With a special mercy for each hour;
All my cares He fain would bear, and cheer me,
He whose name is Counselor and Pow'r.
The protection of His child and treasure
Is a charge that on Himself He laid;
"As your days, your strength shall be in measure,"
This the pledge to me He made.

—Carolina Sandrell Berg

THE DAY GOD EAVESDROPPED

Then those who feared the LORD talked with each other, and the LORD listened and heard. A scroll of remembrance was written in his presence concerning those who feared the LORD and honored his name. "They will be mine," says the LORD Almighty, "in the day when I make up my treasured possession. I will spare them, just as in compassion a man spares his son who serves him. And you will again see the distinction between the righteous and the wicked, between those who serve God and those who do not (Malachi 3:16-18).

AT THE TIME OF THE WRITING OF MALACHI, the nation of Israel had strayed far from God. Those were dark days indeed; sin abounded and unbelief prevailed. The majority of people went their own way, giving little thought to the will of God or the ways of God. They laughed at the prophets and showed utter contempt for the law of God.

But even in the midst of all this darkness God had a people—a remnant, a people who revered His name and sought to do His will. As they saw the spiritual darkness of their day, they drew closer together. There were not many of them, but they were devoted. They would meet in a secret place to encourage and cheer each other and find fellowship with one another.

What specifically went on in those meetings? Malachi tells us that they were engaged in three things: (1) they *talked with one another* about the Lord; (2) they *thought* about Him; (3) they *sang* about Him. Everything they said and did was built around the person of God Himself. In verse 16 of Malachi 3, the prophet tells us how God reacted to all of this. He gave attention to what was happening. He listened very carefully—eavesdropped—listened in on their conversation. He hushed the angels and strained to hear the words of this righteous remnant, much like a parent listening to the noises of a newborn baby in the night.

Have you ever eavesdropped on anyone, listening intently? In that darkened day, when a spiritual awakening was so needed, thanks be to

God, a few people thought about God and His nature. And as they did, the Bible says that God heard. He tuned in to their frequency. He leaned down as close as He could in order not to miss anything, for it was like sweet music to His ears.

In fact, the Lord enjoyed it so much that He had it written down in a book! He calls forth an angel to take notes on our prayers, our testimonies, our conversations. And if they center in Him, a permanent record is established.

Think about it! Kings were making edicts, but God was listening to a handful of Hebrews praising Him. Generals were barking out orders, but God was giving His ear to His people. Judges were speaking in court, handing out decisions, but the Lord was paying attention to His remnant. Politicians were making speeches, but God was not listening to them; His ears were tuned to His faithful children.

In verse 17 God is saying, "In that day when I make up my *jewels,* I am going to remember that crowd and spare them." The word jewel is the word, "segula" in Hebrew and means "God's very own special possession or treasure."

Are you one of God's *segula?* Is He paying special attention to what you say because your life is bound up in Him? The *segula* are those consecrated believers whose sole aim in life is to do the will of the Lord. How does one become a part of God's very own special possession? Let us look a little more carefully at this remnant to find the answer.

First, we are told they remained *true* to God (verse 16). The world had never known such darkness. It was not easy to remain faithful to God. Corruption was everywhere. Atheism was on every side. Filth and profanity and blasphemy were the order of the day. But this remnant said, "Let the world curse God; we will praise His name." They stood for righteousness in a wicked and perverse culture. Enduring the ridicule of family and friends, they met together regularly for worship. And God looked down on the black midnight of that age and saw a light. No, not a light, but several lights, huddled together. And as they talked about Him and thought about Him, He said, "They are going to be my special treasure."

In 1947, a professor at the University of Chicago was scheduled to teach an advanced seminar in astrophysics. At the time he was living in Wisconsin, doing research. He planned to commute twice a week for the class, even though it would be held during the harsh winter months. Registration for the seminar, however, fell far below expectations. Only two students signed up for the class. People expected the professor to cancel the course. But for the sake of these two students, he went ahead with it, traveling 100 miles round trip through back country roads in the dead of winter. His students did their assigned work. Then years later, in 1957, they both won the Nobel Prize for physics. So did the professor in 1983. For effective teachers, there is no such thing as a small class.

For our Father in heaven, there is no such thing as too small a group of believers. He bends close to give special attention to their lives. John Wesley once said, "Give me a hundred men who fear nothing but sin and desire nothing but God, and I will shake the world. I care not a straw whether they be clergymen or laymen; and such alone will overthrow the kingdom of Satan and build up the kingdom of God on earth."

Fredrick the Great was a scoffer, but his great general, Von Zealand, was a devoted Christian. One day at a gathering, the king was making coarse jokes about Christ and the whole palace was ringing with laughter. Von Zealand rose stiffly and said, "Your Majesty, you know I have not feared death. I have fought and won thirty-eight battles for you. I am an old man now and soon I will go to be with the One you are blaspheming—the very One who has redeemed me." With trembling voice King Fredrick replied, "General Von Zealand, I beg your pardon, I beg your pardon!" And the gathering quickly dispersed without a further word being uttered.

Christian courage does not go unnoticed. God in heaven sees it all. And one day the books will be opened and the attitudes and actions of God's people will be read because He has been eavesdropping on His *segula*. And then the rewards will be given.

Secondly, those who are God's special possession are known for *esteeming His name.* This simply means that when they thought about the Lord, they held Him in highest regard. They were in awe of Him. They beheld Him in His majestic splendor; they honored Him by their words and lives. They believed what the prophets had said and what their hearts told them. They remembered the mighty acts of God and looked to His Word. And as a result they visualized the Lord seated upon His throne and the heavenly hosts singing, "I will praise you, O Lord my God, with all my heart; I will glorify your name forever (Psalm 86:12). Isaiah esteemed the Lord and wrote of it in 40:28: "Do you not know? Have you not heard? The LORD is the everlasting God, the Creator of the ends of the earth. He will not grow tired or weary, and his understanding no one can fathom."

There is an interesting story about of Zacchaeus of Jericho fame. When he was well up in years he spent much time in a garden which he bought in Jericho, near the Jerusalem road. Neighbors noticed there was one tree under which Zacchaeus loved to sit and which he touched almost with reverence. A passing stranger one day asked him, "Why carest thou for the old tree?" The aged man lifted his fading eyes, and slowly came the answer: "Because from the boughs of this tree I first saw my Lord and heard His voice."

The third observation concerning this minority had to do with the fact that they spoke about God to *one another.* When they met together they did not spend time gossiping or criticizing others. They did not rehearse their problems or talk about the weather, sports, or current events. They could have, but they chose not to. The days were too grim, so they talked about spiritual matters—about the Lord that they loved. They testified, sharing His blessings and presence to one another.

Have you ever noticed how anyone who is in love will incessantly talk about that thing or person they are in love with? And furthermore, they tend to gravitate to those who share their love. God's special treasure are those who love to get together in order to share the things of God.

Here is a man who gets married. He makes plans for a honeymoon. He buys just one ticket, gives it to his bride and says, "Take off and have a good time." She answers, "But aren't you going?" He replies, "Must I do that to be married?" She is astounded. "Well, no, but I was expecting you to go along." And he answers, "Look, we got married didn't we? I just don't want to be fanatical about this whole affair!" "Well," says his bride, "I don't think it's fanatical for me to ask you to go with me on our honeymoon." The groom replies, "But I've already seen Niagara Falls; I'll go to San Francisco." To this the young bride says, "Look, people who are in love and get married ought to go places together! That's the whole purpose of marriage."

God's people are in love with Him. They love to be together with Him and with each other—to spend time talking about Him. He is the topic of their conversation. Out of these intimate gatherings faith is enlarged and hope burns bright.

What a wonder it is, to think that God bends low to hear what we have to say. It makes you want to measure your words. Psalm 66:19: "But God has surely listened and heard my voice in prayer." Psalm 18:6: "In my distress I called to the LORD; I cried to my God for help. From his temple he heard my voice, my cry came before him, into his ears."

SPIRITUAL SPECTACLES

And Elisha prayed, "O LORD, open his eyes so he may see." Then the LORD opened the servant's eyes, and he looked and saw the hills full of horses and chariots of fire all around Elisha (II Kings 6:17).

IN II KINGS, CHAPTER SIX, we have the record of the Syrian armies' attempts to capture the prophet Elisha. They had his home surrounded. His servant was terrified at the sight of this vast force. He had vision problems. He could see and yet he could not see—like someone who lost his glasses or contacts. He saw the enemy, but not the greater host of God's heavenly army, poised for battle. He could see the DANGER, but not the DELIVERANCE! His physical eyes may have been tested and declared 20/20, but he was badly in need of "spiritual spectacles."

When Jesus was asked by His disciples why He taught the crowds in parables, He answered, "This is why I speak to them in parables: Though seeing, they do not see; though hearing, they do not hear or understand. In them is fulfilled the prophecy of Isaiah: 'You will be ever hearing but never understanding; you will be ever seeing but never perceiving'" (Matthew 13:13,14).

Helen Keller once said, "I have talked with people whose eyes are full of light but who see nothing. They see nothing in the woods or sky, nothing in sports, nothing on the street. Their soul's voyage through this enchanted world is a barren waste."

The greatest and wisest men are those who see further and deeper than others. Jesus saw what blind eyes could not see. And He was therefore calm and joyful, even in the presence of agony and death.

The truest vision is the vision of faith. The world says, "Seeing is believing;" the Gospel says, "Believing is seeing." There is a great spiritual world that we have never seen with our physical eyes. The clearer sight we have of the power of heaven, the less we shall fear the troubles of earth.

There is a minnow-like fish called "Four Eyes" which makes its home in Central and South America. What is unusual about it are its large, bulging eyes. They are so situated on its head that it can spend its time cruising along the water with only the upper half of each eye above the surface. The top half has a water lens which amounts to a set of bifocals, giving him the ability to see in both the upper and lower world. That is the kind of discerning vision we should have as followers of Christ. We need to have our eyes fixed on the needs of those around us and be aware of the snares of the enemy; at the same time we should be careful to look up! John Peterson wrote a little chorus that speaks of this: "Turn your eyes upon Jesus, look full in His wonderful face. And the things of earth will grow strangely dim in the light of His glory and grace."

Elisha's servant was gazing so intently at the Syrian army that he could not see the chariots of fire! Chariots are symbols of God's power. Habakkuk referred to this in 3:8: "Were you angry with the rivers, O LORD? Was your wrath against the streams? Did you rage against the sea when you rode with your horses and your victorious chariots?" Also, Psalm 68:17 seems to buttress this symbol: "The chariots of God are tens of thousands and thousands of thousands."

Do you recall what happened to Elijah? Chariots of fire appeared when he was taken to heaven in a whirlwind. Elisha's servant represents those today who concentrate so much on problems and obstacles that they do not see the power of God. But before we are too harsh on this servant, we need to ask ourselves how we would fare in regard to faith?

- Do we see the chariots of fire when we are facing a serious health problem?
- Do we confidently trust in God when we have been slandered unjustly?
- When we are down to our last dollar, how do we react? Do we believe that God will somehow provide for us?
- When our soul is downcast, do we look up?

As I see it, Elisha's servant represents a good deal of humanity. He was so overcome by the magnitude of the problem that he failed to recognize three important truths.

First of all, please notice that Elisha's servant was blind to the *presence* and *power* of God. When we speak of the presence of God we must be careful to distinguish between the *omnipresence* of God and the *special* presence of God as Father to His children.

The Bible teaches that one of the attributes of God is His omnipresence—it fills the universe. A little girl was once asked, "Why is there but one God?" She answered, "Because His presence fills every place, and there's no room left for any other." If you look carefully at Psalm 139, you will discover that it clearly supports this girl's assertion—wherever you are, God is!

The special presence of God is promised to those who follow Jesus Christ—who know and love Him. Matthew 28:20 and Hebrews 13:5 are two examples. As someone has rightly said, "God is so big that the heavens can't contain Him and small enough to dwell within our hearts."

Elisha lived within the presence of God. That is why he was so victorious. Surrounded by the enemy, it looked as though his fate was sealed. The Syrians had come for him, but there was no terror in Elisha's face, no panic in his heart. With calmness, courage and confidence he replies, "Don't be afraid; those who are with us are more than those who are with them" (vs.16). The Apostle Paul echoed those sentiments when he wrote to the Roman believers, "If God be for us, who can be against us?"

When you feel all alone in your struggles, lift up your eyes; the hosts of heaven are all about you. See the chariots of fire! If you have eyes to see, you will feel yourself enveloped by the protecting and providing care of Almighty God.

Elisha's servant stands as ample proof that even some of God's own people do not practice the presence of God in times of stress. No doubt he believed in God, but when the time came to put his belief to a practical test, he panicked. "Oh, my lord, what shall we do?" he asked. Have you ever felt like this? You believe you are a child of God, that He takes care of people, yet perhaps there are times when you become anxious about your health, business, financial status, etc., and you allow yourself to be weighed down by causeless fears. Do not despair. Help is on the way.

The Bible is filled with examples of men and women who trusted in God's presence. Abraham left family and homeland, not knowing exactly where he was headed, but went forth because he knew God was with him. Moses led the Israelites into the wilderness because he believed that God would be with him. Nehemiah rebuilt the walls of Jerusalem despite the ridicule from his companions because he was convinced that God was going to help him.

An ocean liner left a British port during WWII and headed for a harbor in the United States. Enemy ships were everywhere. The captain was given secret directions charting the route. Added were these instructions: "Keep straight on this course. Turn aside for nothing. If you need help, send a message in code." After a few days at sea the crew spotted an enemy cruiser on the horizon. It appeared to be trailing them. The captain immediately sent a coded message: "Enemy cruiser sighted. What shall I do?" The reply came from an unseen vessel: "Keep straight on. I'm standing by." No friendly ship could be seen, but the captain kept the liner on course until it safely reached port. Within a short time a British submarine glided quietly into the same port. Although it had been out of sight, it had been present all the way.

Elisha's servant had a problem seeing the unseen Presence. He also was blind to God's *protection*. However, the prophet, although greatly outnumbered, felt as though with God one is a majority! There is a bit of humor here, for we are told that the king of Syria sent a whole army to confront one prophet. It seems as though God wants to make a point here: Greater is he that is in us than he that is in the world (I John 4:4). The odds are never in our favor from the viewpoint of the world. But let the hordes come; our God is able!

Two missionaries in Malaysia walked to a distant village for some money which had been sent to a bank for them. When they were returning to their station, darkness overtook them. They prayed and committed themselves to God. Then they lay down to sleep on a lonely hillside. Some weeks later a man came to the mission hospital for treatment. He looked intently at the missionary doctor. Finally he said, "I have seen you before." "No, I don't think we have ever met," the doctor replied. "But I know we have met before," insisted the man. "You were sleeping one night on a hillside. Several of us saw you withdraw some money from the bank. We followed you, intending to rob you when it was dark. But we could not get near you because of all the soldiers that were surrounding you." "Soldiers!" exclaimed the missionary. "There were no soldiers with us!" The bandit replied, "But there were many soldiers there. I saw them with my own eyes, and so did my companions—16 of them, with guns drawn. We simply ran away for your force was too great."

In this case, the Lord opened the eyes of unbelievers to see His power, even though they did not apprehend it. After all, it was not for their benefit, but for the protection of God's people. "The angel of the Lord encamps round about those that fear him, and delivers them" (Psalm 34:7). Look up, my friend and see the chariots of fire!

Not only was Elisha's servant blind to God's presence and protection, he was also unable to see His *provision*. The provision in this case was in the form of deliverance. Notice in verse 18 that the deliverance comes as a result of prayer: "As the enemy came down toward him, Elisha prayed to the Lord, 'Strike these people with blindness.' So he struck them with blindness, as Elisha had asked." Prayer moves the mighty hand of God. He specializes in deliverance. He delivered the Hebrews from Egyptian bondage, David from Goliath, Daniel from the lion's den, and Peter and John from prison.

In II Corinthians 4:4, Paul writes, "The god of this age has blinded the minds of the unbelievers, that the light of the gospel of Christ, who is the image of God, should not dawn on them." But Jesus came to correct our spiritual vision. He spoke of it in Luke 4:18: "The Spirit of the Lord is upon me, because he has anointed me to preach the gospel to the poor; he has sent me to heal the broken-hearted, to preach deliverance to the captives, and recovering of sight to the blind, to set at liberty them that are bruised."

The next time your heart is filled with fear, look up and see the chariots of fire! He has corrective lenses for those whose sight is limited. Don't be short-sighted. See His mighty power available for you.

The Christian's Horizon

What do I see as I look back?
Millions of mercies along life's track;
God's love shining where all was black;
That's what I see, looking back.

What do I see as I look within?
A heart by my Savior redeemed from sin;
A hope, through His grace, heaven's joys to win;
That's what I see, looking to Him.

What do I see looking forth today?
Blessings granted before I pray;
A sheltering arm, a guiding ray,
Today.

What do I see as I look on?
Burdens lifted and trials gone;
A light at even, surpassing dawn;
That's what I see, looking on.

What do I see as I look above?
God's own banner, whose name is love;
Love unspeakable, wonderful love;
That's what I see,
Above!

THE ESSENTIAL ESSENCE

Blessed are those who have learned to acclaim you, who walk in the light of your presence, O LORD (Psalm 89:15).

ADAM WAS THE FIRST TO EXPERIENCE IT—in the Garden. It must have been wonderfully fulfilling and exhilarating. It happened in the cool of the day as he walked and talked with his Creator. But after his act of disobedience, it vanished, never to appear in quite the same way again.

ABRAHAM knew of it personally, even though he lived in a pagan society—in the cradle of civilization. It is still a mystery to us. How did he come to sense it? The answer will have to wait, but one thing is certain—he carried this perception with him the rest of his life and with the passing of time he became more convinced of its reality. It should not be surprising then that he would pass it on to succeeding generations.

MOSES cried out to God for it. It was his firm conviction that unless it accompanied him, he could not go on. Oh, that this longing might truly possess us. It is the prerequisite to effective spiritual leadership and essential to biblical discipleship.

DAVID sang of it often in his Psalms. Especially in those moments when he felt the angel of death closing in on him. Many times he confessed openly that his times of personal victory were dependent on it.

ISAIAH preached and prophesied concerning it. He warned Israel that unless they sought it above all other, they would fall prey to their enemies and perish from the earth.

DANIEL was one of those rare individuals who was so committed to God that even in the face of impending doom, when he felt the lion's breath, he claimed it. The Babylonians were amazed at Daniel's determination to live in light of it.

THE DISCIPLES were not aware of it at first. They had the Second Adam in their midst. The fourth Person who communed with the three in the fiery furnace walked among them. But they were unconvinced until after the Resurrection. It was unleashed upon them in a powerful manner on the day of Pentecost. They were able to live victoriously henceforth because they were sure it was real. All, save one, were willing to die at the hands of cruel men rather than deny it.

SAUL, the "Christ-hater," was wonderfully converted and became THE APOSTLE PAUL, the "Christ-promoter." What else could explain this turn around? Was it not the absolute assurance that it is present in the lives of those who are committed to Jesus Christ?

JESUS CHRIST, the Son of God and the Son of Man, lived perfectly in its glory. Never once did the human Jesus doubt that it emanated from His heavenly Father.

SAINTS OF GOD, down through the church age have believed in its reality. They have been burned at the stake, thrown to the lions, cast into the sea, and even crucified rather than surrender their reliance upon it.

What is it, you ask? What is it that so captures the minds and hearts of men? What is it that would call forth such loyalty and devotion? Why, the answer is clear—"Presence." And not just any presence—God's presence! Angels will not suffice, cherubim are inadequate. For the child of God, this is the *essential essence.* We cannot function without it. We must have it. Or should we say, Him? Anything less will most certainly lead to failure and disappointment.

This "Presence" manifested itself in various ways—a burning bush, symbolizing God's holiness; an earthquake, indicating His awesome power; and a still small voice, demonstrating His love for a prophet who was at the end of his rope. Over and over again the Presence went before the people of God until at last it filled their hearts on the Day of the Holy Spirit's visitation in the Upper Room.

Moses was desperate for it. He knew that he could not be the leader that God expected him to be without the anointing of the Holy One. Exodus 33:12-15 confirms it: "Moses said to the Lord, 'You have been telling me, Lead these people, but you have not let me know whom you will send with me. You have said, I know you by name and you have found favor with me. If you are pleased with me, teach me your ways so I may know you and continue to find favor with you. Remember that this nation is your people.' The Lord replied, 'My Presence will go with you, and I will give you rest.' Then Moses said to him, 'If your presence does not go with us, do not send us up from here.'"

Moses was simply saying to God, "I cannot take these people into Canaan unless You personally are with me. It is too big a task. I need YOU, Lord—not Your representative." And his pleas prevailed. God said, "My Presence shall go with you, and I will give you rest." What a glorious promise! God's commands are His enabling acts because of His divine presence. The Holy Spirit is at work in us and through us to bring peace, joy, and faith, even in the midst of trying times.

In the pioneer days of our country, there was a boy whose home was situated in the backwoods. A school had been opened some miles away from where the boy lived. Part of the way to school led through a dense forest. The boy's father was a strong, brave backwoodsman. He wanted his son to grow up to be like him, so he told his son that he would have to make the journey to school alone. When the lad walked through the dense forest he always expected to meet some wild animal or Indian. With the passing of days and weeks, his fear subsided. Then, one day, late in the afternoon, he came upon a giant bear standing in front of him in the pathway. The bear reared up and growled at him. The boy stood motionless, filled with fear. He knew he could not outrun the beast. Suddenly a shot rang out and the bear fell dead at his feet. Then from the bushes the father emerged. "It's all right son. I've been with you all the time. Every morning I have followed you to school and every afternoon I have been in the shadows watching over you. I kept myself hidden because I wanted you to learn to be brave."

There are times in every person's life when danger stares him in the face. And although God's presence is unseen, it is not any less real. His promises can be trusted, as in Genesis 26:24: "Fear not for I am with thee" (KJV).

God is before me, He will be my guide,
God is behind me, no ill can betide,
God is beside me to comfort and cheer,
God is around me, so why should I fear?

There is much danger in our world today. Life is so uncertain with violence everywhere. Certainly one needs the assurance that he is not "going it alone." How much better to walk through life, convinced of the real presence of Almighty God.

THE RESTORATIVE POWER OF THE SPIRIT

This soul is enriched a hundredfold by the infusion of the Holy Spirit… for the flame of human love or active energy is substituted the intenser flame of Divine Love or Divine Energy. Rather it is not a substitution, but the higher is added to the lower.

—FRANCIS THOMPSON
Health and Holiness, 1905

GUEST OF THE SOUL

But I tell you the truth: It is for your good that I am going away. Unless I go away, the Counselor will not come to you; but if I go, I will send him to you. When he comes, he will convict the world of guilt in regard to sin and righteousness and judgment: in regard to sin, because men do not believe in me; in regard to righteousness, because I am going to the Father, where you can see me no longer; and in regard to judgment, because the prince of this world now stands condemned (John 16:7-11).

DO YOU BELIEVE IN GHOSTS? If you do, you are among a growing number of Americans who are convinced that there are spirits from another realm that operate within our own. Some folks are so caught up in this certitude that they see them everywhere! The New Age movement has spawned a revival of interest and belief in ghosts. On the other hand, there are still the materialists who chose not to believe in anything that cannot be proven in a laboratory experiment. Personally, I do believe in ghosts, chiefly because of what the Bible has to say on the subject. It is full of references to spirit beings—both good and evil. They are usually referred to as *angels* and *demons* (fallen angels). Both groups are very active in the affairs of men. Angels are ministering servants of God. Demons are anything but. They assist Satan in carrying out his evil design.

In the King James Version of the Bible we find the Third Person of the Trinity referred to as the "Holy Ghost." Perhaps those translators were right after all, for the word *ghost* in the old Saxon was the same as the word for "guest." It can certainly be said that He is the "Guest of the soul"—the Holy Guest.

He has come into the world and visits every heart, seeking admission. He may come to the soul without being asked, but He will not go in without being invited. He may be un-welcomed. He may be rejected. But He comes nevertheless. He is in the world like Noah's dove, looking for an abiding place, searching for a heart to land on. He forces Himself upon no one. He waits for the open door and the invitation. He comes gently. He comes in love. He comes on a mission of good will. He comes to exalt Jesus.

There are some things that the Spirit is not. Let me point our some erroneous ideas that many people entertain in regard to Him.

First, the Holy Spirit is not an "It." He is not just a "force," although He certainly has the capacity to cause change in our world. The Holy Spirit is a distinct Personality. The Bible tells us that He can be grieved, lied to, and even rejected. These constitute persona, not an abstract entity.

In the second place, the Spirit is not a substitute for God. He is God! God the Spirit, second Person of the blessed Trinity—coequal with God the Father and God the Son. He was there in the beginning, involved in Creation and in redemption.

Thirdly, the Holy Spirit is not imaginary, but real and relevant. We should never think that because something is invisible it is, therefore, unimportant or weak. Take air for example. Air is invisible, but it can snap a tree in two, or demolish a whole city or, put under pressure, it can bring a large truck to a screeching halt, break up concrete, and even loosen and tighten lug nuts on one's car wheels. Air. That is all, just air. You cannot see it or smell it or hold it, but it keeps us alive. If we go without it for a few minutes, we will be brain-damaged. We cannot live without it! Therefore, the inability to see the Holy Spirit does not negate His reality any more than our inability to see air.

The fourth erroneous idea floating within human minds has to do with the Spirit's work on earth. He is not passive, but active and involved. His activity is basically among two classes of people: Christians and non-Christians. His work among believers constitutes the following: maturation, guidance, sanctification, comfort, and exaltation of Christ. His work among non-Christians includes such things as conviction and revelation. In fact, the Greek word translated in John 16:8 (convict in the NIV) is *elegchein,* a legal term used in cross-examination of a witness, or a man on trial, or an opponent in a debate.

In this verse Jesus says that the Holy Spirit does three things in the world: (1) He *convicts men of sin,* or more specifically, the sin of unbelief. When the Jews crucified Jesus they did not believe they were sinning;

they believed they were doing the will of God—eliminating a blasphemer. But when the story of the crucifixion was later preached as recorded in Acts 2:37, these same men suddenly came under great conviction—the conviction that what they had participated in was the greatest crime in all human history. How does one account for this sudden change of attitude apart from the work of the Holy Spirit? It is he that gives one a sense of sin. And further, how is it that the story of a man crucified as a common criminal in far-off Palestine some 2,000 years ago, can tear at the hearts of people still today? It is the work of the Holy Spirit! (2) The Holy Spirit also *convinces men of righteousness*. He is the great persuader—convincing us that Jesus was and is exactly who He claimed to be—the Holy One—God Himself, without sin, love in all its perfection. When we become convinced of His righteousness, we then see ourselves as unrighteous in comparison. Our mouths are stopped, our eyes are opened. We can only cry out, as did the leper, "Unclean, I am unclean; oh make me clean! If thou wilt, thou canst make me clean." (3) The Spirit *convinces men of judgment*. Why do we feel that we are going to be held accountable for our attitudes and actions? Why this fear of death, of the unknown? Why should we not do what we want? How is it that we know deep down inside that we must answer for our wrongdoing? The answer to these questions is obvious: It is the work of the Holy Spirit! Ecclesiastes 12:14: "God shall bring every work into judgment, with every secret thing, whether it be good or whether it be evil." And Paul echoes this truth in Romans 14:12: "So each of us shall give account of himself to God."

The Spirit's convicting work is prompted by love. He wants us to be free of sin's entanglement, of its dire consequences. Really, when you contemplate it, why should God be concerned with us? We break His laws and crush His heart. We often ignore His Son and go our own way. We spurn His love by turning away from the cross. But all the time God the Holy Spirit keeps on trying to win our affection. Why? It is His work.

A certain salesman had been stealing from his company. He knew it was wrong, but he kept trying to block out what his conscience was saying. He began to seek pleasure nightly, going to bars, drinking, gambling, and being with other women. One night in a motel room, he was sharpening an old fashioned straight razor. He could not find anything to wipe the edge off, so he tore a page out of a Gideon Bible. His eye caught these words: "For the wages of sin is death, but the gift of God is eternal life in Christ Jesus our Lord" (Romans 6:23). Conviction struck his heart. He said to himself, "That's me. I'm dead inside. My life is meaningless and going nowhere." He read that Gideon Bible for two hours before kneeling beside the bed and surrendering his heart to Christ. He made a full confession, but was not prosecuted. Arrangements were made for him to pay back monthly what he had stolen. He began a totally new way of living. How does one account for this? Is it not the ministry of the Holy Spirit?

Yes, I believe in ghosts—especially the Holy Ghost. I believe He is still convicting, convincing and converting the hearts of men and women today. He is also active in the hearts of believers as their "Guest." That is why it is terribly important for us to pause amidst our busy lifestyles and give Him opportunities to minister to us as only He can do. He will make us more alive than we have ever been, bring strength and comfort to our weary souls. Be quick to listen and swift to obey His loving voice.

THE CLEANSING BREEZE

Now no one can look at the sun, bright as it is in the skies after the wind has swept them clean (Job 37:21).

THE PASSAGE ABOVE CONTAINS THE WORDS OF ELIHU TO JOB. There is a certain glory which is obscured by the clouds. But as soon as the wind dispels them, then the glory is seen. The above verse reminds us of one of Jesus' statements in His Sermon on the Mount: "Blessed are the pure in heart, for they shall see God." The sum total of the Christian life is love out of a pure heart (I Timothy 1:5), and the secret of prevailing prayer is to "call on the Lord out of a pure heart (II Timothy 2:22).

Who is sufficient for such purity of heart? Who is it that can move upon our souls to cleanse and purify? Is it not the Holy One Himself? He alone has the power to do for us inwardly what we find impossible—to live a holy life.

Some of our larger cities have been beset with industrial pollution problems. When the atmospheric conditions are just right, when the wind has ceased to blow and an inordinate amount of pollution spews forth from her many stacks, a warning is issued by the local media. Senior citizens and those with respiratory problems of any sort are urged to stay indoors if at all possible until the alert is lifted. Often the contamination is visible to the eye. It is a dangerous environment, to be sure. This situation can exist for hours or even days. But when a breeze begins to move through the area, the contaminants vanish and fresh air returns.

This is a beautiful picture of the work of the Holy Spirit. It is within His power to blow across a nation, church, family, or individual who is contaminated with sin. If we are willing, He can "clear the air," so to speak. That is, He can expel that within us which hinders God's work of grace. The Spirit of God can cleanse the heart and keep it pure.

The aforementioned analogy breaks down, however, at this point: No amount of action on man's part can bring the wind of God, just as there is no technology known to man to cause the wind to visit a polluted community. But, on the other hand, a yielded and seeking heart is all that is needed to call forth the Spirit's willingness and capacity.

O, how sweet is the breeze of God when it blows across a needy soul! It cleanses. It refreshes. It revitalizes. A frequently asked question is, "How can I receive the Holy Spirit's purifying presence?" No pat formula can be given because we are unique individuals and God deals with us as such. However, there are three things that we all have in common: (1) intellect, (2) emotion, and (3) will. If we are to experience the Spirit's work in our lives, our total personality must be involved—how we *think,* how we *feel,* and how we *decide.*

Our minds are important because our actions flow from our thoughts. We need the Spirit to blow across our thought patterns so that they will become like His—pure, resolute, and positive.

The emotions are important as well. We must get beyond merely intellectual conviction when it comes to our belief. The Spirit must be invited to reach down to where we feel. We are emotional beings, created in the image of God, and we have an innate need to sense the presence and reality of Almighty God.

And, of course, the will must be involved. Paul stresses the importance of the will in Romans 6:13: "Do not offer the parts of your body to sin, as instruments of wickedness, but rather offer yourselves to God, as those who have been brought from death to life; and offer the parts of your body to him as instruments of righteousness."

This is the part of our personality that no one else can control—our freedom to decide. Even God will not violate the integrity of this part of us. Nothing can alter the fact that we have the power to say "NO" to God. I was part of His grand design—that we might choose to love Him.

If we meet these conditions the Spirit will breathe on our spirits to remove any and all impurities. As we confess, God forgives. As we yield, God cleanses. As we consecrate, God fills. Our prayer ought to be...

O Lord, please blow across our spirits with refining power and filter out that which is contrary to Your will. Amen.

BLESSED PARACLETE

When the Counselor comes, whom I will send to you from the Father, he will... (John 15:26).

IN JOHN, CHAPTER 15 and following, Jesus lays upon His disciples, a good news – bad news scenario. First the bad news: He tells them that His days on earth are soon to come to an end. Well, you never saw a more distraught group of men anywhere. They had been pinning their hopes on Him and now He is bowing out? Then the good news: He consoles them by telling them that it is expedient for them that He go so that "another Comforter" may come. While they did not grasp the meaning of His words immediately, they would in time.

When Nansen, the Norwegian explorer and zoologist, started on his Artic expedition, he took with him a carrier pigeon, strong and fleet of wing; and after two years—two years in the desolation of the Artic regions, he one day wrote a tiny message and tied it under the pigeon's wing and let it loose to travel two thousand miles to Norway, and oh, what miles, what desolation—not a living creature, just ice, snow, and death. But he took the trembling bird and flung her up from the ship—up into the icy cold. She circled the ship three times and then, straight as an arrow, she shot south—one thousand miles over ice, one thousand miles over the frozen water of ocean, and at last dropped into the lap of the explorer's wife. She knew by the arrival of the bird that it was all right in the dark night of the North. So it was with the coming of the Holy Spirit, the Heavenly Dove. The post-resurrection disciples knew that Christ was alive, for His coming and His manifestation workings were proof of it. He kept His promise. The word Jesus used to describe the Holy Spirit is *paracletos,* translated "Counselor" or "Comforter." It means literally, "one called alongside to help."

On a particularly rough airplane flight, a lady became very frightened. Her face was flush; she was shaking and perspiring noticeably. One of the flight attendants, seeing her condition, immediately went to her aid. She sat with her a while and held her hand, speaking words of encouragement. Then she fetched a glass of water for her and gave her some gum to chew. After a while the turbulence subsided and the flight attendant was able to return to her other duties. The passenger was no longer shaking with fear and enjoyed the rest of the trip—all because someone came to her aid. This is what the ministry of the Holy Spirit is like in our lives. He comes alongside to help us when we are in a state of panic or hopelessness. He admonishes us, encourages us, and restores hope and faith in our lives.

Yes, the Spirit of God has come to us—come to *abide* with us, to *indwell* us, to *teach* us, to *bear witness* in and through us, to *convict the world* through us. No wonder we call Him blessed. He is here that we might listen to Him, commune with Him, be guided, taught, and strengthened by Him. That is why it is so important that we observe the occasional "intermission" in the drama of our life. It is then that He will open the eye of the soul and show the sight of Jesus wonderfully.

The Spirit's work in our lives and in the corporate body of Christ is so broad, so all-encompassing as to almost defy description. It is He that revives and restrains. We simply cannot survive without Him.

A young Italian boy knocked one day at the door of an artist's studio in Rome and when it was opened, exclaimed, "Please, madam, will you give me the master's brush?" The painter was deceased, and the boy, inflamed with a longing to be an artist, wished for the great master's brush. The lady placed the brush in the boy's hand, saying, "This is his brush; try it, my boy." With a flush of earnestness in his face, he tried, but found he could paint no better than if he used his own brush. Then the lady said to him, "You cannot paint like the great master unless you have his spirit."

So it is with those of us who bear the name of Christ. In order to carry on His work, we must have the Spirit's power. If we rely on human effort alone, we will fall far short of what He wants to do in us and through us.

Blessed Spirit, come alongside. I invite You to dwell in every room of my temple. Sweep out the corners, inhabit every place. Guide my thoughts, re-educate my conscience, and teach me how to live and love like Jesus.

When Frank Bottome penned the words to the following hymn, he succeeded in capturing the essence of the joy that abides within the heart of every child of God who meditates upon the wonder of His presence within.

Oh, spread the tidings 'round, wherever man is found,
Wherever human hearts and human woes abound;
Let every Christian tongue proclaim the joyful sound;
The Comforter has come!

The long, long night is past; the morning breaks at last;
And hushed the dreadful wail and fury of the blast,
As o'er the golden hills the day advances fast!
The Comforter has come!

Oh, boundless love divine! How shall this tongue of mine
To wondering mortals tell the matchless grace divine—
That I, a child of hell, should in His image shine!
The Comforter has come!

The Comforter has come! The Comforter has come!
The Holy Ghost from heaven, The Father's promise giv'n!
Oh, spread the tidings round. Wherever man is found:
The Comforter has come!

THE KISS OF LIFE

On the evening of that first day of the week, when the disciples were together, with the doors locked for fear of the Jews, Jesus came and stood among them and said, "Peace be with you!" After he said this, he showed them his hands and side. The disciples were overjoyed when they saw the Lord. Again Jesus said, "Peace be with you! As the Father has sent me, I am sending you." And with that he breathed on them and said, "Receive the Holy Spirit." (John 20:19-22)

SEVERAL YEARS AGO an article appeared in the newspapers describing a series of events that were astonishing. It seems that several people were rescued from the jaws of death because someone performed mouth-to-mouth resuscitation on them, for example, a boy who was accidentally electrocuted as the result of touching a bare wire at a construction site; or the man who suffered cardiac arrest in an airport terminal; or the hiker who tore an artery in his wrist on a jagged rock.

What makes these events so amazing is that in each case an off-duty physician performed CPR, the "Kiss of Life" and, in effect, saved their lives! And what makes it all the more astonishing is that it was the same doctor in each of these crises. Dr. Max Benis, of Sherman Oaks, California, an allergist who just happened to be in the right place at the right time, rescued 19 in the same manner. He performed these acts of heroism at great risk to his own career, especially in light of recent court cases that involved law suits brought against doctors for malpractice.

But as grand as the physician's deeds were, there is another One far greater called "The Great Physician." He daily performs *spiritual* CPR as He breathes upon humanity His "Kiss of Life." The Bible provides at least five examples of when God breathed out His best.

The first divine kiss appears early in the pages of holy writ. In Genesis 2:7 we read, "The Lord God formed the man from the dust of the ground, and breathed into his nostrils the breath of life; and man became a living being." The Hebrew word that is translated *soul* or *being* is *nephesh* and denotes a complete person. All of us derive our lives directly from God. Without His breath we are lifeless and incomplete.

James Kidd, a New York recluse, vanished many years ago, leaving only a hand-written will. It directed that his estate, valued at more than $200,000, be given to anyone who could prove that his soul existed. A college professor from Mount San Antonio Junior College accepted the challenge and eventually presented a foot-thick manuscript to the court of Judge Robert Myers of Phoenix, Arizona, in the summer of 1967. It was supposed to prove the existence of the soul and net the professor all that dough. Well, it was never announced how the case came out. Perhaps the judge is still reading the manuscript. In any case, as far as the existence of the soul is concerned, the matter was settled long ago—and one can read about it in Genesis, chapter one.

No doubt about it. Man is unique. He is what he is because God breathed into his nostrils the breath of life. This "breath" makes man a spiritual being. Consider Job 32:8 if you will, as a proof text: "But it is the spirit in a man, the breath of the Almighty that gives him understanding." We are far more than an animal. God imparted his moral, intellectual, and creative self into us when He breathed into our nostrils. We are made in His image.

John Bishop tells of a man riding his bicycle along the shores of a lake when he heard a boy screaming for help. He was thrashing helplessly in the water, about to drown. So the man swam out and brought him to the beach where for ten minutes he gave him CPR—the "Kiss of Life." When the boy revived, he looked up into the face of his rescuer and said, "Thank you sir, for saving my life." And the man responded, "That's all right, son, just live your life as though it was worth saving." Not bad advice for all of us. In creation God planted His kiss upon us. He had great plans for us. And now it is incumbent upon us to live as though we were worth creating.

The second example of divine exhalation has to do with the inspiration of the Bible. In Paul's second letter to Timothy he wrote, "All scripture is God-breathed" (3:16). And Peter, in his second epistle, wrote, "...men of God spoke from God as they were carried along by the Holy Spirit" (1:21). God breathed out His thoughts upon the minds, hearts, and personalities of certain godly men to give us the Scriptures.

Here is a family living in Michigan. A son grows up and moves to California. Once a month his mother writes him a long letter, revealing the things that are happening at home, as well as the thoughts of her own heart. She tells of the sickness in his family, the death of a neighbor, the birth of a new baby, and the wedding of friends. We call this "human revelation." When God wanted to send a message to His human family, He breathed on holy men of old (prophets and apostles) and inspired them to write it down for all generations. This is called "divine revelation." God revealed how the world was made and then He put His own great thoughts in the Book as well. Thank God for His "kiss of life" upon these men of old. The Bible tells the history of mankind and the story of the Babe who was born to die. It tells of a man's sin and God's great love for sinners. It tells of a man's power of choice and his opportunity for salvation. It tells us about heaven and hell and how to enter one and avoid the other. It tells us how to treat one another. What a marvelous Book! What a glorious message! And no wonder. It is God-breathed, the product of His great heart.

The third kiss of life occurred when Jesus Christ, the Lord of glory, breathed His last breath. Luke recorded it in 23:46: "And when Jesus had cried out with a loud voice, he said, 'Father, into your hands I commit My spirit.' Having said this, he breathed His last." His mission was accomplished. He died that we might live. He kissed the world. Was ever a kiss so loving? When Adam and Eve fell, one might say that Satan gave them the "kiss of death." But Jesus came to revive us! Praise His holy name!

The Vietnam Veteran's Memorial in Washington, D.C., is visited annually by thousands of veterans and their families. One day three men who served together in that campaign were there reading the names of their deceased comrades—56,156 names inscribed on that black stone. Suddenly their eyes fell on their own names! They had been listed as killed in action, a governmental blunder. These men had been thought dead, but were actually very much alive. Satan reckoned us spiritually dead—and, in fact, we once were, according to Ephesians 2:1-10. But

Christ has made us alive! He brought us back from a spiritual grave, from slavery to Satan, from a state of separation from God.

When Jesus told Nicodemus in John chapter 3, "You must be born again," He was telling the truth. Nicodemus was alive physically but dead within, and he knew it. All the religiosity he possessed was a poor substitute for the real thing: LIFE! He needed the breath of the Holy Spirit to fall upon his soul. And so do we. As the song writer put it, "Breath on us breath of God; fill us with life anew."

The fourth example of the "holy kiss" can be found in the Book of Acts, chapter two, when God the Father sent the Holy Spirit to descend upon the Church, the body of Christ. When he breathed upon the corporate body, everything changed. Fearful followers of Christ became bold preachers of the cross. Doubtful disciples became convinced propagators. Pentecost is synonymous with purity and power. Once breathed upon, the Church moved forward to accomplish her mission. Wise is that church today who cries out for the Spirit's empowerment.

Robert Moffat, father-in-law of David Livingstone, was leaving home for the first time. His mother asked him to promise her something. She drew his face down to hers and said, "Robert, you are going out into a wicked world. Begin every day with God." Then she kissed him, and afterwards he testified that that kiss made him a missionary. There is a spiritual analogy to that in the Church. It is the kiss of the living Christ in revival that supplies the motivation and momentum of its missionary zeal. Oh, how we need the Spirit to breathe out upon our church, our nation, and our tasks.

The fifth and last instance of heavenly exhalation has to do with the defeated believer. Paul wrote in Ephesians 5:18: "Be filled with the Spirit." He was writing to believers—those who were weak, carnal, self-centered, and defeated. Paul wrote from personal experience—that it is not enough simply to be breathed on in salvation. We need something more. We need the power of God! We need the Spirit of God to breathe on us in sanctifying power—to make our hearts pure and our witness strong. Without the power of God released in our lives we are like a soldier facing a tank with a bow and arrow. Satan, the trials of life, temptation—these, to name a few, are just too much for us to handle by ourselves. We must have divine assistance—a power that is not native to us, but available to every child of God.

A few years ago, during the Rose Parade of Pasadena, California, one of the large floats suddenly stopped. Those who attended it tried in vain to get it going again. The sponsor of the float was Standard Oil Company. Do you know what the trouble was? It was out of gas! How ironic. Not unlike a Christian who seeks to live a victorious life apart from the Spirit's enabling. When we yield to the Spirit's control, His breath will produce a new power in our lives. *Spirit of the living God, fall fresh on me,* ought to be the prayer that we voice regularly. Then we will be equipped to move forward to accomplish His will.

PROPERLY ATTIRED

I am going to send you what my Father has promised; but stay in the city until you have been clothed with power from on high (Luke 24:49)

LET ME PUT A QUESTION TO YOU. How important do you think it is to have the right clothes on? You are looking for a job, does it matter? You are in a wedding, does it make a difference? You have been invited to address a gathering of dignitaries; will they judge you by the way you are adorned? Madison Avenue would probably say, "Clothes make the man!" And a rousing cheer would arise from retailers from across the world. Andre Agassi, the legendary tennis player, used to say in his commercials, "Image is everything." Then, just how vital is wearing apparel? I suppose it depends to a large extent on the occasion. In Samuel 16:7 we read, "But the LORD said to Samuel, 'Do not consider his appearance or his height, for I have rejected him. The LORD does not look at the things that man looks at. Man looks at the outer appearance, but the LORD looks at the heart.'" This is reference, of course, to Eliab, one of David's brothers, whose appearance was stunning. Appearance is important, but we also know that before we judge a person we must look past what appears to be to see what really is.

One thing we can say with absolute certainty: WE NEED OUR HEARTS ADORNED! And this is the ministry of the Holy Spirit in the lives of believers. In Luke 24:49 the Risen Christ is addressing His disciples. He is about to ascend to His Father and has something very important to say to them. He tells them to tarry in Jerusalem and wait for the coming of the Spirit who will "clothe" them with power. Clothe! This is a vivid verb, to be sure. The Greek word for clothing is enduma, a term from which we derive our English word, "endue." The King James Version puts it, "Tarry...until ye be *endued* with power." But the word *clothed* is stronger, more striking. Let us put this word under the microscope—look at it in more detail.

First of all, notice to *whom* our Lord is speaking. He is addressing His followers! Not to pagans, not to unbelievers. He is preaching to the choir! These were believers who were listening to His words—believers who lacked something in their lives, those who needed supernatural assistance to become all that God had planned for them to be. The power we need is not found in ourselves alone. This is none other than a call to the Spirit-filled life.

The command is two-fold: They are to be His *witnesses,* but not until they have been *clothed* by the Spirit of God. Would a soldier go into battle without his helmet and weapon? Would a football player go onto the gridiron without his pads on? Would a surgeon go into the operating room minus his gown and gloves, say nothing of his specialized training? Before we can be clothed with power from on high, we must first take off and cast away the garments of self-dependence. We must rid ourselves of that which hinders God from truly transforming us into Christ's likeness. Can you imagine someone returning from work with filthy clothes, who has a dinner appointment, deciding to put that nice suit or dress right on over the dirty clothes? Of course not. The Bible has a lot to say about preparing ourselves inwardly to serve Christ. It says a great deal about *putting off* and *putting on.* For example, in Romans 13:12 we read, "Cast off the works of darkness and put on the armor of light." And then in Ephesians 4:24 and 25 Paul urges us to put away the old man and put on the new man of righteousness and holiness.

Consider the many uses of clothing. Chief among them is "concealment." The person who is clothed with the Spirit is not an exhibitionist. He is not trying to promote himself or do God's will in his own strength. On the contrary, he is aware that the Spirit's adornment is the only real power for service.

Another obvious use for clothing is *warmth.* And in a similar manner we need the warmth that only the Spirit can bring to our often cold souls. His fire consumes us—sets us ablaze within. We are often cold to the needs of others—too busy, too indifferent, too apathetic, too callous. Let the garment of the Spirit burn within us, motivating us to "renew our passion" for the lost and lonely. Cars that are kept in heated garages start faster and run better. Would not it, therefore, be prudent to daily "put on" the Spirit's enabling?—after we have dressed for the day to take time to clothe ourselves with His amazing power by looking to His Word and pleading for a fresh outpouring. If we neglect this second adornment, we could start out the door with a naked soul—susceptible to all kinds of spiritual health problems.

Clothing is also used for *protection* from the elements. There are Satanic forces that will oppose our witness. The world is at odds with the Gospel. It has never been the friend to the message of salvation. The presence of the Spirit acts as a buffer and shield against all who oppose our God! On one occasion a British subject was in danger of being unjustly thrown in prison by a foreign power. The American and British representatives wrapped the man in the flags of their respective countries and then dared the authorities to touch him. The message was simple: To assault this subject was to insult the nations that these flags represented and to invite their wrath as well. The foreign power then decided to abandon their plan. When a child of God is attacked, there is a hedge of protection placed over his spirit that no force on earth can risk tampering with.

Still another purpose for clothing is *identification*. It marks the distinction of sex, individuality, career, and ethnic background. Christians are known for how they are dressed, spiritually. They stand out. Their character shines forth. They have put on the distinctive garments of love, compassion, joy, peace, and patience. They glow with His grace.

And then it goes without saying that clothing is for *adornment*. How dull life would be if people chose their clothes with only warmth and protection in view. We want to be as attractive as we can and yet retain a degree of modesty. If we allow the Holy Spirit His rightful place in our lives, He will make our inner life more beautiful and attractive to the unbelieving world.

Lastly, it can be said that clothing is used for *authority*. We are to be clothed with power from on high. Even in worldly affairs clothing symbolizes power, as in the case of a policeman's uniform or a judge's robe. So it is in the life of the Spirit. Elisha was clothed with power when he put on Elijah's mantle. Aaron was clothed with power when he arrayed himself in his sacerdotal garments. Jesus was clothed with power and it flowed out from Him as He touched and healed those afflicted. Paul had parts of his clothing taken and people were healed and delivered from demons when they touched them.

In Deuteronomy 8:4 we are told that the clothes of the people of Israel did not wear out during the forty years of wilderness wandering. And in like manner, the Spirit's power will not diminish in our life as long as we retain Him as manager and not as guest. Do not leave home without Him!

THE BREATH OF GOD

The wind blows wherever it pleases. You hear its sound, but you cannot tell where it comes from or where it is going. So it is with everyone born of the Spirit (John 3:8).

I WENT ON A TREASURE HUNT OF SORTS THE OTHER DAY. I was sifting through the pages of the Bible, seeking to unearth as many symbols of the Breath of God as possible. To my amazement I discovered an almost endless supply—fire, water, oil, rain, rivers, the dew, the dove, and clothing, just to mention a few. Each one of these reveal a significant characteristic of the Holy Spirit's ministry in the world and in the church.

Of all the metaphors used to describe His ministry, none is more revealing than that of the wind. Simply put, wind is air moving across the earth's surface. That is exactly what the Spirit of God does—moves across this planet of ours, searching for receptive hearts. Wind may blow so slowly and gently that it can hardly be felt, like a soft breeze on a warm summer's evening. The Spirit floats quietly against an aching soul, bringing comfort and solace when it is most needed. At times the wind may blow so hard that it smashes buildings and pushes over large trees, not unlike the Holy Spirit as He moves in convicting power against a stubborn heart.

Think about that for a moment. The atmosphere is the life and breath of nature. Take it away and creation becomes one vast tomb without so much as the wind to wail over it. The Holy Spirit is the "atmosphere of the immortal realm," the life and breath of the spiritual universe. Take Him away and the moral world is left in hopeless death. The atmosphere in motion we call wind. In John 3:8 Jesus uses the wind to show the movements of the Spirit. "The wind blows wherever it pleases." It was night when our Lord had this talk with Nicodemus. Perhaps the night winds were heard sighing, giving suggestion which the Great Teacher used. "You hear the sound..." Let us take a closer look at this statement and see what we can learn from it as it applies to the wind.

First, the wind is noted for its *freedom*. It is the untamed element in nature. Rivers are confined to their channels. The ocean is bedfast. But the wind is at home on land or sea. Thus it is with the Third Person of the Trinity. He is everywhere present, as attested to by the Psalmist: "Whiter shall I go from thy Spirit?" (Psalm 139:7). Every man has felt the Spirit's convicting power as surely as he has felt the wind against his face.

Secondly, the wind is *mysterious* in its operation. "You cannot tell where it comes from or where it is going," so says Jesus to Nicodemus. The Spirit of God blows where He will, though often in answer to prayer. Just how He operates is beyond our puny minds. The mystery of His movings is further testimony to His divinity. Like the wind, we stand in awe of Him. Although we do not understand just how He works, we do see the effects of His workings in the lives that He has blown across.

Thirdly, there is the ***resistless power*** of the wind. No other element of nature dare dispute its sway. The giant oak is torn from its place in a moment and hurled skyward by a passing tornado. Cities made solid by the passing centuries are caught up and smashed like a child's toy. Here is a picture of the Holy Spirit moving sometimes as a terrible tempest and yet again in a still small voice. As He brooded over the dark, dead waters at the dawn of creation, giving life to stagnant seas, so He now hovers over the dead of humanity to quicken it to spiritual life. That power has brought millions from every nation and tongue to the foot of the cross. In Acts 2:1-13 we read about the awesome power of the Spirit as He blows in gale force upon the Church. Instead of raining destruction, He fills empty vessels with courage and vigor. His visitation blows away the chaff, producing fruit that is lasting. It was the wind of God that blew across that group of believers, transforming them from weak, uncertain, even fearful disciples to bold, secure, and certain apostles! How does one account for such a change? The answer my friend is "blowin in the wind; the answer is blowin in the wind."

Fourthly, wind cannot be *silenced*. It may rob us of a night's sleep, but we cannot hush it. So also with the Spirit. The eras of the soul are greeted by His warning voice. However, the reader is cautioned to take a warning here as well. The Holy Spirit has no alarms for the dead conscience. The spiritually deaf cannot hear His voice no matter how loud it is.

Lastly, it must be noted that the wind cannot be *aroused*. We are powerless to call it forth. Only God Himself can do it. When the Spirit's voice ceases His movements upon the human heart, it is because His message has been rejected. There is no assurance whatever that He will ever return. Genesis 6:3: "Then the LORD said, 'My Spirit will not contend with man forever.'"

God took the prophet Ezekiel to the Valley of Dry Bones. These bones represented Israel who had lost all hope. They had forgotten about God's power and ability. He was about to blow upon them anew. And the word of the Lord came to Ezekiel: "Then he said to me, Prophesy to the breath; prophesy, son of man, and say to it, This is what the Sovereign LORD says: Come from the four winds, O breath, and breathe into these slain, that they may live."

And live they did! God revived the nation of Israel. He can do the same for any people or individual who will look to Him. Oh, for a mighty outpouring of the Spirit of God today that would reach every heart—every city, town, and congregation. Let us cry to the Lord as did the prophet of old: "Come from the four winds, O Spirit, and breathe new life into our lacking hearts!"

LET'S GO FOR A WALK

If we live in the Spirit, let us also walk in the Spirit (Galatians 5:25).

WALKING HAS BECOME THE EXERCISE OF CHOICE THESE DAYS. Physicians are recommending it because of its positive effect on the cardiovascular system. It is also beneficial to those who desire to lose weight and lower their cholesterol and blood pressure.

They can be seen everywhere, these walkers—in malls, on the street, on the beach, in exercise facilities—young and old alike. Some are out for a casual stroll; others are doing a "power walk." Still others are walking as a means of postoperative therapy. And then there are those who walk just to relieve stress.

The Apostle Paul was interested in walking also, but walking of a different sort—spiritual walking. In Ephesians, chapters 4–6, his theme seems to be just that. He makes use of this word to speak of a believer's conduct, behavior, example, and lifestyle. It is commonly believed that policeman are known by their feet. It is an absolute certainty that Christians are known by theirs! Thus, Paul says believers should "walk worthy of their calling" (Ephesians 4:1). They are to be different from the pagans (Ephesians 4:17). They are to "walk in love" (Ephesians 5:2), as "children of light" (Ephesians 5:8). And they are to walk "carefully" (Ephesians 5:15) and "courageously" (Ephesians 6:15).

If you look carefully at some of Paul's other writings you will find him using this term figuratively time and time again. Perhaps it was because it was such a common mode of transportation in his day. In Romans 6:4 he urges us to walk after the Spirit. It is almost as though he is writing a manual on "How to Walk."

As a matter of fact, it seems that the whole Bible likens the Christian life to that of a walk. Consider the following scriptural references:

- **Genesis 3:8:** "And they heard the voice of the LORD God walking in the garden in the cool of the day."
- **Genesis 5:24:** "And Enoch walked with God."
- **Genesis 6:9:** "…and Noah walked with God."

- **Deuteronomy 13:4:** "You shall walk after the LORD your God, and fear him, and keep his commandments, and obey his voice, and you shall serve him, and cleave unto him."
- **Matthew 9:5:** "For which is easier, to say, 'Thy sins be forgiven thee'; or to say, 'Arise and walk'" (KJV).

If the author was to write a manual on how to walk properly, it would include the following recommendations:

1. ***Be properly attired.*** I read recently about a young man who was walking at twilight in dark clothing. A passing motorist struck him, causing fatal injuries. Walkers should wear bright colors, especially during the hours when visibility is challenged. Wearing apparel is important. It does matter what you put on before starting out the door. This is a dark world that we are called upon to walk in. According to Peter, we should be "clothed with humility" (I Peter 5:5). And Paul urges us to "put on" several things: the armor of light, the whole armor of God, the new man and, above all, Christ.
2. ***Warm up before beginning.*** How sad it is when we begin our day, without first spending some quality time with our Father. We could avoid "cramping up" when we meet that trial or stressful situation.
3. ***Start slowly.*** Sometimes we are guilty of rushing headlong into the day, giving little thought to that still, small voice. If we are not careful, we can get ahead of God.
4. ***Get into a rhythm.*** Consistency, that is what is important. It is better for the heart and lungs in the long run. This is true in the spiritual realm as well. The "up and down" kind of living is not good for the soul. The NIV renders Galatians 5:25 thus: "Since we live by the Spirit, let us keep in touch with the Spirit."
5. ***Be on the alert for danger.*** Wise walkers do. They are always on the lookout for dogs, traffic, cracks in the road or sidewalk, fallen tree limbs or wires. We are sure to encounter Satan's subtle attacks as we journey through life. Peter warned us in his first letter: "Be sober, be vigilant; because your adversary the

devil, as a roaring lion, walketh about, seeking whom he may devour" (I Peter 5:8, KJV). Some walkers carry a large stick to ward off aggressive dogs. Believers carry the sword of the Spirit (which is the Word of God), not so much in their hands as in their hearts. And remember, God always has a leash on the devil. He can scare us but he cannot eat us. He only seeks to.

6. ***Walk with a companion.*** It will make the trip much more pleasant. Spiritually, it can be said that walking in isolation is both dangerous and selfish. The saints of God are referred to as a body and a temple. We need each other for support and encouragement. In Galatians 5:25, the word "walk" is translated from the Greek word, stoicheo, which means, "a row," or "to walk in a line,"—to march, and is used metaphorically of walking in relation to others. We are part of a vast army, standing shoulder to shoulder as we advance.
7. ***Worship as you walk.*** One of the advantages of walking outdoors is to appreciate creation's witness to the glory of God. Hear the birds singing. See the flowers blooming. Cast your eyes upward to behold the grandeur of the heavens. You cannot help but praise God for His goodness. Some walkers employ the use of headphones while they listen to recorded worship choruses and hymns. They may even sing along or silently pray. We cannot survive long on this journey without worship. It is the way we express love and the means of sustaining us.
8. ***Assume the proper posture***—head up, shoulders back, eyes forward. We are children of the King! We know where we are headed. Our destination is fixed. We march with certainty and with a spring in our step. With unbounded energy we walk because we know that we never walk alone. Never!
9. ***Persevere.*** Muscles aching? Feet sore? That is all right. That is the way it is meant to be—a sure sign that you are getting a good work-out, getting in shape. Almost home. No need to quit now. It is just around the bend and over the hill. The Father is watching for us. He has a cool drink waiting and a feast fit for a king.

One of the most rewarding aspects of walking is that you encounter people along the way. This means opportunity—opportunity to meet and make new friends, to spread some cheer as you move along through life. It is amazing how many needs one can encounter on the trail. For example, there is the couple who consistently walks their dog, but never make eye contact, or the elderly gentleman who struggles to walk due to a recent stroke, or the young lady who carries hand weights to build upper body strength, or the man who seldom smiles and never speaks first. Who can say what a friendly word or smile can lead to? As we make our way down the highway of life, we should be alert to opportunities to minister in His name.

One last observation, or should I say, benefit. Walking affords us the occasion to meditate, to clear our heads, to remember, to dream, even to pray. In a sense, walking can be very restful, giving us some time away from the pressures of life. It is "relaxation therapy in motion"—a time to breathe in His promises and exhale His love.

To walk in the Spirit, then, is to be in harmony with His will and purposes—to live a life of obedience, of discipline, of perseverance, and to experience the joy of His presence. How wonderful it is to walk through life with Jesus as our Companion. He walks beside us—all the way!

THE COMPASS THAT NEVER FAILS

But when he, the Spirit of truth comes, he will guide you into all truth. He will not speak on his own; he will speak only what he hears, and he will tell you what is yet to come (John 16:13, NIV).

HAVE YOU EVER BEEN LOST? I mean *really* lost? So lost that there was no hope of ever finding your way? I have. It happened to me many years ago while I was deer hunting in the foothills of the Allegany Mountains, near the border of New York and Pennsylvania. I was on the trail of a large, magnificent-looking buck. Foolishly, I left the hunting party I was with and went off on my own. Foolishly, for three reasons: I was unfamiliar with the territory; I did not possess a compass; it was nearing dusk.

As I moved along off the main trail (I do not know why deer do not stay on the trail!), I began to visually mark the new path I was blazing by fixing my gaze on certain land marks—a large oak tree, a huge boulder, etc. When at last I gave up any hope of finding the deer, I started back toward our base camp. It was nearing dinner time and it was starting to get dark. I looked for the trees and boulders I had seen, but they all looked alike. I began to panic. I had absolutely no idea where I was and the thought of spending a night in the forest on a cold November evening was frightening. I am sure I walked in circles. I began to pray, "Lord, please guide me out of this situation." I walked for what seemed like two hours. It was now fully dark. I was about to give up when suddenly I walked out of the woods into a clearing, not more than a few yards from camp! Coincidence? Luck? Answer to prayer? You decide.

This harrowing experience taught me a very valuable lesson. Never, no never, go into the woods without a compass and/or guide. The whole episode also inspired me to think about how wonderfully the Holy Spirit guides us through this maze we call life. We are often lost mentally when it comes to truth. What should I believe? What is truth and what is error? What course should I set? What is God's will for my life? There are so many voices beckoning to us, so many experts ready to give us advice.

The disciples, at the time Jesus spoke the above scripture, were certainly not an example of surety. They were confused and frightened. They had sat at Jesus' feet and now He was speaking of leaving them. But when He said that He was sending the Comforter and that He would guide them into all truth, that must have been encouraging to them even though they probably did not fully comprehend His words until after Pentecost. But, because these early believers stayed close to the Lord, He kept His promise to them. The Spirit of God descended on their *minds* on that momentous day recorded for us in Acts 2. Their memory, their reasoning, were affected. They had the mind of Christ and began to think and interpret events with enlightened acuity—all because they lived in a state of perpetual obedience.

To Jesus, the Holy Spirit is the Spirit of Truth and His great work is to bring God's truth to us. This is called *revelation*. All truth is God's truth, and the revelation of all truth is the work of the Spirit. Truth is not men's discovery; it is God's gift to us—helping us to understand who He is, who we are, and what His plan is for us. As we study the Scriptures and walk by faith, He reveals His will progressively. The light dawns, the mist lifts, and the Spirit begins to reeducate our conscience, opening our minds to His eternal purposes.

Years ago I took my family to visit Mammoth Cave in Kentucky. We decided to take the long tour and so that meant a guide. We joined a group after getting our tickets and entered this underground marvel. When we reached the "Cathedral," the guide mounted a rock called "The Pulpit," and said he would preach a sermon. It was short. All he said was "Keep close to your guide." We soon found it was a very good sermon, for if we lagged behind or went to some other passageway, we would be lost in the midst of pits and precipices. It is hard to find one's way through this cavern without a guide; it is harder to find one's way through the world without the guidance of God.

The most frightening aspect of this excursion was when our guide assembled us in order to demonstrate what total darkness is like. He cautioned us that he was about to turn off his lantern for about five seconds and for us to remain perfectly still and not to panic. Those five seconds seemed like an eternity. The darkness seemed so intense, far worse than anything I had experienced before—a very uncomfortable feeling. How glad we all were when the light came back on. There was a collective sigh of relief.

Similarly, the darkness that envelops this world of ours can be terrifying as well. But the Holy Guide turns on the lantern of His Word and brings peace and hope to our hearts. In the words of Sue M. Voorhees:

I cannot see the way I go;
I go not knowing why;
But this I know, each step is set
By Him who is Most High;
And so I gladly tread His path,
Nor fear what e're be tide,
Assured that when I win His smile,
I shall be satisfied.

THE RESTORATION EXPERT

The Lord is my shepherd, I shall not want. He makes me lie down in green pastures; he leads me beside quiet waters; he restores my soul (Psalm 23:1-3, KJV).

LET ME FOCUS ON THE WORD "RESTORE." *He restores my soul.* **Restore:** 1. to bring back into existence or use; reestablish. 2. to bring back to an original condition. 3. to put (someone) back in a former position. 4. to make restitution; give back.

In a remote Swiss village stood a beautiful church. It was so beautiful, in fact, that it was known as the Mountain Valley Cathedral. The church was not only beautiful to look at with its high pillars and magnificent stained glass windows, but it had the most beautiful pipe organ in the whole region. People would come from far away to hear the lovely tones of this instrument.

But there was a problem. The columns were still there—the windows dazzled with the sunlight, but there was an eerie silence. The mountain valley no longer echoed the glorious fine-tuned music of the pipe organ. Something had gone wrong with the organ. Musicians and experts from around the world had tried to repair it. Every time a new person would try to fix it the villagers were subjected to sounds of disharmony—awful penetrating noises which polluted the air.

One day an old man appeared at the church door. He spoke with the sexton and after a time the sexton reluctantly agreed to let the old man try his hand at repairing the organ. For two days the stranger worked in almost total silence. The sexton was, in fact, getting a bit nervous. Then, on the third day at high noon, the mountain valley once again was filled with glorious, harmonious music. Farmers dropped their plows, merchants closed their stores. Everyone in town stopped what they were doing and headed for the church. Even the bushes and trees of the mountain tops seemed to respond as the beautiful music echoed once again from ridge to ridge.

After the old man finished his playing, a brave soul asked him how he could have fixed the organ. How could he restore this magnificent instrument even when the world's experts could not? The old man said it was an inside job. "It was I who built this organ fifty years ago. I created it and now I have restored it."

What a beautiful picture of God! It is He who created the universe, and it is He who can, and will, and is in the process of restoring it. And since we are a part of that creation and have been marred by sin, we are also in need of restoration. We need to be once again remade inwardly in the image of God. Right now it is a process. One day the Lord will complete His act of reconstructing this world. He will also complete our salvation by giving us a new body like unto His glorious body. Resurrection Day could also be referred to as "Restoration Day."

The life of a Christian is made up of a series of restorations. In fact, much that is called conversion is nothing more than restoration. And then there are also those times when our spirits are depressed or harassed by circumstances and/or disobedience. We are like sheep who have somehow managed to end up on our backs. We cannot right ourselves by ourselves. We need a Shepherd to help us get on our feet again.

When God restores, He puts us back to a better point than the one from which we had fallen. Restored life is sweeter than life that has never been clouded.

By His sovereign grace, God can bring good out of our failures, and even out of our sins. J. Stuart Holken tells of an old Scottish mansion close to where he had a summer home. The walls of one home were filled with sketches made by distinguished artists. The practice began after a pitcher of soda water accidentally spilled on a freshly decorated wall and left an unsightly stain. At the time, a noted artist, Lloyd Landseer, was a guest in this house. One day when the family went out to the moors, he stayed behind. With a few masterful strokes of a piece of charcoal, that ugly spot became the outline of a beautiful waterfall, bordered by trees and wildlife. He turned that disfigured wall into one of his most successful depictions of Highland life.

So my friend, when we take time from our hectic pace and get alone with God, He will, in like manner, take His divine brush and begin a work of restoration within. But we must make the time.

THE ENLIGHTENING SPLENDOR OF CREATION

Nature is one grand cosmic book describing the power and the majesty of God and bearing on us its title page those memorable words of Genesis which express so beautiful and so sublime a truth: "In the beginning God created heavens and earth...and God created man in His own image."

—JOHN A. O'BRIEN
The Origin of Man, 1947

TOUCHING THE FACE OF GOD

O LORD, our Lord, how majestic is your name in all the earth! You have set your glory above the heavens. From the lips of children and infants you have ordained praise because of your enemies, to silence the foe and the avenger. When I consider your heavens, the works of your fingers, the moon and the stars which you have set in place, what is man that you are mindful of him, the son of man that you care for him? You made him a little lower than the heavenly beings and crowned him with glory and honor. You made him ruler over the works of your hands; you put everything under his feet: all flocks and herds, and the beasts of the field, the birds of the air, and the fish of the sea, all that swim the paths of the sea. O LORD, our Lord, how majestic is your name in all the earth! (Psalm 8)

IN DECEMBER 1941, JOHN GILLESPIE MAGEE, JR., a nineteen-year-old pilot serving with the Royal Canadian Air Force in England, was killed when his Spitfire collided with another aircraft. Among his personal effects was the following poem, written on the back of a letter during the time he was in flight school.

Oh, I have slipped the surety bonds of earth,
And danced the skies on laughter-silvered wings;
Sunward I've climbed and joined the tumbling mirth
Of sunsplit clouds—and done a hundred things
You have not dreamed of—wheeled and soared and swung—
High in the sunlit silence. Hov'ring there,
I've chased the shouting winds along, and flung
My eager craft through footless halls of air.
Up, up the long, delirious, burning blue,
I've topped the windswept heights with easy grace,
Where never lark or even eagle flew.
And, while with silent, lifting mind I've trod
The high un-trespassed sanctity of space,
Put out my hand, and touched the face of God.

Could anyone argue that this man had indeed encountered the Almighty? There is nothing like nature to unfold truth about God—that He is, that He is awesome, that He reveals Himself to us, constantly shouting about His wisdom and power. His creative hand can be seen everywhere. It gives a sense of reverence and mystery to life. Even atheists cannot fully escape this.

The writer's identification with the feelings expressed in Magee's sonnet first burst upon his consciousness when he took his maiden flight. Gazing out the window at 35,000 feet, a feeling of awe overwhelmed him. The sky seemed bluer than he had ever visualized it. The white fluffy clouds, several thousand feet below, formed a vast canopy. They looked so inviting—almost as though they were beckoning us to land. Now and then one could peek through vast holes in the clouds and see mountains, rivers and lakes—the creative handiwork of God from a vantage point not yet experienced. It was a little like surveying a topographical map. The things that seem to loom so large to us here on earth are not even discernable from such a vast height. Little wonder that the Psalmist words came to mind: "When I consider the heavens, the work of your fingers, the moon and the stars, which you have set in place, what is man that you are mindful of him?"

The work of William Beebe seems to echo the words of the Psalmist. Beebe was no armchair scholar. His extensive knowledge of nature was gained from explorations into the jungles of Asia and South America and to the bottom of the ocean in the world's first bathysphere. Beebe had much in common with his friend, Theodore Roosevelt, who also loved nature and exploring. Often, after a visit to Sagamore Hill, Beebe recalled, he and the President went outdoors to see who could first locate the Andromeda galaxy in the constellation Pegasus. Then, gazing at the tiny smudge of distant starlight, Beebe or Roosevelt would say, "That is the spiral galaxy of Andromeda. It is as large as our Milky Way. It is 750,000 light years away. It consists of at least 100 billion stars, each one larger than our sun."

After that thought had sunk in, Roosevelt used to flash his famous toothy grin and say, "Now I think we're small enough." Then the two men would retire, put in their place by the limitless universe, spoken into existence by Almighty God.

And yet the Lord God Almighty, creator of heaven and earth, thought so much of us poor, defiled, insignificant creatures inhabiting this speck of dust that He was willing to give His one and only Son to come and die for us. This is a truth that simply staggers the imagination! The Creator became the Redeemer. From somewhere beyond the galaxies, yea even the universe, came a visitor—not from outer space, but from beyond space. He came to rescue us from Satan's clutches—to do for us what we could not do for ourselves—to set us free!

HEAVEN'S TESTIMONY

The heavens declare the glory of God; and the firmament sheweth his handywork. Day unto day uttereth speech, and night unto night sheweth knowledge. There is no speech nor language, where their work is not heard (Psalm 19:1-3, KJV).

ASTRONOMERS TELL US THAT THE MILKY WAY, the disc-shaped galaxy to which our sun belongs, is a family of more than 100 billion stars. And these scientists say there may be as many as 100 billion other galaxies in the universe. It is also posited that each of these galaxies' billion stars may have hundreds of millions of planets like our earth. All of this from a one-sentence command from God!

Anything may be reproduced on scale model except the universe. The impossibility of making such a model accurately is shown by the fact that, if the earth were represented by a ball only one inch in diameter, the nearest star, Alpha Centaury, would have to be placed nearly 51,000 miles away.

A man looking up at the sky on a clear night sees as much of the universe as a protozoan might see of the ocean in which it drifts. The moon, the planets, and a few thousand stars which are visible to him are as a single drop of water in the boundless sea of the universe.

Our sun is so large that if it were hollow, it would contain more than one million worlds the size of our earth. There are stars in space so large that they could easily hold 500 million suns the size of ours!

To better appreciate the vastness of our ever-expanding universe, consider the speed of light—186,000 miles per second. In one second, light makes 37 round trips across the United States. At this speed, light will pass the moon in one and one-half seconds. It will pass the sun in eight minutes, take four years to the nearest star, 10,000 years to leave our galaxy, and two million years to reach Andromeda, our nearest galaxy!

How is it then that two men can gaze up at the same stars on a cold, crisp, clear night and not see the same thing? Some look at the stars and worship them as gods. Others gaze at the heavens and order their lives according to its movement. Still others study them and see them merely as a combination of certain chemical elements that came into existence as the result of a cosmic explosion billions of years ago.

And then there are those like the Psalmist who praise God who made them, who by faith cling to the biblical account of creation. They do not rob God of the glory due His name.

The Russian astronaut, Gherman Titov, said after his return from outer space, "Some people say there is a God out there…but in my travels around the earth all day long, I looked around and didn't see Him. I saw no God or angels. The rocket was made by our own people. I don't believe in God. I believe in man, his strength, his possibilities, his reason."

However, when some American astronauts were in space, they were so moved by what they beheld that they read the Creation account from Genesis for the whole world to hear.

Perhaps one way to explain this different way of observing the heavens is to liken God's revelation in nature to a concert performed by an orchestra. Some who come to listen hear only the instruments as they express the melody and harmony of the music. But others who come are familiar with the composer and know the words that go with the music. These hear much more than sound.

In much the same way, only those who have a personal relationship with the Creator can really see in all of creation the fullness of what God intended to communicate through it. And together with all the saints, with hearts spilling over with praise, they sing with the Psalmist:

1 Praise the LORD. Praise the LORD from the heavens, praise him in the heights above.
2 Praise him, all his angels, praise him, all his heavenly hosts.
3 Praise him, sun and moon, praise him, all you shining stars.
4 Praise him, you highest heavens and you waters above the skies.
5 Let them praise the name of the LORD, for he commanded and they were created.
6 He set them in place for ever and ever; he gave a decree that will never pass away.

7 Praise the LORD from the earth, you great sea creatures and all ocean depths,
8 lightning and hail, snow and clouds, stormy winds that do his bidding,
9 you mountains and all hills, fruit trees and all cedars,
10 wild animals and all cattle, small creatures and flying birds,
11 kings of the earth and all nations, you princes and all rulers on earth,
12 young men and maidens, old men and children.
13 Let them praise the name of the LORD, for his name alone is exalted; his splendor is above the earth and the heavens.
14 He has raised up for his people a horn, the praise of all his saints, of Israel, the people close to his heart. Praise the LORD.

—Psalm 148:1-14

In keeping with the theme of this book, let me ask you a question: Have you ever taken the time to lie on your back out under the stars on a warm summer evening and gaze up into the heavens? If not, why not? You see, there is stretched out before you a wonderful display of God's power and artistry. It will fill you with reverence, awe, and a sense of how small we are and how grand God is. And that, I believe, was His intent from the beginning.

THE KING OF BIRDS!

Like an eagle that stirs up its nest and hovers over its young, that spreads its wings to catch them and carries them on its pinions, so the Lord alone did lead him (Deuteronomy 32:11,12).

They that wait upon the Lord shall renew their strength; they shall mount up with wings as eagles; they shall run, and not be weary; they shall walk, and not faint (Isaiah 40:31).

"Bless the Lord, O my soul and forget not all his benefits...He satisfies my desires with good things, so that my youth is renewed like the eagle's (Psalm 103:2,5).

HAVE YOU EVER BEEN TO PRARIE DU CHIEN, WISCONSIN? It is right on the Mississippi River, near the border of Iowa. My wife and I visited there because we had been told that it was one of the places where eagles lived and mated. It was a beautiful spring day and we decided to have a picnic lunch in a park that overlooked the river. As we were eating, suddenly we saw them—eagles in flight—sweeping over the palisades—bald eagles at that! These magnificent creatures left us spellbound. There is something majestic and mysterious about our national bird.

The eagle is known as the king of birds. It has some interesting features and traits that we would do well to evaluate and emulate.

First, consider the NEST. It is usually built on the edge of a great precipice. There the mother bird hatches her young and there for a time she nourishes and cherishes them. The nest is made of thorns, jagged stones, and sharp bones. It is covered with wool, feathers and furs from animals she has killed. When she "stirs up" the nest, the eaglets begin to feel like leaving. She also prods them with her sharp talons, and then a day comes when she sweeps them out with her powerful wings and casts them over the ledge of rock. Screaming with terror, they drop like stones. But just as they are about to be dashed to pieces, she swoops down below them and bears them up. She will continue this process until they learn to fly.

In a similar manner, God deals with His people. He cherishes them, but He also challenges them. He protects and provides for them but He also subjects them to the disciplines of disturbance—so that they can learn how to fly!

The eaglet that whimpers, "I can't" dies on the rocks and adds its carcass to the carrion already there. But the eaglet that attempts to fly, when flight seems impossible, soon finds itself "lord of the blue."

Secondly, consider its WINGS. An eagle is built for flight—upward flight. They soar above the storms. They keep flying until they are safe in the sunshine.

In like manner, the child of God should face the darkness of storms with courage and determination. His prayer and faith can penetrate the clouds and bring him into the glory of the Son's presence.

The wings make it possible for the eagle to perform with great speed and strength. Spiritual eagles can perform with equal speed and strength. God has promised to supply it. The believer quickly flees temptation and God's strength is made perfect in his weakness. These wings make it possible for the believer to go swiftly to the aid of others.

In Psalm 103:5 we read about our youth being renewed like that of the eagle. The Psalmist is referring to the molting of birds which, in most cases, takes place annually, in which they cast their old feathers off and get a new plumage.

The third amazing feature of eagles has to do with their EYES. They are known for their keen eyesight. The expression "eagle eye" describes quite accurately one of the unique characteristics of this fascinating bird of prey. The eagle's eyesight is three to four times stronger than that of humans.

Spiritual eagles should have keen eyesight also. They are to keep their eyes centered on Jesus (Hebrews 12:2). They are to overlook the faults in others. They should be quick to see the needs of others as well. And, of course, they should be able to spot the enemy readily. This is often referred to as "spiritual insight."

Another aspect of eagle life has to do with their HABITAT. They build on high ledges and live apart in the high places because they are solitary birds. Spiritual eagles pursue the lofty summits as well—they separate themselves from the principles, values, and standards of the world. They lay up treasures in heaven, not on the earth.

Joseph Parker, a great English preacher once said, "An eagle does not roost in a sparrow's nest." And neither does a child of God! God has designed and empowered us to be like the eagle—ever ascending in our faith.

When we strive to live in the heights, we cannot help but notice several things: (1) It is not crowded, (2) The air is clear, the vision greater, (3) The beauty is breathtaking, and (4) a feeling of exhilaration surges through the one committed to live such a life—success, instead of failure. Perseverance and hard work paid off and we soar like the eagle.

The story is told about a farmer who caught a young eagle and placed it with his chickens. The eaglet ate with them and soon adopted itself to their ways. One day a friend was visiting the farm and noticed the eagle with the chickens in the barnyard. He said to the farmer, "What's that eagle doing in there?" The farmer answered, "O, he doesn't know he's an eagle. He thinks he's a chicken. He eats feed and does everything the chickens do. He'll never fly!" But his friend said, "No, I don't agree. He's still an eagle because he was created to be one. He has the heart of an eagle and one day he will realize it."

The farmer's friend tried to prove it by encouraging the eagle to fly, but unsuccessfully. Finally, one day he took him to the foot of a mountain just as the sun was rising. The instant the eagle got a vision of the rising sun he uttered a wild scream of joy, stretched his wings, and flew off—never to return to the barnyard again.

O, for a vision of Jesus, the Son of Righteousness, that we may "mount up with wings as eagles…"

LEVIATHAN!

How many are your works, O LORD! In wisdom you made them all; the earth is full of your creatures. There is the sea, vast and spacious, teeming with creatures beyond number—living things both large and small. There the ships go to and fro, and the leviathan, which you formed to frolic (Psalm 104:24-26).

I MUST ADMIT THAT I HAVE ALWAYS BEEN FASCINATED by the *leviathan*. From what I am able to deduce, Bible scholars are not quite certain exactly what this creature was—crocodile? hippo? dragon? or some other creature long extinct? I do not know that we will ever know for certain this side of heaven. Whatever it was, it was BIG!

You may be surprised to learn that the largest creature ever to grace the earth is still flourishing. Contrary to popular assumption, the dinosaur cannot lay claim to that title. The largest of those reptiles—the brontosaurus, rarely grew to a length of more than ninety feet and averaged well under 50 tons. These measurements seem modest compared to those of that famous leviathan—the blue whale. Specimens of this sea-going giant have been reported as long as 120 feet—longer than a city block and many weigh close to 120 tons!

Almost everything about this creature is colossal. The blue whale has the biggest nose and the biggest tongue of anything alive, and a mouth so large that a full-grown man can stand erect inside the enormous cavern and still have to stretch his arms to touch the roof of the whale's mouth! So much for the idea that Jonah could not possibly have been swallowed by one.

Despite its size and enormous appetite, the blue whale can swallow nothing larger than a shrimp. Most of its food consists of tiny fish and sea animals no bigger than the head of a pin. The whale does not have to hunt for this food; it merely swims slowly through the water with its huge mouth open. Small sea creatures enter the cavernous mouth and get caught in a brush-like growth of bony hairs that hang from the roof of the whale's mouth. Every so often the whale closes its jaws, expels the water inside, licks the food off the roof of its mouth with a gargantuan tongue, and swallows thousands of tiny morsels.

Although the whale spends its entire life in the ocean, it is not a fish. Rather, it is a warm-blooded mammal that breathes air—just like seals, beavers, otters, and other sea animals. The longest a whale can stay submerged is about half an hour. But this feat is astonishing when we realize that a man, another mammal, holding his breath to the utmost of his endurance, can stay under water for only two or three minutes!

When a whale comes to the surface for a breath of fresh air, it shoots a fountain of vapor into the air that can be seen from miles away. Most people believe that the whale is spouting water from its nostrils, but this is not the case. A whale never deliberately takes water into its breathing passages; if it did, the creature would drown just as surely as a human being would.

Before a whale dives underwater, it fills its lungs with air, and then, when it resurfaces, expels this air with great force. This breath, warmed and moistened by the whale's lungs, condenses upon contact with the outside colder air and forms streams of vapor resembling water. And if the whale happens to exhale or "blow" a short distance below the surface, a considerable amount of water may be carried upward with the escaping air.

There is a great deal of evidence to suggest that some whales are capable of a form of communication. A humpback whale, for instance, emits a series of very low sound waves that travel great distances through water to inform other members of its species of its whereabouts. They are truly amazing creatures!

All of this is a testimony to the creative power of Almighty God. In fact, there is nothing like nature to unfold truth about God. Creation is constantly shouting to us about the wisdom and genius of God. It gives a sense of mystery and awe to life. Even atheists cannot fully escape this. Robert Browning has written a verse about a certain young man who has determined that he is going to build his life without God. He has his philosophies all worked out and none of them include God. But then he admits to an older friend the following:

Just when we are safest, there's a sunset-touch,
A fancy from a flower-bell, someone's death,
A chorus-ending from Euripides.
And that's enough for fifty hopes and fears;
The Grand Perhaps.

And, I might add, the sight of a whale in the wild—this magnificent creature, designed by the Creator to remind us of His power, wisdom, and creativity. Only those who have a personal relationship with the Creator through His Son, Jesus Christ, can really see in all creation the fullness of what God intended to communicate through it. Let nature resonate with the character of God, and man stand in awe of it.

I sing the mighty pow'r of God, that made the mountains rise;
That spread the flowing seas abroad, And built the lofty skies.
I sing the wisdom that ordained The sun to rule the day;
The moon shines full at His command, And all the stars obey.
—Isaac Watts

THE RESURRECTION PLANT

As for you, you were dead in your transgressions and sins, in which you used to live when you followed the ways of this world and of the ruler of the kingdom of the air, the spirit who is now at work in those who are disobedient...But because of his great love for us, God, who is rich in mercy, made us alive with Christ even when we were dead in transgressions—it is by grace you have been saved (Ephesians 2:1,2,4,5).

THE RESURRECTION PLANT, among numerous other botanical wonders, is God's way of providing spiritual lessons from nature—signposts, if you will, of the lengths He has gone to in order to reveal His love to us.

This plant, a desert growth found in arid regions of America and the Near East, owes its name to its extraordinary ability to come to life again from a seemingly dead and shriveled state. Of course, the plant does not really come back from the dead, but from a form of "hibernation" in which it is almost completely inactive. And unlike most other plants which must wait for water, the resurrection plant can move over the land to search for needed moisture!

The name *resurrection plant* is applied to several species, including the Biblical rose of Jericho, which exhibits similar resurrective powers. In the presence of water, a resurrection plant will flourish, sporting green, fernlike leaves. But when moisture is scarce, the plant pulls up its roots and withers into a dry, ball-like mass of apparently dead matter, completely devoid of green coloration. This withered mass is carried along by the wind, and can remain in a dormant state for years if no water is found. But once moisture is located, or after rain, the plant sinks its roots into the wet ground and springs to life again. Its leaves uncurl, again revealing green tissue on their undersides. The plant fares well until the moisture has evaporated, then curls up into a withered ball and roams again in search of water.

How like the Christian is this plant. If one does not drink regularly from the "water of the Word" he can become a shriveled-up soul. Even in this state it is possible to be revived if he will get back to his source of life—prayer and Bible study. And it will soon become evident that his "dormancy" was not death but suspended animation!

I wonder how many believers are like this dried-up plant, devoid of real spiritual power, needing to drink once again from the well that never runs dry.

There is another application that could be made in regard to this most amazing plant. The non-Christian is an example of one who is alive physically, but dead spiritually—dead to the consequences of sin, dead to the love and mercy of God, dead to the provision made for him at Calvary. He wanders from place to place, longing for something to satisfy the thirst within. He drinks from the wells of this world—money, pleasure, knowledge, and religion to name a few. Oh, if only he would drink from the well of salvation found in Jesus Christ, he would spring to new life! Then he could sing from the depths of his soul, the song that Clara T. Williams penned…

All my life long I had panted
For a drink from some cool spring
That I hoped would quench the burning
Of the thirst I felt within.

Well of water, ever springing,
Bread of Life, so rich and free,
Untold wealth that never faileth,
My Redeemer is to me.

Hallelujah! I have found Him
Whom my soul so long has craved!
Jesus satisfies my longings;
Thro' His blood I now am saved.

—Clara T. Williams

SYMPHONY OF PRAISE

The flowers appear on the earth; the time of singing of birds is come, and the voice of the turtle is heard in our land (Song of Solomon 2:12, KJV).

"ESCAPE TO FLORIDA"—that is what the television commercial said. So I did. I bid farewell to the frozen North for a few days—left behind the biting frost, the howling wind, and the bleak landscape. I said goodbye to icy roads and the ever-present threat of the flu.

When I boarded the plane the thermometer registered two degrees below zero and when I deplaned in the land of sunshine, it was 74! The shock was almost too much for my system, but in a very short time I was able to adjust.

Sitting by the pool one day I began to contemplate the many benefits of this "escape to paradise." The green grass, palm trees swaying gently in the warm breeze, white, sandy beaches, and gorgeous flowers were everywhere. I began to ask myself, "What is the one thing above all others that makes me appreciate this flight to the South?" The answer came swiftly as my mind raced back to my first trip to this fair land. It happened on the very first morning of my arrival in sunny Florida. I awoke to a sound I had not heard for months. At first I thought I was dreaming. But there it was again. It was a melody so sweet, so enrapturing that if I was dreaming, I did not want it to end. The window was open and in floated a most pleasant succession of sounds. What was it? Birds! That is right, birds—a sound I dearly missed, one which we often take for granted in the other seasons in Michigan.

One or two of these winged creatures piped forth with their morning call, then soon others joined in, and still others till the full orchestra was pouring out its sympathy of praise, each member seeming to vie with another in trills and roulades that any human singer might well envy. The robin's joyous song, the oriole's liquid trill, and the nervous little house wren with its shrill piccolo obbligato. How wonderfully God has equipped these little songsters, and how joyously they usher in the new-born day.

But alas, how few hear these air-borne singers. The cares of life often drown out their melody. What a difference it would make if we could cease our activity and learn to listen again—I mean really listen. They might even remind us of God's care, for even a sparrow does not fall to the ground without His knowledge.

Bird calls are among the most relaxing and restful sounds in the world. It is possible even in the dead of winter to purchase a tape recording of these happy songsters, then lie back in a favorite easy chair and listen as they serenade. It is not very long until visions of spring begin dancing in one's head. Such therapeutic value. Who can measure it?

There are about 8,600 kinds of birds in the world. And, of all the known creatures on earth, only birds and people sing. Have you ever noticed that for the most part, only the smaller birds are songsters? Think about it! Nary a sweet note issues from the beak of a crow, or an eagle, or even a turkey. Oh yes, one can hear a caw, a screech, and a gobble, but not one single melody. But listen to the canary, the wren, and the lark. Is God trying to tell us something? Could it be that He wants to teach us a basic principle of life? Do not despise the "little things." The sweetest music comes from those who are small in their own estimation and before the Lord.

Years ago a number of skylarks were brought to America from England and set loose in one of the eastern sections of the country. They soon were at home and began to breed. One day an ornithologist was observing their behavior and listening with some interest to their song. He happened to notice an Irish-American laborer working nearby. Suddenly the Irishman stopped his work, put his tools down, took off his cap and gazed skyward, a look of reverence and yet, joy, on his face. It was apparent that he was moved by the sight. No doubt he was reminiscing about days gone by in his native land. He was entranced—memories from his youth flooded his mind—all of this because of association, because of larks. For the bird expert the birds were merely a scientific observation, but for the Irishman it was the recollection of affection and love—an esoteric experience, if you will. In a similar manner, the songs of the Gospel come to the Christian, reminding him of past blessings, present joys, and future hopes.

Birds—God's orchestra. Nature singing. Creatures crooning His glories. Listen carefully; they may be singing your song!

This is my Father's world.
The birds their carols raise;
The morning light, the lily white
Declare their Maker's praise.
This is my Father's world.
He shines in all that's fair;
In the rustling grass I hear Him pass;
He speaks to me everywhere.

—Maltbie D. Babcock

THE CROWN OF CREATION!

I will praise You, for I am fearfully and wonderfully made; Marvelous are Your works, and that my soul knows very well (Psalm 139:14, NKJV).

WHEN I ATTENDED COLLEGE, biology was one of the required courses. To fulfill the criteria of that class meant that each student must present a project of their own choosing. I chose insects, i.e., gathering, identifying, and presenting them to the professor for evaluation. Consequently, one sunny spring day I was dutifully doing just that—scouring my back yard with net in hand, hunting for butterflies.

Suddenly a voice from across my neighbor's fence came my way. She said, "Excuse me, but aren't you studying for the ministry?" I answered in the affirmative, to which she replied, "Well, what on earth do butterflies have to do with that?" I responded, "I'm not sure exactly. I suppose it has to do with the fact that I'm attending a liberal arts institution. They want their graduates to be well-rounded."

However, by the end of the course my answer would have been vastly different. For you see, my reverence for God and my respect for His creative genius had increased immeasurably. Peering into a microscope will do that. Studying the various complex and interrelated systems of the human anatomy will also do that. It is true; we are fearfully and wonderfully made. The study of life in all of its forms enhances one's view of God and His love for us. Sermon ideas come flowing out of creation upon every observation.

Scientists tell us that there are several trillion hard-working cells in every person. A cell is so small that it takes 250 of them placed side by side to equal the diameter of a dot the size of a period at the end of a sentence. Imagine that! Inside the membrane of each cell, swimming around in the cytoplasm, are about 200 wriggling, squirming particles, each one a living and active chemical laboratory, a food and energy factory. We are fearfully and wonderfully made.

These particles are called *mitochondria*. Each one of these would be about 1/50,000 the size of that aforementioned dot. Inside of each of these mitochondria hundreds of small "spheres" are scattered along stalks. Each sphere is a chemical factory, with a "production line" that produces energy and food for the cell. This is such a marvel of smallness and intricate complexity that it stretches one's imagination even to try to think about it. Truly we have an awesome God who made it all—The Master Designer! We are fearfully and wonderfully made.

Consider the heart as well. It is a hard-working marvel. It can keep on beating automatically even if all other nerves were severed. And what a beat! It beats an average of 75 times a minute, 100,000 times a day, 40 million times a year, or 2 and 1/2 billion times in a life of 70 years.

At each beat the average adult heart discharges about four ounces of blood. This amounts to 3,000 gallons a day or 650,000 gallons a year—enough to fill more than 81 tank cars of 8,000 gallons each. We are fearfully and wonderfully made!

The heart does enough work in one hour to lift a 150-pound man to the top of a three story building—enough energy in 12 hours to lift a 65-ton tank car one foot off the ground. We are truly fearfully and wonderfully made.

And what of the marvel of the human brain? Even though a typical brain will forget more than 90 percent of what is learned during an average lifetime, it may still store up as much as ten times more information than is in the Library of Congress, with its 17 million volumes. Only God could design and build such a living computer.

The body's entire structure, from head to foot, is a miracle of precision engineering and production. No matter what portion of human anatomy is considered, one cannot help but be impressed with what a marvelous mechanism each member is. The major organs alone—and there are ten of them—perform such unique feats of electric conduction that it would take volumes to explain each one adequately.

In the fraction of a second that it takes to read one word on this page, the marrow in your bones produces over 100,000 red blood cells. We are fearfully and wonderfully made! Consider what takes place in the average adult of average weight, in a 24-hour period:

- The heart beats 103,689 times
- The blood travels 168,000,000 miles
- Air is inhaled and exhaled 23,040 times
- 438 cubic feet of air is inhaled
- 750 muscles are moved
- 7,000,000 brain cells are exercised

Can you doubt it? Do you not agree? We are fearfully and wonderfully made! If I were asked today what butterflies and ministry have in common, my answer would be something like this: "Oh, biology is the study of living things. And God is all about life. In fact, He created it, willed it into being. And what is more, He sustains it. Biology opens one's eyes to see further and deeper into the mystery of creation and ultimately leads one to praise Him with his whole heart. One cannot help but see that the whole earth is full of His glory."

All creatures of our God and King
Lift up your voice with us and sing,
Alleluia! Alleluia!
Thou burning sun with golden beam,
Thou silver moon with softer gleam!
O praise Him, O praise Him!
Alleluia! Alleluia! Alleluia!

Let all things their Creator bless,
And worship Him in humbleness.
O praise Him! Alleluia!
Praise, praise the Father, praise the Son,
And praise the Spirit, Three in One!
O praise Him, O praise Him!
Alleluia! Alleluia! Alleluia!

God has made us in His image. We are a trinity—body, mind, and spirit. As wonderful as the body is, the mind and spirit of man eclipse's that in that it is unique and splendid. Our Creator has endowed us with certain faculties that are not the property of other animals. We have a mind that is capable of creating music, art, and poetry. We build, we invent, and we discover. The human mind is staggering in what it can absorb and disseminate.

And the spirit of man? It is that part of us that relates to God—that believes, that worships, that prays, that trusts, hopes, and dreams—longing for that time when worship will be exercised in perfection.

We are fearfully and wonderfully made!

THE OBSERVABLE ORACLES OF GOD

The heavens declare his righteousness and all the people see his glory (Psalm 97:6, KJV).

"NATURE IS A SCHOOL-MISTRESS, the soul, the pupil; and whatever one has taught, or the other learned, has come from God—the Teacher of the teacher." These words, written by Tertullian in A.D. 199 must have come in part from his observation of the Master Teacher as well as from the created order. One cannot help but be impressed by the use Jesus made of his surroundings. Some have even gone so far as to suggest that He may have been a farmer instead of a carpenter. However, it could be argued that His use of terms connected with construction and the fact that He was raised in a carpenter's home suggest the latter. In any event, Jesus seems to be the originator of the "object lesson" sermon. He especially delighted in seizing nature to illustrate spiritual truth. If one were to take a careful look at chapters four through ten of Matthew's gospel, he would be struck with our Lord's employment of at least 25 separate references to some aspect of nature: bread, salt, light, birds, lilies, grass, snakes, stones, fish, sheep, wolves, fruit, thistles, seeds, fig trees, sand, rain, wind, foxes, wine, sparrows, water, sawdust, darkness, grapes. This is just a small sampling of what is found throughout the four gospels.

Wise indeed, is that teacher or preacher who follows the example of Christ as he seeks to communicate gospel truths. The handiwork of God affords us an inexhaustible supply of illustrations. For example, consider the employment of wind. It propels, destroys, cleanses, and extinguishes. A follower of Ingersoll, the infamous infidel, once boasted that he would build a barn that "God Almighty could not blow down." So he constructed a great stone structure, and called his neighbors to see it. The following year a great cyclone swept that part of the country, and yes, you guessed it, one of the first buildings to fall into a heap of ruins was this very barn! Ingersoll stood before the wreck silent, and one was heard to say, "It is the finger of God." Personally, I would have said, "It is the *breath* of God." In any case, Ingersoll gave no answer to this statement. In fact, it is said by those who knew him that since that day his infidelity left him.

Have you ever pondered the many applications of fire? It purifies, warms, illuminates, exposes, guides, and melts.

Or what of water? Think of what it symbolizes: cleansing, refreshment, the quenching of thirst, electric power, transportation. The point is, there is an endless supply of spiritual truths that emanates from nature.

Let us take the palm tree as an example of what we can learn from God's creation. In Psalm 92:12, we read, "The righteous shall flourish like a palm tree." Why not a peach tree or a plum tree or an oak tree? There are several reasons why this particular tree is linked with the righteous.

First, palm trees are known to be *breakers of bands*. Farmers seek to anchor their wire fences to the strongest tree they can find, preferably an oak tree. With the passing of time, the bark will grow over the wire. But not so with a palm tree! If you anchor a wire fence to a palm tree, it will not simply grow over the wire; it will swell up and break the bands. That is exactly what Jesus did for us on Calvary when He broke the bands of sin.

In the second place, palm trees are *well-grounded*. Just so with the righteous—grounded in the word of God—grounded in faith. Ephesians 3:17: "That Christ may dwell in your hearts by faith; that ye, being rooted and grounded in love…" (KJV). Paul wrote to the believers at Colosse: "If ye continue in the faith grounded and settled, and be not moved away from the hope of the gospel, which ye have heard…" (KJV). Like the palm tree, the roots of the righteous are firmly planted.

A third fact about palm trees is that they *have life at their cores*. We read in the Bible that "out of the heart are the issues of life." "The heart is deceitful and desperately wicked; who can know it?" David was referred to as "a man after God's own heart." At the core of David was a faith and trust in the great heart of God. And the same can be said of any follower of Christ.

In the fourth place, palm trees *require much water*. The righteous have been cleansed by the washing of the Word (Ephesians 5:26). They drink often from the "well of water"—Christ Himself. He sustains them and imparts life to them. The supply is endless and satisfying.

Fifthly, a palm tree will *bend but not break* when the storms rage. They are made for just that purpose. So it is with the righteous. Paul expressed this thought best when he wrote in II Corinthians 4:8,9: "We are afflicted in every way, but not crushed; perplexed, but not driven to despair; persecuted, but not forsaken; struck down, but not destroyed."

In the sixth place, palm trees *bear fruit the year around.* That is the way of the righteous as well. They are "seasonal" producers of fruit because the Lord who lives in them is not. Listen to what Jesus says in John 15:5: "I am the vine, you are the branches. If a man remains in me and I in him, he will bear much fruit; apart from me you can do nothing."

Lastly, consider this fact regarding these remarkable trees: The fruit of the palm tree *sweetens with age.* O, how true of the righteous. The longer we know Him, the sweeter we grow—in our disposition, and in our love for others. Solomon got it right when he declared, "As the apple tree among the trees of the wood, so is my beloved among the sons. I sat down under his shadow with great delight, and his fruit was sweet to my taste." The righteous not only "taste and see that the Lord is good." They are also sweet to those who taste their godly lives.

Yes, nature has much to teach us if we will take the time and effort to study our surroundings. Everything from trees to toads, flowers to frogs, birds to bears—they all testify to the wonder and love that God longs to plant within us. And school is always in session. Let us pray as did the hymn writer, Clara H. Scott, when she penned these words:

Open my eyes, that I may see
Glimpses of truth Thou hast for me;
Place in my hands the wonderful key
That shall unclasp and set me free.
Silently now I wait for Thee,
Ready, my God, Thy will to see
Open my eyes, illumine me,
Spirit divine!

SO WHAT'S AN ALBEDO?

You are the light of the world. A city on a hill cannot be hidden. Neither do people light a lamp and put it under a bowl. Instead they put it on its stand, and it gives light to everyone in the house. In the same way, let your light shine before men, that they may see your good deeds and praise your Father in heaven (Matthew 5:14-16).

"IT WAS MOONLIGHT. YES, DEFINITELY THE MOONLIGHT!" That was the answer given by a member of an air-rescue squad that helped retrieve a downed Air Force pilot from the cold waters of the Atlantic. It was in response to a question put to him by a member of the press: "What single factor, more than any other, in your estimation aided you in the safe return of the pilot?" The rescuer went on to add that working in darkness hampers greatly the effort put forth by a rescue team. Trying to locate and extricate someone from the vast, dark ocean is so much easier with good visibility.

Tell me reader, can you think of an obvious spiritual parallel? Every believer gives off a certain amount of reflected light which aids greatly in delivering those who are floundering in darkness. It is their *albedo* at work! So what is an albedo? The albedo of an object is the "ratio of light reflected from a surface of that object in proportion to the amount of light it receives." In astronomy it means the reflecting power of a planet.

Planets give off light from the light they receive from the sun. There is a difference in the amount of light they have in proportion to the sun, and in the amount of light which they give off in proportion to the light they receive. For example, the sun is 600,000 times brighter than the moon. Mercury gives off, as far as the earth is concerned, only 13% of the light it receives; the moon, 17%, Mars, 26%, Venus, 50%, Saturn and Jupiter, 62%. The point of these illustrations is this: The albedo of these planets is determined by three things: (1) the *character* or constituent makeup of the recipient of the light; (2) the *distance* that the planet is from the sun; (3) the relative *position* and *distance* of the planet from the sun and the earth.

With all this in mind, should we not be asking ourselves, "What is my Christian albedo?" What amount of spiritual light which I receive from the Son of Righteousness do I reflect upon a world of sin and need all about me? The light of Christ is ours to absorb and ours to reflect. The question is, how much do we absorb and reflect?

When Jesus said, "You are the light of the world," He was saying in effect, "I give you spiritual light." It is our duty, our privilege, and our opportunity to keep whatever amount of it we need for ourselves for our spiritual power and warfare. And, it is also our obligation to give it out to the world of darkness about us.

A little girl sat with her mother in church one Lord's Day morning. She looked with enchantment at the figures in the beautiful stained-glass windows, vivified and glorified by the light which filtered through them. She whispered, "Mommy, who are those people in the windows?" Her mother replied, "They are saints, darling." As they walked from church later, the girl said, "Mommy, now I know who saints are." "That's fine dear," said her mother. "Who are they?" "Well, mommy, saints are people through whom the light shines!" Once again, a child grasps an eternal truth.

As in the case with the planets, our spiritual albedo is also determined by the same three things. First, by our *character*—the level of spiritual maturity we possess. It is not hard to see that some need to get and absorb a great deal more light in order to have as much proportionate power as that possessed by the child of God who seems to radiate the glory of God. For you see, what we are inherently within our character will determine to a great degree not only how much spiritual light we receive and need, but how much we give off! By dwelling close to the glorious Presence, we can overcome all obstacles and be a blessing to others. This character that is formed within us takes time and effort. That is exactly why it is important to occasionally "push the pause button" in order to enjoy the Presence.

Secondly, our Christian albedo is determined by our relative *position* to the Son of Righteousness and to the world. There are certain planets that are not as observable in the night as the moon is in the daylight.

A planet never reflects the light of the sun until it rises above the horizon of the earth. When it gets up high enough to where it can absorb the glorious sunlight, it not only receives, but gives it out! This is one of the great paradoxes of the Christian faith: In the world, yet not in the world. We must rise high enough above the sin and shadows of the world in order to catch the clear sunlight of His glory. At the same time, we must live close enough to this world that the light we receive form Him will pierce into the dark recesses and shadows of sin and doubt and distress all about us. In short, light possessors become light transmitters.

When Jesus said that we must be the light of the world, He meant that we are to be *seen*—our witness must be obvious. We are to make the way clear for others. And we are to be *warning lights,* pointing out the dangers that lead to spiritual destruction and ruin.

It is not necessarily the amount of light that we give off that is important. What is important is the relative position and distance at which we live from where the need may be. We can shine for Him wherever His light is needed—the dens of doubt, the alleys of confusion, and the recesses of ignorance.

A.W. Milne labored as a missionary in a section of New Guinea where there were cannibals. There he died preaching the Gospel. His converts asked permission to place a marker on his grave on which they inscribed, HERE LIE THE REMAINS OF A.W. MILNE. WHEN HE CAME TO US THERE WAS NO LIGHT. WHEN HE DIED THERE WAS NO DARKNESS.

Thank God, Jesus is the Light of the world. Thank God, we are the light of the world. May our light so shine before men, that they may see our good works and glorify our Father who is in heaven.

PLOWING A STRAIGHT FURROW

Since, then, you have been raised with Christ, set your hearts on things above, where Christ is seated at the right hand of God. Set your mind on things above, not on earthly things (Colossians 3:1,2).

IT IS AMAZING THE NUMBER OF LIFE'S LESSONS one can learn from the land. When God created this planet He also built into its systems, principles that are timeless. The earth, and most especially the tilling of it, has so much to teach us if only we will take time to observe its oracles. Blessed indeed are those who have had the good fortune to grow up on a farm or at least spent some of their formative years with grandparents in such a setting. The soil and the growing process are excellent schoolmasters.

I can remember how, as a boy of 10, watching my grandfather plow a field behind a single horse. Sometimes he let me ride on the horse as he plowed and I would imagine that I was the Lone Ranger, chasing the bad guys.

Grandpa would begin by plowing a "back furrow" in the middle of the field. If this back furrow was straight, all the other furrows would be the same. Conversely, if it was crooked, so would all the others be. Grandpa would make a furrow as straight as an arrow. He said the secret was remembering four things: (1) do not look down at the furrow you are plowing; (2) always keep your head up; (3) never look back to see how you are doing; (4) look straight ahead and fix your eyes on some immovable object—such as a rock or tree or fence post.

Now we know that believers are plowmen, but not all plow a straight furrow. In Luke, chapter nine, Jesus speaks about discipleship. All the disciples are believers, but not believers are disciples. To become a believer, little effort is required. We bring nothing but ourselves—not good works, not a moral life, not even our religiosity! We simply come as we are and receive by faith God's free gift of salvation.

But to be a disciple, well that is another matter. Discipleship, from a biblical standpoint, means sacrifice, discipline, separation, suffering, and self-denial. In short, salvation is free, but discipleship costs. In Luke nine, Jesus spoke to two men about discipleship, but they wanted to be exempted, and the reason they gave was that they had family responsibilities—not terribly different from us when you come right down to it. We say that we will get serious about spiritual matters "as soon as we get caught up," or "as soon as we finish school," or "as soon as we get married and/or raise our children." And on and on it goes. The list just keeps getting longer. Are we really any different than these folks Jesus was addressing? The point Jesus is making is that in everything there is a crucial moment. If that moment is missed the thing will most likely not be done at all.

Psychologists tell us that every time we are stirred to action and yet do not act, the less likely we are to act at all. Take one example: sometimes we feel an impulse to write a letter. If we procrastinate, we may never do it. Jesus urges us to act at once when our heart is stirred. His words to the third man state a truth which no one can deny. No plowman ever plowed a straight furrow looking back over his shoulder. There are some whose hearts are in the past. They walk forever looking backwards, thinking of the good old days. One time a minister and his grandson were walking on the beach when they met an elderly man. The preacher tried his best to pass pleasantries with him but the old man was a bit of a grouch and complained bitterly about a recent sunstroke he had experienced. The little boy had been listening, but had not quite picked up the dialogue correctly. And when they left the grumbling old man he turned to his grandfather and said, "Granddad, I hope you never suffer from a sunset."

The believing child of God marches on, not to the sunset but to the dawn! The watchword of the kingdom of God is not, "Backward March!" It is "FORWARD MARCH!"

Exactly how can we make sure that our lives plow a straight furrow? How can we keep from looking back? Well, first of all it requires conviction. We are going to have to be convinced somehow that following Christ is more important than anything else in the world.

Secondly, it will require *commitment*. This involves the total person, moving in the direction He wants us to go, regardless of when or where.

Thirdly, it will require a certain *conduct.* We must live what we believe. Our prayer must be, "Teach Your holy ways, O Lord, and help me to walk in Your truth."

Back to the opening illustration. We cannot plow an acceptable field if we look down at the furrow we are plowing. God and God alone must receive the praise and glory. Pride in self-achievement will mess us all up! We must also keep our heads up. We will lose sight of where we are going if we are always looking at this life only. We simply must stop gazing at its problems, cares, burdens, and trials. It is imperative that we fix our eyes on Jesus, the Author and Finisher of our faith until we cross the finish line. After all, it is God's field that we are plowing. We want His rows to be straight, His grain to stand tall and true, His harvest to yield a hundred-fold.

FROGS IN SPACE

The heavens declare the glory of God; the skies proclaim the work of his hands. Day after day they pour forth speech; night after night they display knowledge. There is no speech or language where their voice is not heard. Their voice goes out into all the earth, their words to the ends of the world. In the heavens he has pitched a tent for the sun, which is like a bridegroom coming forth from his pavilion, like a champion rejoicing to run his course. It rises at one end of the heavens and makes its circuit to the other; nothing is hidden from its heat. (Psalm 19:1-6).

ACCORDING TO REUTERS NEWS AGANCY, June 12, 2003, a Russian cargo rocket, the only remaining supply link to the International Space Station, arrived at the outpost carrying food and recorded sounds of rain and croaking frogs for the homesick crew. Psychologists working with the Russian and U.S. space agencies say the sounds of nature will relax the crew and help them cope with the six-month stint in space.

Russia's Progress cargo vessel and its manned Soyuz were the only remaining ties to the $95 billion ISS since the Columbia space shuttle disaster grounded the U.S. fleet, leaving the outpost to struggle without deliveries from the larger craft.

The Progress M1-10 was packed with some 2,400 kg (5,300 pounds) of supplies for the station, including water, fuel and food, as well as music, recorded nature sounds and letters for U.S. astronaut Edward Lu and Russia's Yuri Malenchenko, on board since April.

The crew, reduced from the usual three astronauts in an effort to save fuel and water, was due to return to earth in October 2003.

The next Progress was scheduled to blast off from Russia's Baikonur base in Kazakhstan in August. Any hitch with either of the Progress or the Soyuz would prove crippling for the ISS which is funded by 16 states.

Since the Columbia shuttle disaster, Russian space officials planned an extra launch for November 20003. The Columbia, NASA's oldest shuttle, disintegrated over Texas in February only minutes before landing, killing all seven astronauts on board.

Frog Music aboard the Russian cargo rocket! Of all things! What will the government think of next? Actually, nature's sounds do have a soothing effect on one's psyche. For example, who has not lain on the beach and listened to the sounds of gentle waves lapping against the surf and not been put at ease? Or, what about a morning dove's coo? Or a babbling brook? Or wind chimes?

No doubt about it, the Lord has created a symphony of sorts—all for our benefit. Let nature's soft melodies quell your troubled mind. No need for headphones, CD's, or any recorded music for that matter. The sounds are all about us. Open your ears and listen to the sweet tones. Observe the relaxing of your tense muscles as creation sings her songs.

Whether thousands of miles away in outer space or by the shores of a lake, the calm repose nature offers frees one temporarily from all care.

Come to think of it, our universe offers serenity of soul that is devoid of sound, also. Visualize if you will, a warm summer evening, gazing at a beautiful sunset. And in the background are palm trees, waving gently in the breeze. Does not the mere thought of it deliver certain peacefulness? Who could improve on a mountain peak rising majestically to praise the One who designed her? How many times have weary souls gazed into a starry sky, only to be caught up in a breathtaking spell, mindful of nothing save the wonder of such a sight? "The heavens declare the glory of God; the skies proclaim the work of his hands. Day after day they pour forth speech; night after night they display knowledge. There is no speech or language where their voice is not heard" (Psalm 19:1-3).

THE REVITALIZING MINISTRY OF MUSIC

Music was as vital as the church edifice itself, more deeply stirring than all the glory of glass or stone. Many a stoic soul, doubtful of the creed, was melted by the music, and fell on his knees before the mystery that no words could speak.

—WILL DURANT
The Age of Faith, 1950

THE GIFT OF GOD

And he hath put a new song in my mouth, even praise unto our God: many shall see it, and fear, and shall trust in the Lord (Psalm 40:3, KJV).

IT IS HARD TO CONCEIVE OF A CULTURE DEVOID OF MUSIC, but a story comes out of Central America that confirms the existence of just such a phenomenon. A missionary couple had entered a region of southern Mexico and begun working with a people group known as the "Chol Indians." The primary task of these missionaries was to translate the New Testament into the language of this tribe. In a short time it was discovered that the Chol Indians did not know how to sing. In fact, they did not even have a word for "singing" in their language. Imagine that—a culture completely destitute of music! However, it was not long before they were introduced to this expression of praise. You see, the Gospel, when embraced, puts a song in one's heart.

Today the Chol church is thriving and the believers not only raise their voices in praise to their Maker, but they have become known throughout that region as the "singing people." Who else could accomplish this but the living God Himself?

Judaism and Christianity are singing religions. No doubt about it. Wherever they gather for worship there will be singing—songs of praise and adoration, songs of victory, songs of testimony, songs calling for commitment and service.

On the other hand, atheism is song-less; agnosticism has nothing to sing about; the various forms of idolatry are not tuneful; even the cults who sing the songs of Zion are guilty of plagiarism; but those who truly love the Lord, say, "O come, let us sing unto the Lord." And when Christ came to this planet, the angels greeted His birth with praise. From the beginning, Christian music has gained in fullness and strength of voice with each passing generation.

There is an old Jewish legend which says that, after God had created the world, He called the angels to Him and asked them what they thought of it, and one of them said, "One thing is lacking; the sound of praise to the Creator." So God created music and it was heard in the whisper of the wind and in the song of the birds; and to man also was given the gift of song. And all down the ages this gift has indeed proved a blessing to multitudes.

But the problem is that many of us are too busy, too preoccupied to hear the voice of creation. We need to shut the computer off, turn off the vacuum cleaner, go outside and listen to nature singing. Hear the pine trees whistle to their Creator as the wind passes by. Listen to the song of the owl and wolf as they serenade the One who made them. Take a trip to mighty Niagara and hear the sounds of falling water as they sing in bass, praises to God.

But if you want to hear the highest expression of praise, tune in to the crown of creation—listen as a redeemed child of God declares his praise to the One who recreated him. As the old gospel songwriter put it, "Holy, Holy, is what the angels sing; and I expect to help them make the courts of heaven ring. But when I sing redemption's story, they will fold their wings, for angels never felt the joy that our salvation brings" (Johnson Oatman Jr., 1894).

The music of the Gospel is so powerful and enduring that even the strongest assaults from the enemy cannot drown it out. The Psalm-singing of the early Christian martyrs as they marched to their deaths in the arena caused the Romans to stand in awe as they witnessed a new and revolutionary force coming into being. And it continues to this day!

Some years ago, the staff of an Armenian Mission was undergoing a severe persecution for their Christian faith—even to the point of the threat of death. They gathered in a room, silently waiting for the end to come. They felt their coronation day had arrived. In fact, they were so convinced of it that the women dressed in white, for they would be seeing the Bridegroom shortly! Outside the compound wall was the frantic, crazy mob, shouting in one breath the praises of Allah and the doom of the Christians. But in spite of the frenzy without, there was an unearthly calm within. None feared, no one complained. In fact, one broke out in song, a hymn in which all joined. The cry of the mob was drowned out by the singing saints as they sang together…

> Peace, perfect peace, our future
> All unknown,
> But Jesus we know, and He is
> On the throne.

The music died, the mob dispersed, the peace of God reigned without, within.

There is something within the human heart that must find expression. That something is the presence of God. That expression is music. We were made to sing! Music is love in search of a word.

The people of God and music are inseparable. It has been that way from the beginning. **Moses** led the congregation of Israel in a song of victory after the Exodus. So far as we know, he was the first choir director in one glorious singspiration! **Miriam**, Moses' sister, followed his lead and sang to the Lord as well. **Deborah**, one of the Judges of Israel, sang a song of praise after the defeat of the Canaanites. **David** played the harp to soothe the lambs under his care and later strummed this same instrument to calm the troubled spirit of King Saul. He went on to compose most of the Psalms that have been such a source of hope and inspiration to millions. **Paul** and **Silas** sang to the Lord while in prison, and in the Book of Revelation, John saw a vision of heaven where the angels and redeemed are pictured as a vast choir, praising the Lamb upon His throne.

The ministry of music is almost impossible to measure. Martin Luther put it well when he said, "I have not pleasure in any man who despises music. It is no invention of ours; it is the gift of God. I place it next to theology."

Many of the great hymns of the church are nothing more than theological statements—hymns such as, "A Mighty Fortress Is Our God," "O For a Thousand Tongues to Sing," "It is Well With My Soul," and "How Great Thou Art."

These and other hymns have served the church well as she seeks to keep on track—to preserve historic orthodox Christian belief. A study of the great majestic hymns of the ages is not unlike an advanced course in theology.

Who can ascertain the positive effect Christian music has had upon the masses? Who can measure their impact and influence? Only eternity will reveal how many dwell in that blessed land due to the words of a hymn or chorus. Who can imagine Moody without Sanky or Graham without Shea? Countless thousands were ushered into the Kingdom of God as they walked to an altar to the strains of "Just as I Am."

Yes, sacred music is a many-splendored thing—the speech of angels, a tonic for the saddened soul, and a call for commitment. It motivates, inspires, encourages, challenges, and affords the child of God a vehicle with which to extol Almighty God. Within the context of worship there are recorded instances wherein music so gripped the hearers that preaching was set aside. The Holy Spirit's power flowed through the combination of tune and lyrics to convict, bless, and console those present. "The Lord is my strength and my shield; my heart trusted in him, and I am helped: therefore my heart greatly rejoiceth; and with my song will I praise him" (Psalm 28:7, KJV). These are the words of the "sweet singer of Israel." Need I say more?

MELODY-MAKING

Speaking to yourselves in psalms and hymns and spiritual songs, singing and making melody in your heart to the Lord (Ephesians 5:19, KJV).

IT HAPPENED IN THE SPRING OF '96. It should not have surprised me, but it did. I did not see it coming, although I should have. I had been warned about it many times—too much preaching, teaching, and especially singing. That is right, you guessed it. I lost the use of my voice temporarily. I mean I lost it completely! This was not a case of laryngitis. This was a serious case of muteness.

So off to my family physician I hurried. After he examined me, he said, "You have a small growth on your vocal cords. I'm sending you to a specialist. He'll remove it. Not to worry; it's common among those of your profession. Your vocal cords are tired and they are rebelling."

I asked my congregation to remember me in prayer as I headed for the specialist. When he examined me he could not see any evidence of a growth whatsoever. Praise The Lord! He did say that my vocal cords were quite red and that I should cut back on my activities for a while. He also encouraged me not to sing along with the congregation for a few weeks and definitely stay away from solos and participation with the choir.

But how does a singing pastor do that? It is a little bit like asking a canary to stop chirping. They were made to sing and so was I! The preacher's number one asset is his voice. If he has to lay that aside for any length of time, it would be a disaster. Can you imagine a carpenter without a hammer? Or a golf pro without clubs? Now you have the picture.

Well, I did cut back a little. It was very difficult, but I really had no choice. Eventually my ability to speak came back. But it was several months before I really could resume singing. That was the hard part. Making a melody to the Lord is such a part of worship—not just in the house of God, but in the secret place as well.

The use of music in worship cannot be overestimated. Lifting a hymn or praise chorus to the Lord causes one's spirit to soar. In so doing we are reminded of the glorious promises of His Word. And even if our voice is silenced, we can make melodies "in our heart." How often has the Lord manifested Himself to us in a special sense while we were singing a love song to Him?

Now I am well aware that there are some religious groups that do not make use of music in their worship services at all. I respect their position, but I certainly do not share it. The Old and New Testaments testify to the grand use of music as both Jews and Christians sought to express their love to God. A casual glance at a hymnbook will reveal how music is both God-directed and man-directed.

Have you ever been discouraged? Try singing, "He is Able." Sad? What about, "It is Well With my Soul." Need some guidance? Break out with, "He Leadeth Me." Anxious? Try, "I Know Whom I Have Believed." Whatever the need, we can find a song to sing. And the great thing about making music to the Lord is that you do not even have to be able to carry a tune! It is the heart that really counts. I remember Ronald (an alias) from my home church. He sang in the choir. He sang loudly, with gusto. He sang way off-key, but his face was aglow with the joy of the Lord. He was in harmony with God, if not the rest of the choir. And even though he probably should have limited his singing to the shower, his radiant countenance was a blessing to all who knew him. Satan himself cannot silence the song within unless we give him permission.

In the period following the Reformation, singing in churches was confined mostly to psalms. It was thought wrong and even sinful to make up new hymns. One man who helped change all this was Isaac Watts. By the age of seven, he was composing so many poems that his father became irritated with him and ordered him to stop. But Isaac refused. The music was within. So his father took him to the woodshed one day to "spank the poetry out of him." But poetry was too deeply ingrained in Isaac for that.

When he was eighteen, Isaac complained to his father that the hymns in the church service were uninspiring. "Well," said his father, "if you think you can improve on them, go ahead and try." And try he did! He wrote a hymn which was sung the following Sunday. And during the next two years he wrote a new hymn for each service. At first his hymns met with opposition. People considered them too emotional, but Isaac wrote on. Today his hymns are sung in churches throughout the world. The Lord guided his pen to write such never-to-be-forgotten hymns as, "When I survey the Wondrous Cross," and "Joy to the World."

There's something about a song for the Lord
That stirs the heart within.
That reaches out to touch a life
Burdened down with sin.
It's the Spirit of God breathing on the words
And flowing through the tune,
That captures the soul and brings relief
To those headed for sure doom.

Oh, sing a song of worship and praise
To the One seated on the Throne.
For His love and care have reached us here
To assure that we're never alone.
Let our voice be raised in endless praise,
To the Grandest Composer of all.
He has set us free, we are not the same,
We have answered His loving call.

BAND LESSONS

Praise the LORD. Praise God in his sanctuary; praise him in his mighty heavens. Praise him for his acts of power; praise him for his surpassing greatness. Praise him with sounding of the trumpet, praise him with the harp and lyre, praise him with tambourine and dancing, praise him with the strings and flute, praise him with the clash of cymbals. Let everything that has breath praise the LORD. Praise the LORD (Psalm 150:1-6).

MUSIC CLASS WAS REQUIRED when I was in grammar school. Like countless pilgrims before me, I was introduced to that little black thing called a recorder. I remember at the time wanting desperately to move on to the trumpet, but was told that I had to learn the basics. There would be plenty of time later for a trumpet. Even though I was greatly disappointed, I can honestly say that upon reflection, that music class opened up to me a whole new world. Music would become an integral part of my life, and the lessons I would learn from participation in it would benefit me for years to come.

By the seventh grade I felt I was ready for the big move up. I approached the music teacher and said that I wanted to play in the junior high band. He welcomed my interest but said that the only position open was French horn. French horn? I wanted to play the trumpet or drums! But he said it was the French horn or nothing. So I humbled myself, began taking lessons, and shortly thereafter found myself in junior high band.

By the time next year rolled around I was asked to move up to the senior high band. They were in need of French horn players. As an eighth grader, to be accorded this opportunity was quite an honor. This promotion was not so much about talent as it was about desperation.

I was too small for football and basketball so the next most popular thing on campus was the band! Oh, how I loved that uniform—concerts, traveling to competitions, marching in parades and at football games. Those were grand days to be sure. But without a doubt, the most advantageous aspect of this participation was in the life principles I learned. Let me share a few with you.

LESSON ONE: PRACTICE! It always showed up in the performance. It contributed to a sense of self-confidence. So it is with our relationship with the Lord. Spending daily time in God's Word, memorizing key passages, contributes greatly to our growth in Him and usefulness to Him. After all, a true musician wants to be at his best. One time a committee asked Enrico Caruso, the great tenor, to sing at a concert that would benefit charity. The chairman said, "Of course, Mr. Caruso, as this is a charity affair we would not expect much from you. Your name alone will draw a crowd and you can merely sing some song requiring little effort or skill." Caruso drew himself up and replied, "Gentlemen, Caruso never does less than his best." And something tells me that Caruso practiced often in an effort to be constantly at his best. O, may the Lord help us to have that same attitude in our service to Him…being prepared at all times, so that we might be at our best when the Lord calls upon us.

LESSON TWO: INSTRUMENT MAINTENANCE. Keeping it clean, polished, protected from the elements. Spiritually speaking, the same could be said of the human instrument through which God wants to convey His love. We must keep ourselves unspotted from the world. The best sounds emanate from that equipment which is kept in the best condition possible.

LESSON THREE: TUNE UP TO THE DESIGNATED APPOINTEE. This person, (usually the concert master) or instrument became our standard. The Bible is the standard by which we measure our behavior and belief. When we stray from it our lives produce a dissonance that is unpleasant and unproductive.

LESSON FOUR: KEEP YOUR EYES ON THE CONDUCTOR. If you do not, you may lag behind or rush ahead. Timing is extremely important. So it is in the spiritual realm. We must "turn our eyes upon Jesus, look full in His wonderful face, and the things of earth will grow strangely dim in the light of His glory and grace." A good orchestra strives for balance and unity. So does a church.

LESSON FIVE: FOLLOW THE MUSIC. Rest when it is called for, keep the sound level in accordance with the composer's wishes.

There are times when softness is called for; there are times when loudness is appropriate. Again, God's Instruction Book, when followed, will produce a life of sweet harmony.

LESSON SIX: REMEMBER THAT YOU ARE A PART OF THE WHOLE. A concert will not be what it is intended to be without everyone participating. No single member should despise himself. Do not be like the piccolo player who did just that. Halfway through a rehearsal, with trumpets blaring, drums rolling, and violins singing their rich melody, the piccolo player muttered to himself, "What good am I doing? I might as well not be playing. Nobody can hear me anyway." So he placed his instrument to his lips but made no sound. Within moments the conductor cried, "Stop the music! Stop the music! Where's the piccolo?" Perhaps many people did not realize that the piccolo was missing, but the conductor did. We play chiefly to please him. And if we achieve that, the audience benefits greatly. So it is in the Christian life. We strive to please the Master. He is glorified and others benefit. God knows when we do not play the part assigned to us, even if others do not.

The church is like one grand orchestra, tuned to Christ, its head, playing for Him. He is our audience as well as our director. Our music will be beautiful and harmonious as we keep focused on Him. He is our tuning fork. His Word is our sheet music, and the song we play is directed heavenward. We make lovely music together. We are not jealous or envious of one another because He is a part of us. The score we play? "Rhapsody in White."

SINGING WITH GRACE

Let the word of Christ dwell in you richly in all wisdom, teaching and admonishing one another in psalms and hymns and spiritual songs, singing with grace in your hearts to the Lord (Colossians 3:16, KJV).

JOHN WESLEY, THE FATHER OF METHODISM, believed that congregational singing was an extremely important element of worship. It sets the tone for what is to follow. It prepares the heart. It establishes a mood of receptivity. In the year 1742, Wesley gave instructions on the fine art of singing to his lay preachers (Works, Volume 14, page 346). Perhaps these same rules should be posted on the front of every hymnal in our churches today.

1. SING ALL. *See that you join with the congregation as frequently as you can.* Let not a slight degree of weakness or weariness hinder you. If it is a cross to you, take it up and you will find a blessing. This is none other than a reminder that congregational singing is an expression of "corporate" worship. We are the body of Christ, the temple of God, the called together ones. Our singing is a witness to that very fact—a witness not only to those who visit us but to the community at large. Let the term "singing Methodists" become our byword!
2. SING LUSTILY. *Beware of singing as if you were half asleep; but lift up your voice with strength.* Enthusiasm! That is the key thought here. Perhaps Mr. Wesley had Ecclesiastes 9:10 in mind: "Whatever your hand finds to do, do it with all your might." Or perhaps he was inspired by Colossians 3:23: "Whatever you do, work at it with all your heart, as working for the Lord, not for men." Apparently Wesley believed that anything worth doing for the Lord is worth doing well.
3. SING MODESTLY. *Do not bawl so as to be heard above or distinct from the rest; but strive to unite your voices together so as to make one clear, melodious sound.* At first glance, this may seem to contradict the above, but not so. This is a warning against

exhibitionism, against egotism, and a call for unity, harmony, and togetherness.

In 1765, John Fawcett was called to pastor a very small congregation at Wainsgate, England. He labored for seven years, but his salary was so meager that he and his wife had difficulty making ends meet. Though the congregation was composed mainly of poor people, they compensated for this lack by their faithfulness and warm fellowship. One day Dr. Fawcett received a call from a much larger church and, after much prayer and consideration, agreed to accept their invitation. As his few possessions were being placed into a wagon, many of his parishioners gathered to say goodbye. Touched by this outpouring of love, Fawcett and his wife said to those assembled, "Unload the wagon. We cannot break these wonderful ties of fellowship."

This experience served as the inspiration for Fawcett's now famous hymn, "Blest Be the Tie That Binds." Each time hymns of this nature are sung in churches throughout the world, unity is fostered, a united front is presented.

Taking this a step further, consider music's contribution to the church at large. It has an international appeal, crossing cultural and language barriers. The hymnbook is the greatest argument for church unity that exists today. For example, *Holy, Holy, Holy, Lord God Almighty,* was written by Hamber, an Anglican. *Jesus, Lover of My Soul,* was written by Toplady, a Calvinist. Doddridge, a Congregationalist, wrote, *O Happy Day.* Faber, a Roman Catholic, wrote, *There's a Wideness in God's Mercy*. And Whittier, a Quaker, wrote, *Eternal Goodness.*

And on and on we could cite—the numerous faith communities represented in our hymnals. Little wonder then that the Spirit of God will cause the walls to fall down as we gather together at various interdenominational meetings and sing our great Redeemer's praise.

4. SING IN TIME. *Whatever time is sung, be sure to keep with it. Do not run before nor stay behind it.* Not bad advice in anything

we do for the Lord. He is our Master Conductor. The sounds that our lives make will be pleasant to His ears as we seek to keep in step with His will and way.

5. SING SPIRITUALLY. *Have an eye to God in every word you sing. In order to do this, attend strictly to the sense of what you sing and see that your heart is not carried away with the sound, but offered to God carefully.* In others words, we must think about what we are singing. Each time we pick up a hymnbook or chorus book in church we should ask ourselves, "Do I really mean what I am singing? Do I intend to live these words? Is this coming from my heart or am I just going through the motions?" When we sing, "I'll Go Where You Want Me to Go, Dear Lord," do we honestly mean it? When we hear of a neighbor in need, do we respond?

   We sing "I Love to Tell the Story" and cannot remember when we last shared our testimony with anyone.

   We join our voices together to sing "Trusting Jesus" and fall apart when a crisis comes our way.

   This is not singing from the heart, but from the vocal cords only. The sincerity of our devotion is demonstrated by what we do. Music from the heart is that which involves hands and feet as well as mouths.

Precious Lord, help us to sing out of sincerity. You deserve our very best. May we be aware of the great thoughts expressed in Christian music and commit ourselves to give substance to them for Thy name's sake. Amen.

COME, PLAY A TUNE

Praise the Lord with harp: sing unto him with the psaltery and an instrument of ten strings (Psalm 33:2, KJV).

I will sing a new song unto thee, O God: upon a psaltery and an instrument of ten strings will I sing praise unto thee (Psalm 144:9, KJV).

MARK TWAIN HAD A BAD HABIT of spicing his conversation with profanity. Twain's wife, a delicate, refined woman, often became very upset with his rough language. She tried in many ways to cure him of it, but to no avail. On one occasion she tried a shock technique. When Twain arrived at home from a trip, he was greeted at the door with a string of profanity from his wife. From the lips of this delicate, refined woman, he heard everything he had ever said of a profane nature. Twain stood quietly, listening, until she had finished. Then he said, "My dear, you have the words, but not the music."

This is what often happens to us in our worship experience. We have the words but not the music—not enough soul, not enough enthusiasm flowing into it. Consequently, not enough joy, contagious joy, flowing out of it.

Genuine praise to God issues from a heart that is in tune with His—a melody of sorts that rises to His throne and brings Him the glory that He alone deserves.

Someone has found that the words praise or rejoice in their various forms appears no less than 600 times in the Bible. Why should we praise the Lord? Let me suggest several reasons, some apparent, some not:

1. Because He is worthy of it. After all, it is He who created us and the world we enjoy. He also provided for our inner re-creation. And if that is not enough, He lives within us—hearing and answering our prayers, forgiving us when we fail, encouraging us when we are weak and afraid. And to top it all off, He is preparing a place for us to enjoy His presence throughout eternity.

2. Because God desires us to praise Him—continually and in everything, as a witness and encouragement to our fellow travelers.
3. Because praise is powerful in its effect. Nehemiah was right when he said, "The joy of the Lord is our strength."
4. Because our outlook on life is changed. Philippians 4:8: "Finally, brothers, whatever is true, whatever is noble, whatever is right, whatever is pure, whatever is lovely, whatever is admirable—if anything is excellent or praiseworthy, think about such things."
5. Because praise helps our faith to grow. Our focus from self and our problems is shifted to God and His power.

The Bible declares that "God inhabits the praises of His people." So, then, there is a sense in which we can determine the degree to which God is present in our gatherings as we focus on praise. A praising church is an attractive church. The atmosphere is charged. Others are drawn to the positive, uplifting surroundings.

The Psalmist declared, "I will sing a new song to Thee, O God; upon a ten-stringed harp I will play to Thee" (Psalm 144:9, KJV). An old man at a prayer meeting prayed like this: "O Lord, we will praise Thee with an instrument of ten strings." Folks in the service wondered what the ten strings were and they soon found out. The old saint prayed on: "We shall praise Thee with THIS instrument of ten strings. It was as if he was suggesting that we can be to God a human harp of praise!

Uncertainty exists as to the exact number of musical instruments mentioned in the Bible, but we do know that the music performed on them was of a joyful nature (see I Samuel 10:5 and Amos 6:5).

Bible instruments fall into three main categories: stringed, wind, and percussion. Those most often appearing in Scripture are: harp, lyre, organ, psaltery, sackbut, dulcimer, flute, horn, trumpet, timbrel, sistrim, cymbal, bell, and triangle.

The harp is the first to be mentioned in the Bible (Genesis) and was invented by Jubal. The most common form was made up of ten strings. We have been designed in such a manner as to cause us to praise our Maker with our whole being—all ten strings. For example, we have **two eyes**. How do we honor God with our eyes? By looking to Him for salvation. As the prophet said, "Look unto me, and be ye saved, all the ends of the earth: for I am God and there is none else" (Isaiah 45:22, KJV). We also look to Him for endurance, as the writer to the Hebrews instructs us: "Looking unto Jesus, the author and finisher of our faith" (12:2, KJV). We also look to the Word of God for hope and help. "Open my eyes that I might behold wondrous things in Your law" (Psalm 119:37). We have eyes to see God's creation which reveals His glory, majesty, and power. And insofar as evil is concerned, we are encouraged to look away from it and focus on our God.

We also possess **two ears** whereby we can listen to the Lord's voice. Recently the London Times stated that there are about 4,000 autistic children in England. These unfortunate ones usually do not react to messages received and transmitted from the eyes and ears to the brain. Consequently, they live in a world where words have little or no meaning. This is a terrible affliction, to be sure. But there is something far worse than this. Jesus spoke of it when He said, "Hearing, they hear not, neither do they understand." They are spiritually autistic!

An ungodly tavern keeper who liked music decided to attend one of John Wesley's meetings to hear the singing. He had resolved, however, not to listen to the sermon. So he sat with his head down and his fingers in his ears. But when God wants to speak to a man's soul, He will have His way! A fly flew on the man's nose and when he attempted to drive it away, he heard nine words that forever changed his life: "HE THAT HATH EARS TO HEAR, LET HIM HEAR!" From that moment on he had no rest in his soul. He returned the next night, listened intently, and was converted.

The voice of God can be heard in a variety of ways and means. We should have our ears attuned to hear from God. He has something He wants to say to us—something personal and relevant to our lives. "How great you are, O Sovereign Lord! There is no one like you, and there is no God but you, as we have heard with our own ears" (II Samuel 7:22). But to hear God will require something on our part. We will have to draw aside from the world and give Him an opportunity to speak.

Strings five and six on this human instrument point to **two hands** with which to praise Him—hands to lift in prayer, hands and fingers to turn the pages of His Word, hands to reach out and touch someone in need, hands to lift up the fallen. These are the instruments of blessing. I am told that the letters O.H.M.S., printed on British government stationary, mean, "On Her Majesty's Service!" So, too, every child of the heavenly Ruler should remember that they also bear a similar seal (Ephesians 4:30) which marks them as a special ambassador of Christ to a needy world. We must summon up our best for we are on the King's business!

We have been blessed with **two feet** with which to praise God by walking according to His ways. When we walk the road of obedience, the highway of holiness, the narrow way, we are truly walking in the King's highway. We take the road less traveled. Our feet are shod with the gospel of peace. How beautiful are the feet of those who take glad tidings to those in search of truth.

String number nine: our **tongue**! "Let the redeemed of the Lord say so" (Psalm 107:2). Our tongues have turned from cursing to singing His praises, from gossiping to gospel-sharing, from lying to truth-spreading. Two businessmen lived side-by-side in a suburb. One was a professing Christian and the other an unbeliever. They rode the same commuter train to work every Monday through Friday on their way to work. Several years were thus spent in pleasant, neighborly associations, talking about sports, current events, the weather, their respective families, and business. And then the unbeliever took desperately ill. His wife became very concerned about his spiritual state and at first did not know where to turn. Finally she asked her husband, "John, would you let me call a good Christian to come and talk to you?" "No," he replied. "There's nothing they can offer. My neighbor is supposed to be a good Christian and we have ridden many miles together. He's never recommended his faith to me. If his religion is not worth talking about, it can't be worth dying by." Let the redeemed of the Lord say so!

The tenth and final string is our **mind**. How do we praise the Lord with our mind? May I suggest at least four ways:

- By meditating on His Word
- By developing an attitude of gratitude
- By dwelling on His attributes
- By remembering His mighty acts on behalf of men

Meditation has almost become a lost art. Perhaps we have let the Eastern religionists scare us away from it. Meditation in the biblical sense is simply feeding upon the Word and digesting its meaning. But that takes time, does it not? And that is the whole point of this book—to pause long enough to dwell on what the Lord wants to reveal to us. Someone has rightly observed, "It is not in the bees touching the flowers that gathers the honey, but their abiding for a time on them and drawing out the sweet nectar that is vital."

So, also, it is not he who reads most, but rather he who meditates upon divine truths that will produce the choicest, wisest, and strongest Christian.

An instrument of ten strings! May we keep it in tune to the only One who has perfect pitch. May the Lord play upon it for His delight. Let Him strum out melodies of exaltation that harmonize with His will.

Two eyes, two ears, two hands, two feet, one tongue and one mind—ten strings. Let them praise God together in one glorious anthem!

SONGS IN THE NIGHT

By day the Lord directs his love, at night his song is with me—a prayer to the God of my life (Psalm 42:8).

I WONDER HOW MANY POETS AND WRITERS WERE INSPIRED by the above verse and others like it? It is easy to sing when the way is clear, when the sun is shining brightly and all is fair. But when the path grows dark and hope has been nearly smothered by trouble, it is difficult to break out in song. And yet, is not this the true test of faith—the ability to sing though the way is grim? The saints have sung their sweetest when the thorn has pierced their hearts. Sorrow and trouble produce songs in the night.

Picture, if you will, Paul and Silas in prison. Their plight is recorded in Acts chapter 16. See them languishing in their cell. They had been dragged before the magistrates and accused of teaching illegal customs to the citizens of Philippi. The magistrates, giving in to the mob, found them guilty and had them stripped and beaten with rods until they could barely move. Then they were thrown into the inner prison with their feet in stocks.

There they were. Cut off from their supporters, in a dark, damp, rat-infested jail, bodies wracked with pain, unable to move about. What was their reaction? Did they complain and curse the night? No, quite the contrary. In fact, they did a very strange thing. They began singing. That is right, singing. The beating had not reached their hearts and, therefore, their vocal cords. If Satan expected his assault on the missionaries to dampen their spirits, he was in for one huge disappointment. Though their bodies were imprisoned, their spirits soared heavenward. They still had a song—a song in the night—a song of praise. What exactly did they sing? No one knows for sure. Some have suggested, "Through It All," or "I'm Gonna Keep on Singing." The truth is, they probably sang one of the many psalms which were written for just such an occasion. Those walls had never heard such sounds before. So loud were they, that the prisoners throughout the jail heard them. What a testimony! Then God let go with an earthquake that canceled the work of the devil. The cell doors flew open and the anchor pins slipped out of the walls. Even the stocks were broken. No one was hurt, everyone was set free.

There is no doubt in my mind but what this incident has served as an inspiration for countless numbers of saints from Martin Luther, who translated the Bible into German from his incarceration in Wartburg Castle, to John Bunyan, as he wrote Pilgrim's Progress from the Bedford Jail. Is it not true that the brook would lose its song if we removed the rocks? Trials and troubles of all kinds do not drown out the song of the redeemed; they only serve to enhance it.

George Matheson, who was engaged to be married, learned he would soon be totally blind. When his fiancé was told of his plight she responded by saying, "I cannot marry a blind man." She left him and his dreams shattered. He thought of taking his life at first. But instead, he took hold of himself and wrote the moving hymn, "O Love That Wilt Not Let Me Go."

A native pastor in Africa took a foreign friend to visit a large leper colony. When they entered the colony, they had to put on sterile robes and medicated boots. They walked past the little homes and gardens to the great temple. Permission had been given to hold a service there for the Christians. One by one the lepers came limping into the temple. Their swollen faces wore happy smiles! When the lepers had all gathered, the leader asked, "What shall we sing? What is your most loved hymn?" The foreigner thought these lepers would call for "I Must Tell Jesus All of My Troubles." To his surprise, the request was quite different. The song the lepers loved best was one by Eliza E. Hewitt:

> Singing I go along life's road,
> Praising the Lord, praising the Lord;
> Singing I go along life's road,
> For Jesus has lifted my load!

I have stood at the bedside of dying Christians and heard them softly sing their way to Glory. Regardless of the circumstances, the melody of the Master is forever in the heart and no force, however strong, can completely obliterate it.

We have a song that Jesus gave us, it was sent from heaven above; there never was a sweeter melody; it's the melody of love. And it is so deep that it cannot be silenced by men or devils.

OUT OF THE MOUTH OF BABES

From the lips of children and infants you have ordained praise because of your enemies, to silence the foe and the avenger (Psalm 8:2).

IT WAS A COLD JANUARY DAY, a good day to visit the mall and engage in one of my favorite pastimes—people watching, while my wife engaged in one of her favorite activities—shopping! I was sitting on a bench with some other lonesome-looking men, who were also waiting for their wives, when I heard the most beautiful song my ears have ever had the privilege of entertaining. I turned to see the origin of this sweet melody when my eyes fell upon a little girl of four or five. There she was, walking with her tiny hand in her mother's, oblivious to her surroundings, singing at the top of her lungs, "Jesus loves me, this I know, for the Bible tells me so. Little ones to him belong, they are weak but He is strong. Yes, Jesus loves me, yes, Jesus loves me; yes, Jesus loves me, the Bible tells me so." Over and over she repeated the lyrics to the amusement of the mall shoppers, totally uninhibited by their stares. It was quite a moment. Innocence on display. Or should I say, faith exposed. It is true, out of the mouth of babes God has ordained praise.

This experience reminded me of something I once read about Karl Barth, the renowned German theologian who dominated the theology of the 20th century. In 1962, six years before his death, Barth made his only visit to the United States. One evening he lectured at Union Theological Seminary in Richmond, Virginia. After the lecture he met with students in the coffee shop for some informal dialogue. A student asked him if there was any way he could summarize his vast theological findings. He wanted to know what Barth thought was the essence of the Christian faith. The great theologian paused for a moment. No doubt the others waited for some profound, intellectual insight. Then Barth answered deliberately, "Yes, I can summarize in a few words my understanding of the Christian faith. Let me put it this way: 'Jesus loves me this I know, for the Bible tells me so.'"

This was an absolutely overwhelming moment for his hearers. There sat the most renowned theologian of the age expressing his final conclusion in words he learned at his mother's knees. A little girl in a mall and a theological giant had something in common—they both understood the essence of Christianity. We are reminded in the Bible to become as children so that we can enter the kingdom. The core of our faith may be understood in the simplicity of a childhood song.

John Wesley in his young days took his sermons and read them to an old domestic servant. He told her to stop him every time he said something she did not understand. His manuscripts became masses of changes, alterations, erasures, and additions. But they were able to be understood, and that was his main concern. The childhood hymn, "Jesus Loves Me," is also easily understood, so much so that its message may be overlooked.

Jesus loves me this I know. Stated more simply, "I know Jesus loves me." One of the foremost human needs is to know that we are loved. When someone says, "I love you," something wonderful happens inside. Self-doubt, despair, and loneliness are chased away. Our failures are covered and a feeling of self-acceptance sweeps over us. To be loved, "warts and all," is a blessing indeed. And how much more a blessing to be loved by God Himself! He looked beyond our faults and saw our need. He set His love upon us. He went to extreme lengths to demonstrate it, even the cross.

For the Bible tells me so. I have yet to hear a sinner sing this song from his heart. Even though it is true for him, he feels a certain reluctance to declare it for sin is in the way. In fact, the unbeliever asks, "How can one know beyond any doubt that God loves them?" He wants to debate and put down those who sing this simple, yet profound song. The reason the Christian knows he is loved is because the Bible declares it to be so. This word was not found somewhere under a rock. It was not dictated to David or Moses or Paul. Rather, it was "breathed upon" holy men of old who, in turn, preserved it and passed it on to succeeding generations.

The Bible is not a science text, although it does contain a great deal of scientific information. It is not an encyclopedia, although it does include a vast amount of knowledge on almost any subject. It is not an answer book or textbook on psychology, but in its pages are principles by which we can live happier and healthier lives. The Bible has as its primary goal the revelation of God's nature and plan for humanity and its central message is "God loves His creatures, even His sinning creatures." And those who believe it have embraced this central message with passion.

Little ones to Him belong. I once heard a definition of a Christian that has stayed with me: "One who believes, behaves, and belongs." Have you ever felt as if you did not belong—that you did not have a place, a standing, a family? You can belong to Jesus. If you are a Christian, you DO belong to Him. If you are not, you CAN belong to Him. When believers feel small or insignificant, they can take this as their hope and comfort: "I BELONG TO HIM!" Our worth flows out of our relationship with Him. We are favored, set apart as His special possession—adopted into His glorious family. We were once orphans, all of us, but our wonderful Lord had it in mind eons ago to take us into His house. Listen as He invites us in: "Behold I stand at the door and knock. If any man hears my voice and opens the door I will come in and have fellowship with him." He comes into our house (dwelling place of the spirit) and then takes us in His! And all that is His is now ours as well. Harriet Buell, in her poem, A Child of the King, captured this well in stanza three:

I once was an outcast stranger on earth,
A sinner by choice, and an alien by birth;
But I've been adopted, my name's written down,
An heir to a mansion, a robe and a crown.
I'm a child of the King, A child of the King;
With Jesus my Savior, I'm a child of the King.

They are weak but He is strong. Yes, it is true. We often hate to admit it, but we are weak—weak in our devotion, in our testimony, in our battle with temptation and the enemy. But God does not leave us in our weakness to struggle alone with forces beyond our ability to cope. Have you ever felt His hand on your shoulder—a supportive touch to let you know that in spite of shortcomings you are loved, you are strengthened? Usually it comes via a brother or sister in the Lord. Jesus specializes in using others to convey His power and love. Do you remember the time when you felt so all alone and helpless? Then the phone rang and on the other end was a friend who just called to talk. That friend said just the right thing at just the right time, enough to carry you through another day. Later, as you reflected on it, you knew in your soul that it was God speaking through that friend. His strength is perfect when our strength is gone. He carries us when we cannot carry on.

Lois Pifer in the web site, *Sermon Illustrations,* relates the following: "A few weeks ago, I was tested on my faith that 'All things are possible with God' (Mark 10:27 NIV). I had been studying Genesis, and specifically reading about Abraham and Sarah, and Abraham's test with the sacrifice of Isaac. At the time, I thought to myself, 'I hope I am prepared for the test when it comes.' I just didn't expect it so soon.

One early morning, two weeks later, I had put a cup of water into the microwave to heat. When I took the cup out, the boiling water shot into my face, burning my eyes and face. I was sure that I had lost my sight, because all I could see was light—no image at all. My husband rushed me to the emergency room. On the way, I remembered, 'This is a test.'

I started praying, and I put the situation into God's hands. An incredible peace came over me, and I knew that in some way I would be okay. Either God would heal my eyes, or He would make it possible for me to deal with my circumstances. As it turned out, my burns were just first degree, and I have healed completely. Our bodies are amazing, and especially our eyes. God is so good!"

Let us thank God for His peace that surpasses all understanding (Philippians 4:7), which comes from His promise that "all things work together for good to those who love God" (Romans 8:28 NKJV).

"Jesus loves me, this I know, for the Bible tells me so. Little ones to

Him belong. They are weak but He is strong." A simple children's hymn with profound spiritual implications. Let it become your theme song, sung from the heart. Sing it loudly as you walk through the crowded streets of life.

SOOTHING THE SAVAGE BEAST

Whenever the spirit from God came upon Saul, David would take his harp and play. Then relief would come to Saul; he would feel better, and the evil spirit would leave him (I Samuel 16:23).

THERE CAN BE NO ARGUMENT concerning music's soothing effect upon the troubled spirit of a man. Even David understood the power of a pleasing, harmonious melody. Today, more than ever, therapists realize the relaxing, stress-reducing dynamics of sound. Consequently, physicians, dentists, psychiatrists, and teachers, to name just a few, are availing themselves of the sway of song.

The state of Georgia believes so strongly in the ability of music to shape our lives that beginning in July 1998, newborns have been bathed in music by Beethoven, Mozart, Handel, Schubert, and Bach. This all came on the heels of new research showing a link between listening to classical music and enhanced brain development in infants. Previous studies have shown that complicated compositions of the Masters can improve mathematical and logic skills in older children. And there is evidence that even babies inside the womb may benefit from the soothing sounds of the classics.

Don Campbell, the author of *The Mozart Effect,* said, "It's my hope that teachers and parents will use music just like they use good food and vegetables—that there's a place for it in their diet. We know that it improves the quality of life from an aesthetic standpoint. And we're at the place where we can say it helps intelligence. We know it helps health, and it can help us orchestrate a better mind and body."

With all of this in mind, just think of the impact of spiritual music upon the minds and hearts of little ones. We have known for a long time that learning and repeating choruses and hymns has a powerful effect upon Christians, from cradle to grave. God-centered hymnology especially helps fortify and enhance one's faith. Exposing toddlers to spiritual music can certainly not hurt. It will fill the mind with thoughts and feelings that will run deeper than the deepest problem. It will educate the soul and bring a sense of well-being that we desperately need in our fast-paced, stress-ridden society.

If music can chase away the demons, can it not also call forth the highest and best within us as we seek to praise God with all our heart? Have you not left a worship service where praise music so buoyed your soul that it carried you aloft for days, in spite of setbacks? Or what of the time, when alone with God, you began to sing a tribute to His glorious name? Yes, music can calm the savage beast. But it can do much more than that. It can refresh, revive, and renew. It simply has that kind of power.

Psalm 46, which was the inspiration for Luther's "A Mighty Fortress Is Our God," has played an important role in sustaining men and women down through the ages. When Sergius the hermit was leading his countrymen and barbarian hordes were overrunning his land, this Psalm was a source of strength and courage. Over and over the godly hermit recited it and then led his revived men in a charge that drove the invaders back and brought ultimate victory. Throughout the ages men have been stirred by the realization the Eternal God is available to them and that nothing, literally nothing, can overwhelm or destroy those that live in this faith.

So then, play on your harp, David! Blow your trumpets, Levites! Sing your anthems, choir! And we will join you in lifting our voices and hearts to the One who alone deserves our praise. Let the melody invade our troubled world with songs of hope and glory until every creature has heard of His everlasting love.

Sing unto the LORD a new song, for he has done marvelous things;
his right hand and his holy arm have gotten me the victory.

—Psalm 98:1

A TRUE MASTERPIECE

Shout for joy to the LORD, all the earth, burst into jubilant song with music; make music to the LORD with the harp, with the harp and the sound of singing, with trumpets and the blast of the ram's horn—shout for joy before the LORD, the King. Let the sea resound, and everything in it, the world, and all who live in it. Let the rivers clap their hands, let the mountains sing together for joy; let them sing before the LORD, for he comes to judge the earth. He will judge the world in righteousness and the peoples with equity (Psalm 98:4-9).

THE MOST DIFFICULT AND CHALLENGING MUSIC that I have ever been associated with is Handel's *Messiah.* My first exposure to this great work was as a young man. I joined a combined community choir and spent what seemed like countless rehearsals in an attempt to perform my role as a bass. The reward was well worth the time and energy expended. The sense of satisfaction felt was overwhelming as we concluded the concert.

The next time was several years later when I was a seminary student. Both experiences convinced me that, though difficult, this piece was by far the most inspiring music ever penned. What makes it so? Perhaps it is because the composer was so in tune with God and so committed to basing it upon Scripture.

Messiah is far and away George Frederic Handel's most highly esteemed and popular work. It has become one of the most renowned pieces of English sacred music. Unlike the majority of his work, which was popular during his lifetime and then fell into obscurity, *Messiah* has endured and is performed throughout the world, especially during the advent season.

The year 1741 was very depressing for Handel. His latest opera failed. His Italian opera company in London was disbanded. That same year Queen Caroline passed away and the commissions Handel had received for composing music for royal occasions all but dried up. A stroke experienced several years prior not only affected him physically, but affected his music as well. It seemed like he had lost the genius that made his music so popular.

Late that year Charles Jennens, a poet known by few, sent Handel a manuscript with a request that Handel set it to music. When Handel read the copy, the words gripped him. Suddenly he came alive. Immediately he began to put the words to music. He labored all through that night and much of the following day. In fact, he worked day and night for twenty two more days, barely stopping to eat or sleep.

When his composition was finished he sensed that it would be a true masterpiece. His *Messiah* was performed the following year and was an immediate success.

The words that Jennens wrote that inspired Handel and lifted him out of the pit of despair were about the Savior: "He was despised and rejected of men. He looked for someone to have pity on him, but there was no man. He trusted in God. God did not leave his soul in hell. I know that my Redeemer lives. Rejoice. Hallelujah!"

Describing his feelings when the "Hallelujah Chorus" burst on his mind, Handel said, "I did think I did see all heaven before me and the great God Himself!"

I would dare to suggest that it was the period of disappointment and despair that prepared Handel in heart and spirit to write this masterpiece of musical genius. How grateful we are that he invested his pain wisely.

An intimate friend of Handel's called upon him just as he was in the middle of setting the words of "He Was Despised" to music and found the great composer sobbing—so greatly had this passage affected him.

On March 23, 1743, when the *Messiah* was first performed in London, the king was present in the audience. It was reported that all were so deeply moved by the "Hallelujah Chorus," that with the impressive words, "For the Lord God omnipotent reigneth," the whole audience, including the king, sprang to their feet, and remained standing through the entire chorus. From that time to this, it has always been the custom to stand during the chorus wherever it is performed. With spontaneous joy the soul stands to salute Him who cometh in the name of the Lord.

Surely the Spirit of God descended upon Handel as he labored over this work. It has stood the test of time and to this day remains a true "spiritual" masterpiece.

Is there any doubt about the power of music to console, inspire, and sustain one's spirit? I think not. Next to the Word of God, it probably has affected more people than any other medium. It can calm the troubled soul, lift the disheartened, and motivate the seeker to achieve beyond his highest dreams. And when it is coupled with the written Word of God, for the glory of God, there is no limit as to its influence.

See the Lord now as He places His mighty hands
Upon the trembling ones of a disconsolate man.
Watch as fingers move swiftly across the page
Creating music that does engage.
A masterpiece ensues,
And hence it moves;
Spirit-breath imparts rich melodies
That reach the hardest heart
And glory is accorded to the One
Who inspires with His part.

THE WELLSPRINGS OF JOY

Rejoice in the Lord always. I will say it again: Rejoice! (Philippians 4:4)

JOHN PIERPONT DIED A FAILURE, or some say. In 1866, at the age of 81, he came to the end of his days as a government clerk in Washington, D.C., with a long string of personal defeats.

Things began well enough. He graduated from Yale, which his grandfather had helped found, and chose education as his profession with some enthusiasm. His teaching career was cut short after he was soundly criticized for being too easy on his students. As a result, he turned away from education to the legal world for training.

He failed as a lawyer because he was too generous to his clients and too concerned about justice to take the cases that brought good fees.

The next career he took up was that of a dry-goods merchant. He was a failure as a businessman because he did not charge enough for his goods to make a profit and he was too liberal with credit.

In the meantime he had been writing poetry and, although it was published, he did not collect enough royalties to make a living. And so he decided to enter the ministry. He went off to Harvard Divinity School and was ordained in a church in Boston. But his position on prohibition against slavery got him crosswinds with the influential members of his congregation and, as a result, he was forced to resign.

Politics seemed a place where he could make some difference, and he was nominated as the Abolition Party candidate for governor of Massachusetts. He lost. Undaunted, Pierpont ran for Congress under the banner of the Free Soil Party. He lost again.

The Civil War came along and he volunteered as a chaplain for the 22nd Regiment of the Massachusetts Volunteers. Two weeks later he quit, having found the task too much of a strain on his health. He was 76 years old.

Someone found him an obscure job in the back offices of the Treasury Department in Washington, and he finished the last five years of his life as a menial file clerk. He was not very good at that either because his heart was not in it.

Yes, John Pierpont died a failure, or so some say. He had accomplished nothing significant in his lifetime—that is, nothing he set out to do. There is a small memorial stone marking his grave in Mount Auburn Cemetery in Cambridge, Massachusetts. The words in the granite read: "POET, PREACHER, PHILOSOPHER, PHILANTHROPIST."

From this distance in time, one might insist that he was not, in fact, a failure in any sense of that word. His commitment to social justice, his desire to be a loving human being, his active engagement in the great issues of his time, and his faith in the power of the human mind—these are not failures. And much of what he thought of as defeat became success. Education was reformed, legal processes were improved, credit laws were changed, and, above all, slavery was abolished once and for all.

This is not an uncommon story. Many 19th century reformers had similar lives, similar failures and successes. In one very important sense, John Pierpont was not a failure. Every year, come December, we celebrate his success. We carry in our hearts and minds a lifelong memorial to him. It is a song. Not a song about Jesus or angels or even Santa Claus or Frosty. It is a terribly simple song about the simple joy of whizzing through the cold white dark of wintertime. It is a song about a sleigh pulled by one horse. It is a song about laughter and singing. No more. No less. John Pierpont wrote "Jingle Bells."

To write a song that stands for the simplest joys in life—a song that millions of people around the world know, about something they have never done but can imagine, well, that my friends is anything but failure.

One snowy afternoon in the deep of a Massachusetts winter, John Pierpont penned the lines of Jingle Bells as a small gift for his family, friends and congregation, and in so doing left behind a permanent gift—the gift of joy. Would you not like to leave a legacy of joy to the world or a least to your family and friends? I know I would. You see, joy oils the machinery of life. It greases the axles of the world. It is medicine to the wounded soul and despondent spirit. Joy dries up tears and is contagious. It has an attracting quality about it, and as someone has aptly put it, it is "love smiling."

Both Old and New Testaments speak of the important role that joy plays in our lives: "The joy of the Lord is your strength" (Nehemiah 8:10). "With joy you shall draw water out of the wells of salvation" (Isaiah 12:3). "These things have I spoken to you, that my joy might remain in you, and that your joy might be full" (John 15:11). "Rejoice in the Lord always; again I say, rejoice!" (Philippians 4:4).

Paul has much to tell us about joy, in spite of the fact he suffered greatly for his faith. The letter to the Philippians is absolutely overflowing with joy. Joy is the key word throughout. Chapter after chapter is filled with the things that brought delight to his soul.

In chapter 1:15-18, he rejoices that the Gospel is being preached, even if it is being declared by those whose motives are impure.

In 2:17 and 18, Paul faces possible execution, but says that if by his death other's faith was deepened, he would be full of joy.

In 4:1, the Philippian believers are one source of Paul's joy. When he thinks of them his heart is warmed; when he writes to them, his spirit is refreshed.

What exactly is Christian joy? In order for us to define what it is, we must explain what it is not.

First of all, joy is not synonymous with fun and games. Pleasure seekers do not find joy. Joy is something different, something deeper. What pleasure seekers do find is something that makes them feel good for a limited time.

Also, joy is not the ability to always tell funny stories or be the life of the party. Laughter has its benefits, to be sure. But it usually will not suffice during a time of crisis. In fact, it may even seem inconsiderate and downright rude.

Neither is joy the same as being carefree. Some believe that vacations are recipes for joy. But they are often merely temporary excursions from stressful situations. Those who espouse this belief see joy only in escapist terms. True joy can be the Christian's portion any time, in any place, under any strain. It was so for Jesus; it was so for Paul; it can be so for any of us.

Lastly, joy is not the same as happiness. Happenings can lead to happiness. Joy is birthed as a result of a loving relationship. Sad is that person who bases his joy strictly on beneficial circumstances. The events of life are like waves on the sea. They come and they go, depending on the direction and force of the wind.

If you were to ask a psychologist what joy is all about, he would say something like this: "Joy is a state of mind into which four ingredients enter: The first ingredient is a sense of being loved. The second is the ability to accept your situation is life. The third is a sense that you have something worth having, e.g., a spouse, children, a friend, a hobby, a career. The fourth ingredient is the sense that you are giving away something worth giving. Giving is a great source of joy. Giving oneself to others is tremendously rewarding. Mothers know this. They give themselves endlessly to make their children happy. Joy is like jam. It sticks to you as you try to spread it."

If you take the time to examine this four-fold formula for joy through a Christian's eyes, you could see how completely it is fulfilled in a relationship with the Lord Jesus Christ. For example, does the believer not know that he/she is loved? Paul spoke of this in Galatians 2:20: "He loved me and gave himself for me." The love of God led Him to adopt us into His very own family as we responded to His gracious invitation.

And then there is the issue of accepting our situation in life. This is something the Christian can do because he knows what other folks do not know—that all of his circumstances are planned out for him by his loving heavenly Father and that they will eventually work out for his good (Romans 8:28). This makes contentment possible in any situation. Remember, Paul was in prison when he said, "I have learned in whatever state I am in, therewith to be content."

In the third place, there is the issue of having something worth having. Now look at what Paul wrote in Philippians 3:8: "I count all things to be loss, for the excellency of the knowledge of Christ Jesus my Lord, for whom I suffered the loss of all things and count them but garbage, that I may gain Christ, and may be found in Him." Paul has

Someone worth having and He brings him such joy that even the things he lost to gain Him seem worthless.

When a man courts a girl, what does he want? He simply wants a love relationship with her; it is to that end that he eventually proposes marriage. The marriage relationship is not a means to an end, but is itself the source of joy which makes it worthwhile!

The Christian says with Paul, "I have Jesus. I have the glorious reality of knowing Him and that is enough for me. He is the Pearl of Great Price. I will let anything go in order to hold onto it."

The fourth and last ingredient necessary for real joy to be present in one's life is giving something worth giving. And what is it that we possess as children of God that is worth giving away? Is it not our faith? As we share our knowledge of Christ with others a certain exultation sweeps over us. We have given the greatest gift possible, something supremely worth giving.

These, then, are the wellsprings of joy—belonging, contentment, possessing something priceless, and giving ourselves away. Think of them, my fellow Christian, and rejoice! You will be singing your way through life. Melodies of satisfaction will flow from within you. And like John Pierpont, you too will be able to leave a legacy of joy behind for others to enjoy!

FRIENDSHIPS

I awoke this morning with devout thanksgiving for my friends, the old and the new. Shall I not call God, the Beautiful, who daily showeth himself so to me in his gifts.

—RALPH WALDO EMERSON
Friendship Essays, 1844

ONE SOUL IN TWO BODIES

As the Father has loved me, so have I loved you. Now remain in my love. If you obey my commands you will remain in my love, just as I have obeyed my Father's commands and remain in his love. I have told you this so that my joy may be in you and that your joy may be complete. My command is this: Love each other as I have loved you. Greater love has no one than this, that he lay down his life for his friends. You are my friends if you do what I command. I no longer call you servants because a servant does not know his master's business. Instead, I have called you friends, for everything that I learned from my Father I have made known to you (John 15:9-15).

TAKING TIME TO REFLECT UPON OUR FRIENDSHIPS will bring consolation and encouragement to our soul. Sitting alone quietly and dwelling on one of life's most precious possessions will do wonders for the inner man. It will lift the sunken spirit, calm the troubled soul, and bring bright hope in the midst of gloom. Sad indeed is that individual who is too busy to recount his friends.

The story is told about a pastor who was making some hospital calls when a nurse stopped him in the hallway and asked him if he would look in on a certain patient who she said was very near death. The pastor asked if any relatives were with him and she responded that he had none. The pastor entered his room and read the name tag at the foot of the bed:

SAMUEL DAVIS
AGE 91
COMMENTS: NO FAMILY, NO FRIENDS

The poorest man on earth has to be the one who has no friends. Would it not be horrible if we had to say, "I don't have a friend in all the world." Friendship is a beautiful and blessed thing. When you find a friend, you find a pearl of great price. Someone once asked a great author for the secret of his success and he replied, "I had a friend."

During the Civil War, thousands of appeals for pardon came to President Abraham Lincoln from soldiers involved in military discipline. Each appeal was, as a rule, supported by letters from influential people. One day a single sheet came to his desk, an appeal from a soldier absent of any supporting documentation. "What!" exclaimed Lincoln, "has this man no friends?" One of his aides answered, "No, sir, not one." "Then," said Lincoln, "I will be his friend." And quickly he affixed his signature to the pardon.

What is a friend? Lots of definitions have been offered. "Someone who knows all about you and still loves you." "The one who comes in when the whole world goes out." "Someone with whom you dare to be yourself." "Someone who tells you the truth even when it hurts." Aristotle said it best: "Friendship is a single soul dwelling in two bodies." The Bible affords us several excellent examples of this kind of relationship: David and Jonathan, Ruth and Naomi; Paul and Silas.

Without a doubt, Jesus is the greatest friend of all because He fulfills all of the aforementioned descriptions of friendship perfectly.

Abraham was called "the friend of God." What a tremendous thing to have said about one. It is an everlasting tribute and memorial to his character and his relationship with God. II Chronicles 20:7: "Are you not our God, who drove out the inhabitants of this land before your people Israel, and gave it to the seed of Abraham your friend?" Isaiah 41:8: "But thou, Israel, art my servant, Jacob whom I have chosen, the seed of Abraham my friend." James 2:23: "And the Scripture was fulfilled which saith, Abraham believed God, and it was reckoned to him as righteousness: and he was called the friend of God" (KJV). No one else in all the Bible is called "the friend of God." The only other person that even comes close to it is Moses. In Exodus 33:11 we read, "Thus the Lord used to speak to Moses, face to face as a man speaks to his friend" (KJV).

What an epitaph! Would you not like that to be inscribed on your tombstone? "______________, THE FRIEND OF GOD."

What was it about the life of Abraham that would give him such a reputation? Is there some secret or special characteristic that he possessed? Yes, and it is found in the phrase, "Abraham believed God," found in Genesis 15:6, Romans 4:3, Galatians 3:6, James 2:23, and Hebrews 11:8,17. Abraham trusted his future to God. He obeyed his call even though he was unsure as to where it would lead. He trusted God with the present while he was sojourning in Canaan, often a hostile and certainly strange land. He trusted God with his dearest possession, his son, Isaac. In fact, the trip to Mount Moriah was the sternest test of his loyalty to God!

Let me share with you what I believe are the main elements that go into the making of friendships.

First of all, true friends love and trust one another. A friend of God is one who rests his soul on the promises of God. Until we trust Christ for salvation, we are strangers and aliens to the things of God. In fact, we are at enmity with God. When we trust Jesus Christ as our personal Savior, then and only then do we become a friend of God. One man, after he had been a Christian for only one week, told his pastor, "I'm only twenty-four years old, but I want to tell you that I've had more happiness packed into my life in this one week than in all the twenty-four years of my life." He had become a friend of God.

Also, true friends read the letters they receive from one another. How inconsiderate and rude it would be to receive a letter from a dear friend and yet not even bother to open it. True friends are eager to read words of encouragement, advice, love, and support. God, the greatest friend of all, has sent us a love letter. It is called the Holy Bible. We read it for a lift, a challenge. Truly it is our road map through life.

Again, true friends communicate often—sharing joys, burdens, desires. We can "have a little talk with Jesus" anytime we feel the need. He delights in our conversations and bids us come to Him, for He can meet the deepest needs of our hearts.

True friends also delight to meet each other's needs and are willing to sacrifice to do so. On one occasion, Sadhu Sundar Singh, the great evangelist of India, and a companion were traveling through a pass high in the Himalayan Mountains. At one point they came across a body lying in the snow. Sundar Singh wanted to stop and help this poor creature, but his companion refused, saying, "We will both lose our lives if we burden ourselves with him." But Sundar Singh would not think of leaving the man to die in the ice and snow. As his companion bid him farewell, Sundar Singh lifted the man onto his back. With great exertion he bore the man onward. Gradually the heat from Sundar Singh's body began to warm up the poor fellow and he revived. Soon both were walking together, side by side. Catching up with his former companion, they found him dead—frozen in the cold. In the case of Sundar Singh, he was willing to lose his life on behalf of another, and in the process found it; in the case of his callous companion, he sought to save his life but lost it. Jesus, the friend of sinners, sacrificed Himself on our behalf. This is the hallmark of true friendship.

It is also true that friends pay their debts. Can we call ourselves a friend of God and yet withhold what rightfully belongs to Him? Is He not the source of all our benefits? We owe Him our best—our talents, our time, our possessions—indeed, our very lives.

True friends give gifts to each other. Is there any question as to whether or not God has gifted us? Abraham believed God and God reckoned it as righteousness—the gift of salvation. And then there is the matter of material possessions. We do not really begin to give to God until after we have tithed. Freewill offerings are those which are above and beyond the tenth. A man wanted to teach his little girl to tithe, so he took a ten dollar bill in his hand and said to her, "Jesus came down from heaven. He had no nice home, no car to ride in, often no place to sleep. He went about doing good and finally He died on a cross for us to save us and take us to heaven. Now we ought to give Him some of this money out of gratitude, so we'll keep nine dollars for ourselves and give Jesus one." Suddenly the little girl started to cry. "What's the matter?" asked her father. She answered, "Is that all Jesus gets?" Giving among friends is a two-way street.

Lastly, true friends stand up for each other. They are known as "defenders of character." They do not go AWOL when times get tough. Shoulder to shoulder, back to back, they protect one another against those who would attack.

"Friendship—the greatest love, the greatest usefulness, the most open communication, the noblest sufferings, the severest truth, the heartiest counsel, and the greatest union of minds of which brave men and women are capable" (Jeremy Taylor). One soul in two bodies—worth attaining, worth keeping, and worth fighting for.

A SWEET AROMA

Ointment and perfume rejoice the heart: so doth the sweetness of a man's friend by hearty counsel (Proverbs 27:9, KJV).

AFTER THE CLOSE OF WORLD WAR I, the king and queen of Belgium wanted to honor President Herbert Hoover for the aid they had received during the war from the United States. After considering the various available honors, they offered Hoover his choice of three decorations. He refused them all, saying, "You have stood at the gateway of civilization and held back the tide of aggression, while we have only shared with you what we had to give. For that one does not ask for honors." The king and queen responded, "He is our very great friend." Desiring to adequately express their appreciation for his efforts, they created a new order to which Hoover alone belonged called, "Friend of the Belgian People."

Friends are often the difference between one person's success and another's failure. Charles Haddon Spurgeon, the great English preacher, said, "Friendship is one of the sweetest joys of life. Many might have failed beneath the bitterness of their trial had they not found a friend." There is a special feeling we get from our friends that makes us want to be with them, even just to enjoy simple things. It is always difficult to leave a good friend.

The Apostle Paul had a good friend, Onesiphorus, who was devoted to keeping Paul's spirits high. He visited him and refreshed him while he was imprisoned in a Roman jail (II Timothy 1:16).

When Paul wrote to the Philippian church he told them how he looked forward to being with them because he remembered their fellowship. Friends hold certain things in common. Jehu and Jehonadab (II Kings 10) provide an interesting look at friendship from this perspective. When Jehu met his friend Jehonadab, he asked, "Is thine heart right, as my heart is with thine heart?" These two friends were going to war to fight a common enemy but, of course, there was more to this relationship than a common foe. To enjoy any friend we need more in common with him than hating the same people.

John Wesley, the founder of Methodism, brought revival to England with his preaching. At the end of his sermons Wesley gave an invitation by using the words of Jehu, then, holding out his hand, he invited sinners to respond, saying, "If your heart is like my heart, then take my hand." Thousands took his hand to show they were taking Christ as Savior. Wesley and the sinner were one in Christ—that made them friends.

Of all the things that a friend can contribute to you, none is greater than to have an interest in your spiritual well-being. Job sought that kind of friend in the midst of his trials when he cried out, "Oh that one might plead for a man with God, as a man pleadeth for his neighbor!" (Job 16:21) Later in his experience Job practiced the same when he prayed for his three friends and God spared them (Job 42:10). How much better is a friend who will help us spiritually than the false friend who leads us away from God (Deuteronomy 13:6).

By the pool of Bethesda, Jesus met the man who had been sick for thirty-eight years, having no one to put him into the pool. The man did not have a friend! What a contrast with the paralyzed man in Luke chapter 5, who had four concerned friends to carry him to Jesus. Unable to get him through the door of the house because of the crowd, they made their way to the roof and let him down to Jesus through a hole. We all need friends who pray and take an interest in our spiritual lives; friends like the poet who wrote these lines:

I like to think that we are friends
Because God has planned it so.
I like to think it pleased Him
To see our friendship grow.
Perhaps that is why so many times
I say a little prayer
That He will always bless you
And the friendship that we share.

—Anonymous

A REFRESHING PERSON

May the Lord show mercy to the household of Onesiphorus because he often refreshed me and was not ashamed of my chains. On the contrary, when he was in Rome, he searched hard for me until he found me. May the Lord grant that he will find mercy from the Lord on that day! You know very well in how many ways he helped me in Ephesus (II Timothy 1:16-18).

JACKIE ROBINSON was the first African American to play baseball in the major leagues. Breaking baseball's color barrier, he faced hostile crowds in every stadium. While playing one day in his home stadium in Brooklyn, he committed an error. The fans began to boo him. He stood at second base, humiliated, while the crowd jeered on. Then, without saying a word, shortstop Pee Wee Reese went over and stood next to Jackie. He put his arm around him and faced the crowd. Suddenly the fans grew quiet. Robinson later said that arm around his shoulder saved his career.

Pee Wee Reese had a forerunner in the person of Onesiphorus. He stood by the Apostle Paul, who was in prison at the time, when all others had deserted him. Of all the definitions of friendship, none can surpass that given in II Timothy 1:16-18. In this brief passage Paul says four things about his friend, Onesiphorus: (1) he refreshed him; (2) he was loyal to him; (3) he persisted in his quest to find him; (4) he was a help to him.

When Paul says that Onesiphorus "refreshed" him, he was saying a great deal. The Greek word translated "refresh" means *to cause one to breathe more easily, to give one rest, to encourage, cheer up, relieve, comfort, revive, like a breath of fresh air.* J.B. Phillips renders it thusly: "Many times did that man put fresh heart into me." In short, it may be said that Onesiphorus was devoted to keeping Paul's spirit's high.

Just how he carried out this bracing ministry is not stated, but we can speculate, based on what we know of the context. Perhaps it was by his very presence—the power of his personality, the influence of his faith and love. Then again, Onesiphorus may have raised Paul's spirits by bringing him good news regarding the churches that he had helped to birth. Or it could be that he reminded the apostle of God's promises and capped it all off by having prayer with him.

On the other hand, perhaps Paul may simply have had something more practical in mind—the supply of food, drink, and literature. Whatever the case, this is one instance where name and nature coincide. Onesiphorus literally means *bringer of help*.

The fact that Onesiphorus was not ashamed of Paul's chains certainly speaks of loyalty, an important element of friendship. Solomon wrote, "A friend loveth at all times" (Proverbs 17:17, KJV). Some friends are dependable, always around when you need them. In fact, a good friend makes a point of it.

Sam Davis was a Confederate spy, executed at Pulaski, Tennessee, for his crime. When captured by the Union Army he had in his possession some papers of vital importance. After examining the case closely, the officers in charge knew he must have had an accomplice in securing the documents. Davis was court-martialed, led out before the firing squad and blindfolded. Then the officer in charge put forward a proposition: "If you will give us the name of the man who furnished you this information, you will be set free." Sam Davis did not hesitate in his reply: "If I had a thousand lives I would give them all before I would betray a friend!"

When Onesiphorus arrived in Rome, we are told that he searched everywhere to find his friend, Paul. That is what true friends do. They do not quit when the going gets tough. They persist. They keep at it until friendship is honored.

A teenager had decided to quit high school, saying he was fed up with it all. His father was trying to convince him to stay with it. "Son," he said, "you just can't quit now. All the people who are remembered in history didn't quit. Abe Lincoln didn't quit. Thomas Edison didn't quit. Douglas MacArthur didn't quit. Elmo Cringle didn't quit." "Who?" his son burst in. "Who is Elmo Cringle?" "That's my point, son. You don't remember him because he quit!"

Onesiphorus did not quit either. That is what made him such a special friend to Paul. While the other believers were hiding, Onesiphorus was diligently searching. The following is attributed to "Gentleman Jim Corbett," who held the heavyweight boxing title for five years at the end of the 19th century: "Fight one more round. When your feet are so tired that you have to shuffle back to the center of the ring, fight one more round. When your arms are so tired that you can hardly lift your hands to come on guard, fight one more round. When your nose is bleeding and your eyes are black and you are so tired that you wish your opponent would crack you on the jaw and put you to sleep, fight one more round, remembering that the man who fights one more round is never whipped."

This then is friendship on its highest level; and friendship rises to its highest point only when the two comrades are followers of Jesus Christ. Who but His followers can be certain that their friendship will last forever? And where can hearts and minds be at one so utterly as those that are at one with God and Christ? Built together on the Rock of Ages, they cherish hopes, interests, convictions, and personal ideals which are fundamentally the same. And this is because the same Lord is He by whom they live and in whom they hope to die.

MAN'S GREATEST OPPORTUNITY

And the Scripture was fulfilled which says, "And Abraham believed God, and it was reckoned to him as righteousness," and he was called the friend of God. (James 2:23).

DURING THE REIGN OF QUEEN VICTORIA, a London doctor visited a 72-year-old lady named Maria Vincent. Her husband had abandoned her some years earlier. She was poor and lived in humble surroundings and was undernourished. She did not have either warm clothes or wood for a fire. The doctor could not believe that her friends would allow her to live in such a state. When asked about it, Maria said she had no friends. Later in the discussion she corrected herself. She admitted that there might be one, but was sure that she had forgotten all about her. The doctor pressed her for the identity of the friend. Finally he was told that it was the Queen herself. Maria said that the two of them were childhood friends.

The doctor left, not sure that he believed Maria, but when he arrived home he wrote the Queen a letter in which he related the entire incident. A few days later, to his astonishment, he received a letter from the Queen corroborating the story. The Queen had not forgotten her friend from childhood. Enclosed in the letter was enough money to provide for all of Maria's needs. For the remaining years of her life Maria Vincent lived comfortably as a friend of the Queen.

Perhaps you can think of an individual with whom you would like to be good friends—a wealthy businessman, a noted politician, a famous entertainment personality, or a renown professional athlete. If one is impressed with the status of an individual to the point of dreaming of becoming his friend, it should be remembered that each of us has an opportunity to become friends with Someone who is more powerful, richer, and more interesting than anyone. We can become a friend of God!

Since the creation of man God has sought the opportunity to enjoy man's fellowship. Even after our first parents disobeyed God, He sought them out (Genesis 3:8,9). Throughout the pages of the Old Testament we read about men who knew God and enjoyed intimate fellowship with Him—men like Moses and David and Isaiah. Three times the Bible tells us that Abraham was a friend of God.

During the earthly life of Jesus, He was called a friend of publicans and sinners (Matthew 11:19). And He told His disciples that He considered them His special friends (John 15:15).

The Apostle Paul tells us more about God's desire for friends when he explains Jesus' death on Calvary: "...that God was reconciling the world to himself in Christ, not counting men's sins against them. And he has committed to us the message of reconciliation. We are therefore Christ's ambassadors, as though God were making his appeal through us. We implore you on Christ's behalf: Be reconciled to God. God made him who had no sin to be sin for us, so that in him we might become the righteousness of God" (II Corinthians 5:19-21).

Abraham's relationship with God presents a sterling example of what true, godly friendship is all about. First and foremost, a friend of God knows Him personally. The Bible records Abraham's conversations with God—conversations regarding the covenant and about Abraham's growing knowledge about the nature of God. Today many people know about God, they are acquainted with some Scripture verses. They know that Jesus died for the sins of the world. They know that He arose from the dead. In other words, they are aware of certain facts about God, but they do not really have a relationship with Him. Millions of Americans know a great deal about the President—that is, about his age, his political background, his family, his hobbies, etc. But he is not their friend. Friendship is the result of intimate contact, of shared joys and concerns. What is a friend of God? It is one who knows Him personally.

A second way to describe friendship with God would include loving Him. Abraham loved God and proved it by serving Him. He was not perfect in his performance, but his heart was set to do His will. He wanted, above all else, to please God. Sometimes we get a distorted idea about what love is. One night a man decided to show his wife how much he loved her. After dinner he began to recite romantic poetry, telling her he would climb high mountains to be near her, swim wide oceans, cross deserts in the burning heat of the day, and even sit at her window to sing love songs in the moonlight. After listening to him go on for some time she asked, "But will you wash the dishes?" If we love God, we will do more than sing or talk about it. We will demonstrate it by our actions. Abraham validated his love for God by obeying His commands. He left his native land; he sojourned in a land that he was unfamiliar with; he was even willing to sacrifice his son, Isaac. What is a friend of God? It is one who truly loves Him.

A friend of God also shares his interests, just as two human friends might share a common interest. This was true of Abraham and God. It was the nation of Israel that Abraham was to father in accord with God's wishes. What are the interests of God? How can we discover them for ourselves? They are clearly outlined in the pages of the Bible: missions and evangelism, discipleship, building the church, seeing to the needs of the poor and suffering. The New Testament tells of forty people, each suffering from the same disease, who were healed by Jesus. Of this number, thirty-four were either brought to Jesus by friends, or Jesus was taken to them. In only six cases out of forty did the sufferers find the way to Jesus without assistance. Of the vast number of people who find their way to Jesus today, most of them reach Him because the friends of Jesus are concerned about the welfare of their souls.

Here is another hallmark of friendship with God—fellowship! The mark of a great man of God is his prayer life. Abraham was a man of prayer. He listened as God spoke. We find it difficult to listen in our fast-paced culture because it takes a commitment of time to do so. We are too preoccupied with other concerns. If we do not "push that pause button" on occasion, we will never know what it is to dialogue with our Father. Abraham talked with God about a variety of things. He held an on-going conversation with Him daily.

There are some other ways to fellowship with the Father as well. We can experience the presence of God as we behold His creative hand. Nature communicates His grandeur, His majesty, His power, His love. We feel God's closeness at such times as these.

We can also fellowship with God as we search His Word and as we worship with like-minded believers. In Revelation 3:20, He calls to us: "Here I am! I stand at the door and knock. If anyone hears my voice and opens the door, I will come in and eat with him, and he with me." What a wonderful promise. These are the words of our blessed Lord! He calls us to His table, to dine with Him. What an awesome privilege and delight.

One last test of one who claims to be a friend of God: loyalty to His cause. There were times in Abraham's life when his example was not the best, but in the arena of loyalty, he was a champion. In terms of "staying by the stuff," Abraham shone. True friends stand by each other no matter what. Our ancient foe will test us in this matter. He wants to divert our attention away from the cause of Christ. But the Spirit of God will ever call us back, reminding us of our commitment to follow Him to the end.

One Sunday an 8-year-old Mexican boy named Pedro, after hearing the minister preach on Simon of Cyrene, approached him and said, "You asked what we would do if we had been in the crowd when Jesus fell under the weight of His cross. I'm sure I would have been happy to help carry it!" The boy had recently received Christ, although his parents were antagonistic to the gospel. To test him the minister said, "Yes, but if you had helped the Lord, the cruel Roman soldiers would probably have beaten you with whips." Without hesitation the boy answered, "I don't care! I love Him! I'd have done it just the same."

Two weeks later the pastor stood at the door of the church, greeting the people as they left the service. When Pedro came by, he patted him affectionately on his shoulder. Shrinking back with a little groan, he pleaded, "Please don't do that. My back is very sore." Since he had barely touched him, the minister was puzzled. He took him to a nearby cloakroom and asked him to remove his shirt. Criss-crossing his back from his neck to his waist were huge red welts. "Who did that?" the preacher asked angrily. "My mother," said Pedro. "She whipped me because I came to church." That Mexican boy proved he was willing to stand up for the One in whom he had put his trust. He was a friend of God.

STAYING IN TOUCH

When the LORD finished speaking to Moses on Mount Sinai, he gave him the two tablets of the Testimony, the tablets of stone inscribed by the finger of God (Exodus 31:18).

THE BEST FRIENDS ARE THOSE WHO KEEP IN TOUCH, over the years and across the miles—it matters not. Their contact is not limited by schedules or busyness. In fact, the true test of friendship is just this: the consistency of communication.

There is nothing like hearing from a friend, especially when you least expect it, or when you are experiencing one of those "low moments" in your life. Friends remember you and communicate their love at both ends of the experience spectrum, that is, when you have achieved a level of success and when you are in some difficulty. Of course, the best kind of communication is close up and personal, but that is not always possible given the distance factor. However, a phone call or note can be equally meaningful. Simply put, friends keep in touch.

The ministry of letters or e-mail cannot be overestimated. They have an advantage over a phone call in that they can be slowly digested over a cup of coffee. They can be read again and again and saved for that gloomy day when one desperately needs to hear from a friend.

Jesus, the Friend of sinners, has delivered a series of letters to us. They are contained in a book called the Holy Bible. They are meant to be cherished and read often. These letters are unique—one of a kind. Consider the following characteristics: (1) they were written by men who were breathed upon by the Breath of God; (2) they are eternal; (3) they are errorless; (4) they are relevant, regardless of the age in which they are read; (5) they are changeless (like their Author); (6) they are indestructible.

Letters written by outstanding historical figures can bring a handsome price at auction, but who can place a value on the writings of The Friend? Who can begin to estimate the worth of words that bring salvation, comfort, encouragement, direction, and strength? From the time on Mount Sinai, when God wrote on the tablets of stone with His finger, He had it in His heart to write us a love letter that would eventually be written on our hearts. And what a letter it is!

The longest and simplest love letter ever written by man was the work of a Parisian painter named Marcel de Leclure in 1875. The addressed was Magdalene de Villalore, his aristocratic light of love. The missive contained the phrase, jevous aime, "I love you," 1,875,000 times. However, this lover did not write this with his own hand. He hired a scribe. Never was love made manifest by as great an expenditure of time and effort—or was it? The Lover of our souls, the best Friend a man can have, surpassed this by far. The exploits of God on our behalf have been written down in a Book. We have only to read it. The words leap off the pages with a constant shout as God repeatedly reminds us of His great love.

Have you ever given thought to writing a letter to God? What I mean is a literal letter, filled with your own thoughts about how much He means to you, expressing the gratitude of your heart for His never-ending love. Why not take some moments to do that today? You will find it to be an act of worship that will solidify your faith and give you new courage and strength.

Dear Lord, thank you for keeping in touch.
From the moment I arose today I sensed Your wonderful presence.
You touched me with that beam of sunlight that came
streaming through the window.
I felt Your warmth and was reminded of Your repeated embraces.
Then a mocking bird sang its repertoire, and once again I became
aware of the many ways You transmit Your gifts to me.

I spent a few choice moments in Your Word and
was amazed to feel Your breath upon me.
I have read Your letters so often that they are now a part of me.

How awesome are Your thoughts, O Lord.

Your law is the delight of my life.
Thank You, Father, for your abiding nearness.
Thank You, Lord Jesus, for opening the way.
And thank you, Spirit, for convincing me that all of this is true!

A TALE OF GREAT LOVE

Greater love has no man than this, that a man lay down his life for his friends (John 15:13).

ONE OF THE MOST AMAZING EXAMPLES OF SACRIFICIAL LOVE is found in Charles Dickens' *Tale of Two Cities,* where Sidney Carton dies for Charles Darney. The setting is the French Revolution. Darney, the young Frenchman, has been condemned to die by the guillotine. Sidney Carton is a dissipated English lawyer who has wasted great gifts and quenched high potential in riotous living. It seems as if he cares for no one other than himself. But when he hears about the plight of his friend, he determines to save him by laying down his own life—not for the love he has for the man, but for the sake of the man's wife and child. To that end Carton gains admission to the dungeon on the night before the execution is to take place. He changes garments with the condemned man and the next day is led out and put to death as Charles Darney.

Before Carton went to the dungeon, he had entered the courtyard and remained there for a few moments alone, looking up at the light in the window of Darney's daughter's room. He was led by the light of love, but it led straight to a dungeon and thence to his execution.

As we see him ascending the steps to the place of death, his hands bound behind his back, taking his last look at the world, these words of our Savior come to mind, "Greater love has no man, than this, that a man lay down his life for his friends." We all like to think of ourselves as rising to the occasion when a time of great crisis arises as in the above story. We all hope to emulate what the heroes of faith did. But as great as they were, Jesus says, "you are my friends if you do whatever I command you." It is very easy to think of the sacrifice implied in "laying down one's life" as dying for another in one moment of time. Though that may occasionally occur, the context shows this sacrifice within the framework of friendship. True friendship occurs over months and years, not just in one moment in time.

True friends are eager to help and willing to spend themselves ungrudgingly, without counting the cost. Friends open their hearts and minds to each other without secrecy, which one would not do for a mere acquaintance. True friends allow the other to see right in and know them as they really are. Friends share what they have learned. Finally, and most importantly, a friend trusts the one who believes in him, and risks that the other will never doubt his loyalty but look upon him with proven confidence.

Though the principle given by Christ is applicable to all friendships, He has one specific friendship as His primary focus: ours with Him, or more generally, ours with God. Proverbs 18:24 says, "A man of many companions may come to ruin, but there is a friend who sticks closer than a brother." That Friend is Jesus of Nazareth, but He made it very clear that if we are His friends, we will show it in our obedience to His commands. But before we can obey, we must trust that what He says is true.

Take a moment to evaluate yourself. Are you as open and frank with Him as He is with you through His Word? Often our prayers are stiff and formal, not truly honest. And sometimes we become bored in His presence and soon have nothing to say to Him. Is it not true that we do not trust Him as fully as we should? That we are often quick to doubt Him? That we easily grow suspicious of Him? That we lose heart of fear that He has forgotten us? That He is not really trying or is unequal to the task of shepherding us into His kingdom?

Though he has never failed us, we are so quick to suspect and blame Him. He is the best Friend anyone could ever have.

I've found a Friend, O such a friend! He loved me ere I knew Him;
He drew me with the cords of love, and thus He bound me to Him;
And round my heart still closely twine those ties which naught can sever,
For I am His, and He is mine, forever and forever.
I've found a Friend, O such a friend! He bled, He died to save me;
And not alone the gift of life, but His own Self He gave me!
Naught that I have mine own I call, I'll hold it for the Giver,

My heart, my strength, my life, my all are His, and His forever.
I've found a Friend, O such a friend! All pow'r to Him is given,
To guard me on my onward course, and bring me safe to heaven.
The eternal glories gleam afar, to nerve my faint endeavor;
So now to watch, to work, to war, and then to rest forever.
I've found a Friend, O such a friend! So kind and true and tender,
So wise a Counselor and Guide, so mighty a Defender!
From Him who loves me now so well what power my soul can sever?
Shall life or death, shall earth or hell? No! I am His forever.

—James G Small

A FRIEND TO THE END

A man of many companions may come to ruin, but there is a friend who sticks closer than a brother (Proverbs 18:24).

I HAVE ALWAYS BEEN A FAN OF PAUL HARVEY. I remember as a young man listening to him daily as I drove home from work. I believe it was a combination of tale and delivery that kept me tuned in. He had an unusual way of captivating the audience and, of course, the stories were beyond interesting—they were simply mesmerizing.

One story in particular captured my attention because it was not at all what I had expected (which, come to think of it is quite true of many of his stories). It is a tale of two peculiar friends with a very unusual twist.

As I recall, Jim and Jack were their names. They were best of friends, completely devoted to one another and inseparable. So, naturally when Jim lost both of his legs in a railroad accident, Jack did what all true friends would do—he did everything he could to help his friend.

Jim thought his career with the railroad was over because of his handicap. But the company gave him another job. They made him a signalman. His outpost was to be a lonely little stop, more than 200 miles from anywhere. But how could he do even this job when it required him to go daily to the signal tower? That is where his friend Jack came in. He went along with Jim to do whatever he could. The lengths of self-sacrifice to which Jack was willing to go is nothing short of phenomenal.

Here was Jim, with no legs, barely out of the hospital, with a new job in a remote area. He had a little shack to live in, about 150 yards from the signal tower. He was still dealing with the trauma of losing both of his legs and knew he had to make several adjustments with respect to his new assignment. Add to that the fact that he was far away from the aid of those who specialize in the psychological aspect of his recovery. Thankfully, he had Jack to assist him. He could help him until he was able to do the tasks on his own, but it would take some time.

At first Jack stayed around just for company—someone to talk to. He also helped with some of the mundane tasks, like sweeping out the shack, pumping water from the well, tending the garden, those kinds of things.

Then Jack's duties expanded. They simply had to if the job was to be done. He would push Jim on a little trolley that led from the shack to the signal tower several times a day and stand there while Jim operated the switches. Eventually, Jack got so familiar with Jim's schedule that he began to walk out and operate the levers in sequence all by himself.

As time passed, Jack was able to do all the duties required by the railroad, although officially he was not employed by the railroad. There was a lot to do each day, but Jack simply did it without complaining. After all, he was Jim's friend and that is what friends do. It was supposed to be just for a while, until Jim could manage for himself, but the weeks turned into months and the months into years. For more than nine years Jack kept at his duties—everything from cleaning the house to tending the garden to trudging out to the signal tower each day, until one day he came down with a bad case of tuberculosis from which he never recovered. His death left a huge hole in Jim's heart.

In all those years Jack had never thrown a switch incorrectly. In nine years there was not one accident or even a narrow miss on the Port Elizabeth main line—not with Jack at the controls.

Jack is buried in Cape Colony, South Africa, not far from the outpost where he worked for almost a decade, for the love of his friend, Jim. His grave is a silent testament to selfless love. But here is the amazing part of this story. Jack, who was so devoted to his friend—who cleaned house and pumped water, who tended the garden and manned the switch tower for all those years, was not a man at all. Jack was a baboon!

It has been said that a dog is man's best friend, but in this case, Jack's love far outweighs any shown by a canine.

Now, if an animal can demonstrate this kind of devotion, how much more a man? God has placed within us a far greater capacity for expressing love to our fellow man. And I choose to believe that we are never more like God than when we give ourselves away for the sake of others.

Self-centeredness often blocks the way, but it is still true that true friendship entails the greatest usefulness, the most open communications, the noblest sufferings, the severest truth, the heartiest counsel, and the greatest union of minds of which brave men and women are capable. And this capability arises within us when we are in union with the greatest Friend anyone can possess.

WHEN FRIENDSHIP CAME ALIVE!

Perfume and incense bring joy to the heart, and the pleasantness of one's friend springs from his earnest counsel (Proverbs 27:9).

MY WIFE AND I LEARNED THE MEANING OF TRUE FRIENDSHIP as never before several years ago when our oldest son, Mark, experienced a life-threatening Illness.

It was shortly after 11 p.m. We had retired for the evening and were just drifting off to sleep when the telephone rang. When the telephone rings at that time of the evening in a parsonage, it generally means trouble or crisis of some type. But little did we know that this time it would involve one of our sons. When I picked up the receiver, it was the voice of a surgeon on the other end, informing us in a southern, difficult to understand drawl, that Mark, a student at Asbury College, near Lexington, Kentucky, was in St. Joseph's Hospital in Lexington. He went on to say that surgery had been performed to remove his appendix, which had burst. He assured us that Mark came through the surgery just fine and that he was in recovery. It was not until the next day that we learned just how serious it was.

After hanging up, I explained the situation to my wife. We looked at each other, numb for a moment. We both felt very strongly that we should go to be with him as soon as possible. So the decision was made to pack a few things as quickly as possible and leave for Kentucky—an eight hour drive. We also decided that a phone call to the lay leader of our church was in order, regardless of the hour. I made the call while Jeanine packed.

When I informed the lay leader of the situation and our plans, he told me to sit tight for a few minutes until he called back. True to his word, Dick called within fifteen minutes. He said, "We're going to fly you down to Lexington. The decision has been made. My wife and I will pick you up and take you to Chicago's O'Hare airport in about fifteen minutes. Reservations have been made. We want you to get there as soon as possible."

We experienced first hand the meaning of true Christian friendship that evening. When a friend hears about someone else's need, he does not immediately think of himself. He responds with action! Words and sympathy are fine, but true friendship goes a step further.

On the way to Chicago (about a three hour drive in a downpour) this wonderful couple engaged us in comforting and reassuring conversation. That is what friends do. By the time we reached O'Hare, we felt as though somehow everything would work out. God would take care of our son. A sense of peace swept over our hearts as we boarded the plane.

Prior to leaving Kalamazoo we had placed a call to a friend of ours in Kentucky, explaining the situation. She agreed to meet us at the airport and chauffeur us to the hospital—another example of the fact that friends do not think about inconvenience; they are focused in on the need at the time.

Mark was in a regular patient room by the time we arrived at St. Joseph's. It was then that we learned that he was full of poison as a result of his ruptured appendix, so they left his incision open in order for the poison to drain out. His temperature had shot up to a dangerously high degree. Consequently the ordeal had taken its toll on him, leaving him very weak. But his life had been spared due to the gracious hand of God.

And as the television pitchmen often say after the initial presentation, "And there's more!" Fast forward a few years and the same couple again came to our rescue. It was while the author was very ill and needed a helping hand. A decision had been made on his behalf to consult with doctors at the Mayo Clinic in Rochester, Minnesota. These dear friends insisted on driving my wife and I to the clinic, a distance of several hundred miles. And they also were willing to stay with us or come back several days later to chauffeur us back home.

The memory of the kindness shown to us during those stressful days lingers to this day. It reminds me of something that I read years ago: "Most people walk in and out of your life, but only friends leave footprints on your heart."

Yes, friends are wonderful. But Christian friends are, without question, the best because they combine prayer with action. It is that extra dimension that really makes all the difference.

When we place our trust in Christ, we enter into some unique relationships. First of all, we are adopted into the family of God. He becomes our Father (John1:12). The Apostle John, in his first epistle, reaffirms this blessing when he writes, "Behold, what manner of love the Father has bestowed upon us, that we should be called the children of God" (3:1, KJV).

As God's children, we enjoy a second unique relationship; we have a family tie with everyone else who knows the Lord, regardless of denomination or even location. In other words, we have a vast multitude of brothers and sisters in Christ that we can count on for support and encouragement.

In addition, we are made members of one body. We have all been made to drink into one Spirit (I Corinthians 12:13). And, as such, we have a special relationship with one another. Paul wrote, "As we have, therefore, opportunity, let us do good to all men, especially to those who are of the household of faith" (Galatians 6:10).

Thank God for Christian friends who, from time to time, refresh our spirits by their acts of kindness and love. They are more precious than silver and gold. They are God's way of taking care of us. Push that pause button. Take time to develop as many friendships as you can. Friends will be God's arms holding you up when you feel as though you are falling.

THE INESTIMABLE INFLUENCE OF CHRISTIAN LITERATURE

In books cherubim expand their wings, the soul of the student may ascend and look around from pole to pole...In them the most high and incomprehensible God Himself is contained and worshiped.

—RICHARD DEBURY
Philobibion, 1473

LITERARY LUNACY

A good book is the precious life-blood of a master spirit, embalmed and treasured up on purpose to a life beyond life.

—JOHN MILTON, *Aeropagitica,* 1644

WHEN WAS THE LAST TIME YOU READ A GOOD BOOK? If your answer fell within the last year, you are in a very select group indeed! Studies show that most Americans do not read even one book a year! Now it is hard to believe, even if it is true, that we have become a video-oriented society. There are hopeful signs on the horizon, however. Book stores are springing up all over the land and there seems to be a renewed interest in reading. Perhaps this is statement to those technocrats who endeavor to convince us that there is no future apart from computers.

Christians are, by new nature, readers. Everything we hold dear—our doctrinal positions, our personal convictions, our vision for what is yet to be, is based upon a book. And not just any book. It is God's Book that we find occupying most of our attention. Little wonder, for it contains all the basics that we need for growth and stability. Andrew Bonar, a great man of God, lived by three rules: (1) Not to speak to any person before speaking to Jesus Christ., (2) Not to do anything with his hands until he had been on his knees, (3) Not to read the paper until he had read his Bible.

As a pastor, I have had the opportunity to be involved in discipling others, in group settings and one-on-one. It has been my pleasure to share the fundamentals needed to develop as a believer, that is, Bible study, devotions, church attendance, fellowship with other Christians, faith-sharing, and prayer. These are the roots upon which grow the healthiest fruits. I have observed that most discipleship material available today pays little attention to the role of Christian literature. Those who ignore this vital aspect may be guilty of literary lunacy!

I believe it is important to expose oneself to the great Christian classics, such as *Pilgrim's Progress, In His Steps,* and *Mere Christianity.*

Mark Twain was right when he said, "The man who does not read good books has no advantage over the man who can't read them." Reading, in general, has certain advantages over other forms of enlightenment.

One of the important battles of today is between books and television. Television presents a tremendous emotional impact, but a picture does not always present a clear thought. Television depends upon an instant response, whereas literature affords us opportunity to review again and again what is being presented. Television is making us descend into something like the global village that Marshal Mcluhan warns us about, where there "will be no more sharpness of elegance to the life of human beings, but instead a great blob of emotional reactions."

Books give us the tools with which to think, to resist the dehumanization of language and the remaking of words in propaganda. "The greatest gift is the passion for reading. It is cheap, it consoles, it distracts, it excites, it gives you knowledge of the world and experience of a wide kind. It is moral illumination" (Elizabeth Hardwick).

William Carey, that great missionary, was inspired by reading the Voyages of Captain Cook. And it was reading Carey's letters that Henry Martyn first thought of the claims of India. Buchaman's Star in the East moved Dr. Judson to missionary work, and eventually sent him to Burma.

Who can estimate the impact that Christian literature has had upon the pilgrim, or even the seeker, for that matter? How many have been led to Christ as a result of reading a testimony or biography? How many have sought and received consolation, encouragement, and enlightenment while perusing the pages of some noble publication? One day heaven will celebrate the use of the pen in the plan of God.

Over 200 years ago, an old Puritan doctor wrote a book entitled, *The Bruised Reed.* A copy of it was sold by a poor peddler to a young man by the name of Richard Baxter. Upon reading it, he was soundly converted to Christ. Baxter, in turn, wrote the monumental book *A Call to the Unconverted.* This book came into the possession of another young man, Phillip Doddridge by name. Doddridge wrote *The Rise and Progress of Religion.* This work came into the hands of William Wilberforce, and he was converted. Wilberforce was a bright and shining light in the

British Empire, and he set in motion a social reform which freed all the slaves in that Empire. In turn he wrote a book entitled *A Practical View of Christianity.* It cheered the faith and fired the zeal of a minister, the Reverend Leigh Richmond. He, in turn, wrote a book entitled *The Dairyman's Daughter.* A man in the bleak north of Scotland was greatly influenced by this volume, and he became a mighty champion of truth until all Scotland rang with the eloquence of Thomas Chalmers.

I rest my case.

THE DISCERNING READER

Finally, brothers, whatever is true, whatever is noble, whatever is right, whatever is pure, whatever is lovely, whatever is admirable—if anything is excellent or praiseworthy—think about such things (Philippians 4:8).

SOMERSET MAUGHAM once wrote, "To acquire the habit of reading is to construct for yourself a refuge from almost all the miseries of life." This quote, of necessity, needs qualifying. It is the habit of reading good literature that provides a safe haven for the mind—that which is positive, noble, and uplifting in nature. For example, if one reads only the daily newspaper, he might develop a pessimistic view of the world, seeing it only as a place filled with hatred, prejudice, fear, and self-centeredness. A good deal of what we think about is the result of our exposure to the media, especially television and the printed page. That is why Philippians 4:8 is so vital to our mental and spiritual health. Whatever enters our mind will eventually shape us. If we think long enough about that which has found entrance, it will ultimately become a passion, and an action in our lives. In short, we will begin to "act it out." Consequently, one must be made to dwell upon good things, excellent things. Any one of us could sit down and think about enough problems to have a nervous breakdown. If we constantly fill our minds with the negative, destructive issues of life, we will reap mental disaster.

A young college girl who was an outstanding student volunteered to be a counselor at a summer camp for girls. Despite her abilities she was assigned to work in the kitchen. One day the camp manager happened upon her while she was mopping the floor. Astounded, she said, "What a shame that a young lady of your intellect should have to do this." The young lady turned and looked at the manager and replied, "Oh, that's all right. You see, I don't have to think about mopping while I'm doing it." You and I can keep our souls out of the dust, no matter what our task, if we center our thoughts on those things which are true, honest, just, pure, and lovely.

Over a century and a half ago, Daniel Webster made the following statement: "If religious books are not widely circulated among the masses in this country, I do not know what is going to become of our nation. If truth be not diffused, error will be. If the evangelical volume does not reach every community, the pages of a corrupt and licentious literature will." In the light of modern American culture, these words have a strangely prophetic ring to them.

The Book of Acts tells about a group of people who burned over $10,000 worth of books (19:19) because they were textbooks on the art of practicing sorcery—books that were godless, that hurt people's relationship with God. These people understood the power of words to distort truth, especially when under the influence of the evil one.

It is distressing to enter a hospital room and find cheap novels and magazines there. What we put into our minds will shape and move us. When we read suggestive magazines and novels that dwell on sexual immorality, we program our minds in that direction. On the other hand, when we immerse ourselves in wholesome literature, especially Christian literature, we are moved in a direction that is pleasing to God. Occasionally, one can find Christian literature boldly displayed in a doctor's or dentist's waiting room. It is there both to feed the spiritually inquiring mind and to provide inspiration and help for the pilgrim.

Here is a call for us to fill our minds with that which beckons us to a higher level of living—the life of stability, of service, or excellence.

May God grant us the gift of discernment to understand the power of the media and to be receptors of truth, truth that will set us free and enable us to glorify God in all that we do.

THE READER'S PRAYER

Gracious Father, thank you for breathing upon men and women throughout history, inspiring them to set down Your thoughts for our benefit. Praise You for the gifts of sight, reading, illumination and imagination—the four posts upon which are built the libraries of the mind.

This morning I read a portion from the Book of books. I read it carefully, prayerfully, thoughtfully, expectantly, and with great anticipation. And, just as in other times, You came to me and breathed yet again upon my needy soul. I felt refreshed and prepared to meet the challenges of another day.

Dear Lord, Your book is too wonderful for me to express in mere words. It is Your Spirit communing with mine. Help me to look through it, not at it, that I might see the world through Your loving eyes.

I praise You, Almighty God, for the world of literature—a most remarkable creation, outlasting monuments, nations, and even civilizations—writings still as fresh as the day they were penned—still speaking to men's hearts by men centuries dead.

Who but You, Lord, could number those whose lives have been transformed and enriched through Christian literature? You have raised up those across the ages, beginning with the early church fathers and including such contemporary scholars as C.S. Lewis and Francis Schaeffer, to be Your spokesmen—men whose writings have inspired millions. In some cases, messages came to us from human souls we never saw who lived far away in another time. Yet there on those parchments, they speak to us, teach us, comfort us, and open their hearts to us as brothers and sisters.

When I consider the practical impact of Christian literature to the weary pilgrim, my heart overflows with praise for...

- *Biographies that inspire us in the direction of imitation.*
- *Hymnals that act as channels of truth and aids to worship*
- *Tracts that capture the attention and open the door of salvation.*
- *Devotional books that rouse a response in us which cannot be awakened through any other means.*
- *Periodicals that keep us abreast of current issues and needs.*
- *Bible helps, such as dictionaries, commentaries, and encyclopedias,*

enabling us to better understand the customs, languages, and places found in holy writ.

- *Theological writings that explain basic doctrinal concepts, such as the nature of God, man, sin, and the work of Christ in our stead.*
- *Christian book stores that make available to us a myriad of spiritual aids.*
- *Church libraries that serve as pure oases that quench the searching soul.*
- *The internet that affords instant information on a variety of subjects, both sacred and secular.*

These are really the work of Your hand. You are behind it all, moving Your children to lay down truth so that they might have an even clearer understanding of just Who you are. Lord, we are indebted to You for the writings of godly men and women who have given to us their most precious thoughts and poured their souls into ours.

Your image is inscribed on pages in order that it may be engraved on our hearts. Help us to see that our lives are like open books, written a chapter at a time. Upon the pages are imprinted our collective searchings and experiences, many of which come to us by way of sacred writings.

Thank You, Lord God, for the books and for the Book! Help us to continually digest Your truth and impart it to all who have open and teachable minds. In the name of the Author and Finisher of our faith. Amen.

A TINY MORSEL'S GREAT EFFECT

And the gospel must first be published among all nations (Mark 13:10, KJV).

EVER SINCE JOHANNES GUTENBERG INVENTED THE PRINTING PRESS, God has been pleased to use the printed word as a means of getting His Word into the hands and hearts of men. The impact of printing is comparable to the development of writing and the invention of the alphabet, as far as its effects on the society.

In general, knowledge came closer to the hands of the people since printed books could be sold for a fraction of the cost of illuminated manuscripts. There were also more copies of each book available so that more people could discuss them. Within 50 to 60 years the entire library of "classical" knowledge had been printed on the new presses (Eisenstein, 1969; 52). The spread of works also led to the creation of copies by other parties than the original author, leading to the formulation of copyright laws. Furthermore, as the books spread into the hands of the people, Latin was gradually replaced by the national languages. This development was one of the keys to the creation of modern nations.

John Wesley saw the importance of the printed page and wrote hundreds of tracts which he distributed in large quantities as he traveled across England on horseback. Think of the number of souls who were touched in some way as a result of Mr. Wesley's endeavors.

One of the oldest Christian organizations in the United States, and one that has veered little from its original purpose, is the American Sunday School Union. It was founded in Philadelphia almost two centuries ago to promote the establishment of new Sunday schools. A group of Philadelphia citizens founded the organization in a schoolroom on May 13, 1817. Francis Scott Key, author of "The Star-Spangled Banner," helped to launch it. Within ten years it had become the foremost publisher of children's literature. In its first century, more than 100,000 Sunday schools were established.

Years ago, a man in Chicago died, leaving $50,000 to the American Sunday School Union, stipulating that the interest was to be used exclusively for its missionary work. During the eleven years in which the Union had the income from this fund it started 819 Sunday schools, 6,150 Bibles and tracts were distributed, 3,676 persons were converted, and 61 new churches were planted.

Many stories could be shared which testify to the power of a few words. One such concerns the conversation of Hitler's bodyguard, Kurt Wagner. He adored Hitler and reverenced him as a god. At the end of the war, with Hitler's suicide in a Berlin bunker, Wagner's faith was shattered and he planned a suicide as well. Going for a final cup of coffee, he picked up a discarded gospel tract and read it, first carelessly and then with great interest. As a result of reading this tract, he sought out a godly pastor who led him to Christ. Wagner was transformed from a hardened man into a peace-loving man and he became a new creation in Christ.

Tract distribution works, and every Christian should be a consistent distributor of the Word of Life in some form or other. After all, the cults and false religions of this world employ this means with a degree of success. Our generation is hungry for the Word of Life. We must feed them. A tract is only a tiny morsel, but what wonders it can accomplish when it falls into the hands of a hungry soul. It is like the seed that falls upon good ground and takes root, springing up to bear much fruit. But the seed in itself is powerless and without value apart from the soil. It can only be brought into contact with the soil through the sower. And that is where you and I come in. We have the printed page that is available to us. We should make use of it while we can.

Even more amazing yet are stories that come to us by way of fragments of truth—like the minister in England who was with a Christian lady who lay dying. He asked her the circumstances surrounding her conversion to Christ. She gave him a piece of paper torn from an American journal containing part of one of C.H. Spurgeon's sermons. The scrap had been wrapped around a package that came to her from Australia. She read the words of Spurgeon and they were the means of leading her to Christ. Think of it! A sermon preached in England, printed in America, in some way ending up in Australia, a part of it used as wrapping paper there, coming back to England—all of this became the means of this woman's entrance into the kingdom of God! Only God could superintend such a series of events. The prophet Zechariah wrote, "For who hath despised the day of small things? For they shall rejoice..." (4:10, KJV).

It would seem from Scripture that God delights in taking the "small things," the despised things of this world, and displaying His awesome power through them, as in the case of the loaves and fishes, or David facing off against Goliath, or Gideon's 300 doing battle against thousands of Midianites. Or better yet, who could have imagined that twelve men would turn the world upside down?

Yes, a tiny morsel, a tract, a scrap of paper, a few words hastily scribbled on a prison wall, when used by the Holy Spirit, can forever change the course of one's life. Thank God for the seed of His Word, no matter how small or insignificant it might appear to be.

TEACHING TOOLS

Every man who knows how to read has it in his power to magnify himself, to multiply the ways in which he exists, to make his life full, significant, and interesting (Aldous Huxley).

HOW DOES ONE MEASURE THE IMPACT THAT CHRISTIAN LITERATURE CAN HAVE upon one's spiritual development? In the early days of my spiritual journey I was greatly influenced by the biographies of noble believers such as Martin Luther, John Wesley, and John Bunyan, to name a few. They served to bolster my new faith and challenge my thinking.

And then there were poets such as Edgar Guest and Annie Johnson Flint. They were favorites of my first pastor and, without question, they were quoted somewhere in his sermon every Sunday.

No doubt about the fact that literature is a powerful force in shaping who we are. The written word not only sways our emotions, it also acts as an important teaching device. I recall reading about a mother, concerned over the envious spirit of her high school daughter toward one of her classmates who had been chosen over her for special recognition. The mother wanted to impart a moral lesson, so she told her the following story that she had heard in a literature class many years before:

> A statue was erected to a Grecian champion for his exploits in the public games. But another Greek, a rival of the honored athlete, so burned with hot jealousy that he vowed that he would destroy that statue. Every night he sneaked out in the dark and chipped away at its base to weaken it and make it tipple. He finally succeeded. But when it fell, it toppled on Him! He died, a victim of his own envy.

Do you see what a teaching tool literature can be? Literature, ancient and modern, offer a huge source of inspirational material that can help shape one's soul. Of course, it is true that the Bible is the believer's primary source of instruction in righteousness, but along with the Scriptures are works that can be said to be "inspired" in another sense. They act as supplements and windows to the Word.

And what of the effect of poetry? It can bring an idea into focus with more beauty and power than the usual prose. For example, in Tennyson's Enoch Arden, an incident illustrates the folly of blindly putting our finger on some verse in the Bible for guidance in finding God's will. Because Enoch had been gone at sea for a long time, his wife, Annie, wondered if he had been shipwrecked and drowned, in which case she would be free to marry her would-be suitor. Unable to sleep one night, she prayed for a sign:

> Started from bed, and struck herself a light,
> Then desperately seized the holy Book,
> Suddenly put her finger on a text,
> "Under the palm-tree." That was nothing to her;
> No meaning there: she closed the Book and slept;
> When lo! He Enoch sitting on a height,
> Under a palm-tree, over him the Sun;
> "He is gone," she thought, "He is happy, he is singing
> 'Hosanna in the highest'" yonder shines
> The Sun of Righteousness, and those be palms
> Whereof the happy people strowing cried
> "Hosanna in the Highest!"

When Annie awoke she concluded that Enoch was in heaven so she consented to marriage. But Enoch was not dead. He returned only to see his wife and her new husband—all this tragedy due to Annie's so-called "guidance" from the Bible.

And then there is the issue of allegory. Can anyone doubt its power to move troubled souls to believe God's promises? Such is the way with Pilgrim's Progress. A speaker on a nursing home team wanted to remind the patients of the promises of God in His Word. So he told how, in Bunyan's classic, both Christian and Hopeful, after imprisonment for several days in Doubting Castle by Great Despair, suddenly thought:

> ...What a fool...am I, thus to lie in a stinking Dungeon, when I may as well walk at liberty. I have a Key in my bosom called Promise, that will, I am persuaded, open any lock in Doubting Castle. Then said Hopeful, "That's good news, good brother; pluck it out of thy bosom and try."
>
> Then Christian pulled it out of his bosom, and began to try at the dungeon door, whose bolt...came out. Then he went to the outward door that leads into the Castle yard, and with his Key opened that door also... Then they went on, and so were safe because they were out of his jurisdiction.

Another form of literature that reinforces the truth of the Bible is found in fables. A fable is a nonfactual story in which truth is imparted by having animals, birds, trees and such, speak and act like people. Aesop's Fables is a classic.

Asked to write a short article for the church youth newsletter on the theme of boastfulness, a high-schooler began…

> An ant climbed on an elephant's back and asked for a ride over the bridge. After they had crossed, ant exclaimed, "My, didn't we shake that bridge!"

Then a little further on in the article he used another fable to get across his point:

> Two ducks and a frog had to leave their home pond when it began to dry up. The ducks could easily fly to another location, but wishing to transport frog friend, they decided to fly with a stick between their two bills, with the frog hanging on to the stick with his mouth. A farmer looking up at the flying trio remarked, "Isn't that a clever idea! I wonder who thought of it?" The frog, to his peril, said, "I did."

The high-schooler added, “Boastfulness, like pride, goeth before a fall—and sometimes the fall can be so great that recovery is impossible!”

These forms of literature, along with many others, can serve to bolster God’s truth. Wise is that person who spends his quiet time with his Bible, devotional book, hymnbook, and other forms of writing at his disposal. He will be the richer for it.

BY ALL MEANS

To the weak I became weak, to win the weak. I have become all things to all men so that by all possible means I might save some (I Corinthians 9:22).

ONLY HEAVEN WILL REVEAL THE NUMBER OF SOULS that made it to the celestial shores because someone cared enough to distribute Christian literature to those without knowledge and, therefore, without hope.

Richard Wurmbrand, in his book, *In the Face of Surrender*, tells of a time when his ministry decided to spread the gospel in Communist countries. But how could they manage to do that since these nations were closed to the distribution of the good news? They took as their cue the statement made by the Apostle Paul in I Corinthians 9:22. His purpose became theirs: to save souls "by all possible means."

While they respected the communist laws, they interpreted them in light of the Bible's mandate, which they believed superseded such laws. To give just a few examples, they threw thousands of plastic bags into the Bering Straits separating Alaska from the USSR. They did the same into the Black Sea near the shores of the Ukraine, and into the sea between the Greek islands and Albania. Each tightly sealed bag contained the Gospel in the local language and a brochure showing the way of salvation. Along with this they placed some chewing gum to entice even the worst Communist policeman to open the bag. They also enclosed pieces of straw to make the bag float on the water. Waves brought the bags to shore. Wurmbrand's organization had studied the currents in the sea to be sure they would arrive as they had planned. The method worked.

When Albania finally opened up to religion a few years ago, Wurmbrand's ministry heard from a man who had found one of these bags. He read the enclosed literature and was converted to Christ. And from then on he watched the shores to find others, which he distributed to family and friends. Eventually he was discovered doing this by the Communist authorities and spent nine years in jail for this "crime."

When asked if he was angry at the Wurmbrand Ministries because of his incarceration, he answered, "Not at all. It was my decision and it was worth it."

Wurmbrand's Ministry also flew the message of Christ in balloons from West to East Germany, and from South to North Korea. People found Christ by all means—even poor means.

As the ministry grew, they smuggled Bibles and Christian literature by land, by sea, by tourists, by diplomats—by any means they could devise. They also smuggled in printing presses piece by piece, which were assembled and sometimes put to work literally underground. The work entailed tremendous risks, but the rewards outweighed them by far. They were relentless in their endeavor. As a result, bookstores, print shops, and missions centers were created in Romania, Hungary, Russia, Ethiopia, and China.

All of this took place because a few believers were convinced that Christian literature can have a life-changing affect in the hearts of those who are receptive to it. It is impossible to overestimate the power of the printed word. The Albanian who found Christ did not require a whole Bible, much less volumes of theology. He was saved and sustained by only one gospel message while imprisoned for Christ.

This story and others like it puts to shame those of us who possess large quantities of Christian literature and yet do not take sufficient time to read as we should. There are many in foreign lands who would give almost anything to possess a whole Bible. May we learn to treasure and avail ourselves of all material that would strengthen our faith. And may we be willing to share this wonderful Gospel "by all means possible."

THE ART OF MEDITATION

Meditation is like a needle after which comes a thread of gold, composed of affections, prayers, and resolutions.

—ST. ALPHONSUS (1696-1787)
Veritable Epouse de J.C.

REFLECTION

Reflect on what I am saying, for the Lord will give you insight into all this (II Timothy 2:7).

ON SPECIAL OCCASIONS, the writer and his wife would have dinner at a restaurant called *Reflections* in Traverse City, Michigan. It was aptly named because it overlooked East Bay of Lake Michigan. The view was spectacular. We always tried to get a table near the windows, which surrounded the dining room. They could just as easily have called this restaurant "Windows," except there was already one by that name on West Bay.

As we gazed at the scene before us—the various colors of the water, the sky, the surrounding hills, we could not help but ponder the wonder of God's creative power. No doubt the restaurant's name had more to do with the window's reflections, but when nature displays her wares, thoughts of our Lord come to mind. And that is the way it is meant to be. The atmosphere was conducive to meditation. Fresh flowers at each table, soft, classical music to dine by, and a view that was simply magnificent. Pondering was Providential for us.

Meditation. It is almost a lost art. Think about it for a moment. A good Thesaurus lists several synonyms for meditation: *ponder, reflect, reason, muse, mull, weight.* But this type of exercise demands a great deal from those who find it difficult to pause for a time. Why? Because it takes effort, mental energy, and a deliberate commitment of time. Our minds are too cluttered with the cares of life. It means setting aside the incidental in favor of the essential. Is it really worth it? Paul reminds us that taking time to reflect on the lessons learned from soldiers, athletes, and farmers is extremely beneficial in terms of our ability to endure hardship. For example, the soldier portrays a sense of *priority.* The athlete models *discipline.* The farmer is the pattern for *perseverance.*

If one is to be a growing disciple of Christ, all three of the above qualities are absolutely essential.

When a young person is about to "sign up" for a hitch in the armed services, the recruiter not doubt says, "Do you understand the commitment you are about to make? It will mean you will leave all other pursuits behind. From this day forward you will become the property of the government for the next four years!" In a similar manner, the disciple of Christ must place himself at the complete disposal of the Kingdom of God. "Seek ye first the kingdom of God and his righteousness," Matthew writes (6:33, KJV).

Athletes have to keep their emotions, instincts, and reactions under control in order to compete according to the rules. Those who do not, soon find themselves on the bench or out of the competition altogether. So, too, the disciple must live under orders and within certain boundaries. He must always remember the formula: FACTS (The Word) PRODUCE FAITH, OUT OF WHICH FEELINGS EXPLODE! Discipline! That is the key to victory.

Paul also uses the farmer as an example of endurance. The disciples, like the farmer, must work long and hard, often under adverse conditions and persevere, perhaps for long times, with little reward for the sake of being faithful to Jesus as Lord.

"Reflect," Paul urges the reader. Turn it over in your mind. Observe life's lessons. If you do, when you come to the bump in the road, you will be able to ride right on over it.

Popular author and speaker Ken Blanchard tells a powerful story about Red, a corporate president, who, as a young man, learned an important and life-changing lesson. Red had just graduated from college and was offered an opportunity to interview for a position with a firm in New York City. As the job involved moving his wife and small child from Texas to New York, he wanted to talk the decision over with someone before accepting it, but his father had died and Red did not feel he had anyone to turn to. On impulse, he telephoned an old friend of the family, someone his father had suggested he turn to if he ever needed good advice. The friend said he would be happy to give Red advice about the job offer under the condition that the young man take whatever advice he was given. "You might want to think about it for a couple of days before hearing my suggestion," he was told.

Two days later Red called the man back and said he was ready to listen to his counsel. "Go on to New York City and have the interview," the older man said. "But I want you to go up there in a very special way. I want you to go on a train and I want you to get a private compartment. Don't take anything to write with, anything to listen to, or anything to read. And don't talk to anyone except to put in your order for dinner with the porter. When you get to New York call me and I will tell you what to do next."

Red followed the advice precisely. The trip took two days. As he had taken nothing with him and kept entirely to himself, he quickly became bored. It soon dawned on him what was happening. He was being forced into quiet time. He could do nothing but think and meditate. About three hours outside New York City he broke the rules and asked for a pencil and paper. Until the train stopped, he wrote the culmination of all his meditation.

Red called the family friend from the train station. "I know what you wanted," he said. "You wanted me to think. And now I know what to do. I don't need anymore help."

"I didn't think you would, Red," came the reply. "Good luck."

Now, years later, Red heads a corporation in California. And he has always made it a policy to take a couple of days periodically to be alone. He goes where there is no phone, no television, no computer, and no people. He goes to be alone with his thoughts, to meditate and listen. He dreams, he plans, he evaluates. He is convinced that this practice has helped make him successful.

Those who draw water from the wellspring of meditation know that God draws close to their hearts. The thirst for direction is quenched. The seeking mind is refreshed. So let down the bucket and enjoy!

PONDERINGS

When the angels had left them and gone into heaven, the shepherds said to one another, "Let's go to Bethlehem and see this thing that has happened, which the Lord has told us about." So they hurried off and found Mary and Joseph, and the baby, who was lying in the manger. When they had seen him, they spread the word concerning what had been told them about this child, and all who heard it were amazed at what the shepherds said to them. But Mary treasured up all these things and pondered them in her heart (Luke 2:15-19).

DID YOU EVER HAVE SOMETHING THAT TOOK PLACE in your life that was so dramatic, so life-transforming, so significant, that you could not get it out of your mind? In fact, from time to time you still hearken back to that moment mentally, even though many years have passed? It might the memory of your first date or perhaps your wedding day. And then again, it might have been that time when certain feelings overwhelmed you at the birth of your first child. It could even be memories of a spiritual nature—your conversion experience or baptism. Whatever the case, it was worth remembering and meditating upon. Mary, the mother of our Lord, had one of those moments that would forever affect her life. Luke tells us in verse 19 of chapter 2 that Mary "treasured up all these things and pondered them in her heart."

That is another way of saying that she stored up those precious memories in her heart. She weighed them over and over again in her mind, thinking deeply about their significance. She would draw upon them many times later in life.

So much had happened to Mary in the last few months that she hardly had time to sit and think about it. Now, at last, she takes time to reflect upon everything she had seen, heard, and experienced.

What are the "things" she treasured in her heart? We can only speculate, of course. But some things seem to jump out from this account in Luke. For example, consider the appearance of Gabriel and his announcement to her. He told her five astounding things: (1) Among all the women of the world, God had selected her to bear His Son—she was "highly favored." (2) The Lord would be with her and she would become pregnant by the power of the Holy Spirit. (3) When the child would be born, she was to give him the name Jesus (Joshua), which means "Savior." (4) This child would be great and be called the "Son of the Most High," a clear reference to deity. (5) He would be given the throne of David and would reign forever. His kingdom would never end. These are five amazing revelations that must have astounded Mary, to say the least.

Is it not also possible that part of Mary's pondering might have included her visit to Elisabeth when John the Baptist leaped for joy in Elisabeth's womb (Luke 1:39-44)? Or perhaps she thought about the long, hard, trip to Bethlehem, the lodging in a stable, the visit of the shepherds, their story, their reaction, their sense of awe and act of worship. In any event, these were, in part, memories to be called up from time to time.

Consider her feelings in regard to Joseph. She loved and appreciated him deeply. It had not been easy for him and she knew it. There was a lot of trust in their relationship. Even when Joseph thought Mary had wronged him, there was no desire on his part to punish or humiliate her (Matthew 1:18-21). He had an inner strength that Mary must have admired and thought about frequently. This gives all of us pause to reflect on how much our spouses mean to us and how blessed we are to be recipients of their love.

It is true that Mary would nurture great love for her son Jesus and for his half-brothers and sisters yet to be born, but her love for Joseph was a special kind. It was a love born out of mutual respect and shared values.

The church focuses a good deal of attention on Mary, as well it should, but let us not forget Joseph. He was special to Mary. In the Jewish home it was the father who had the primary responsibility for the religious instruction of the children. If the elders in the temple marveled at Jesus' knowledge of the Scriptures at age twelve, then I say that Joseph did his job well.

Psychologists tell us that our earthly father gives us our clearest impression of the nature of God. If our father was harsh, we may well see God in the same way. If he was gentle and kind, our image of God likely will be similar. Is it possible that Jesus' concept of His heavenly Father as loving, merciful, and kind was modeled by Joseph? No wonder Mary loved Joseph. Surely her love for him was one of the things she treasured and pondered in her heart.

And speaking of pondering, what about the unique birth of Jesus? He had no human father. Mary had never known a man. Perhaps it went beyond pondering to absolute amazement. We are impressed by the star over the stable and the singing of the angels. But neither of these is as impressive as the birth of a child—and not just any child—the Son of the Highest!

Could there possibly be an atheist in a maternity ward? Could any mother ever hold her newborn infant in her arms for the first time without feeling something miraculous has occurred? Henry Ward Beecher said, "I think that the most wonderful book that could be written would be a book in which an angel should write all the thoughts that pass through a faithful mother's mind from the time she first heard the cry of her child."

I wonder as Mary held this tiny infant in her arms, what thoughts went through her mind—*How can he make atonement for her sins and the sins of her people?* The angel had called Him great, but He lay there on her bosom, weak and wailing as any other babe. He was to sit upon the throne of David; yet he was cradled in manger.

Many years ago, during the Great War, a day was dawning on a battlefield in northern France, through a fog so thick that no one could see more than a few yards from the trenches. In the night the Germans had drawn back their lines a little and the French had gone forward. But between the two positions a lonely farmhouse was still standing. As the sun rose, heavy guns began to boom. But suddenly, on both sides, the firing ceased and there fell a strange, deaf silence. For there in the green meadow, crawling on its hand and knees was a little baby. It appeared perfectly happy and contented and the baby's laugh was heard as it clutched a dandelion. Not a shot was fired that day!

And when the Babe of Bethlehem lay in his mother's arms, it signaled the entrance of the Prince of Peace into a hostile world. His coming would eventually cause men to cease their hatred as they looked by faith to Him.

Certainly Mary pondered these things in her heart—the love of her husband and the miracle that lay in a manger before her. Yet I see one more thing that she meditated on—the nearness of God.

Here was God's own Son lying before her. Did she fully comprehend all that was taking place? Probably not, but I am sure that something deep and mysterious must have been moving within Mary's soul as she gazed upon baby Jesus. Perhaps the words of Isaiah came to her mind: "For unto us a child is born, unto us a son is given; and the government shall be upon his shoulders. And his name shall be called Wonderful Counselor, the mighty God, the everlasting Father, the Prince of Peace."

Somehow all the power and purpose of Almighty God had been focused on that little stable in Bethlehem. If Moses took off his shoes in front of the burning bush because the ground upon which he stood was holy, and if Isaiah cried out, "Woe is me for I am a man of unclean lips and dwell in the midst of a people of unclean lips," on that day when he first beheld the glory of God in the Temple, how Mary's heart must have burned within her as she held the God-Man in her arms and looked into those holy eyes.

Surely Mary pondered all those years later at Calvary as she witnessed her son dying for the world's sin. Do you suppose she thought about the time when she kissed His face for the first time there in the manger and now realized that she had kissed the face of God? Or what of those hands that she often held and now looked upon with spikes driven through—those some hands that healed and blessed?

I wonder also if she thought about His first words, only later to discover that He spoke like no other man—words of life, of liberty, of love. He became the greatest teacher the world has ever known. And now she hears Him speak His last words—words of forgiveness and hope.

As she gazed upon His bleeding brow, do you think memories of

His head upon her breast flooded her mind? A mother would never forget those cherished memories of childhood.

No doubt Mary thought about the time when He took His first steps, later to walk across Palestine, preaching and teaching the Good News—walking into places of danger for love's sake, and finally taking the dreadful journey called "The Way of Suffering."

What do you treasure in your mind? What memories have you stored away that you might draw upon in times of trouble, doubt, and temptation? Pondering is worthwhile, but it takes time and discipline. Let me encourage you to close out the world for a while. Let your mind go back to those eventful moments when God was so real and close to you. Let them inspire you to continue on your journey.

THE PAUSE THAT REFRESHES

Blessed is the man who does not walk in the counsel of the wicked or stand in the way of sinners or sit in the seat of mockers. But his delight is in the law of the LORD, and on his law he meditates day and night (Psalm 1:1,2).

IT TAKES AN INVESTMENT OF TIME, but it is worth it. It requires concentration, but the rewards are plenteous. It takes a good deal of determination, but the endeavor really pays off. What am I referring to? Why the *art of meditation,* of course. It is on the endangered species list in much of Western culture. Look at your own life. How easy is it for you to find the time to sit and read a passage of Scripture, let alone think deeply about its significance for your life? Come on now, be honest. We are a driven generation, driven to succeed and success demands time—time to act, to move, to produce. Meditation? We will have to leave it to those who are into Eastern religions.

However, we do have a problem when we develop this lifestyle as a follower of Christ. What do we do with verses like Psalm 1:2 that call us to reflect upon the great thoughts and acts of Almighty God? The Living Bible's rendering of the above verse crystallizes the concept of meditation: "But they delight in doing everything God wants them to, and day and night are always meditating on his laws and thinking about ways to follow him more closely."

In many of the Psalms, the word *Selah* appears. It has several probable meanings and uses one of which is as follows: "to pause, to be silent and think about the words and how they reveal truth for the soul." It is used many times at the end of certain sections or strophes which report a high spiritual experience. It is as if the writer is saying to the reader, "Hush! This is awesome truth; think carefully about what is being transmitted to you. Be still and know that these are holy words."

Several years ago, I was introduced to "scriptural praying." My devotional life took on an entirely different meaning. For the first time in my life I began to experience the value of meditation. I began to realize afresh that the Bible is the best devotional book ever written. Scripture praying is simply taking time to pause and think about each word or phrase in a passage. What is God saying to me? What should my response be? As truth was unfolded to me by the Holy Spirit, my prayer might at that moment include praise, petition, confession, or intercession, depending upon the context. Let us take this approach to Colossians 1:3-6 and see how it works as an example.

> We always thank God, the Father of our Lord Jesus Christ, when we pray for you, because we have heard of your faith in Christ Jesus and of the love you have for all the saints–the faith and love that spring from the hope that is stored up for you in heaven and that you have already heard about in the word of truth, the gospel that has come to you. All over the world this gospel is bearing fruit and growing, just as it has been doing among you since the day you heard it and understood God's grace in all its truth.

Points to Ponder (verses 3 and 4):

- How thankful am I for the impact of my brothers and sisters in Christ?
- Do I faithfully intercede for others in the body of Christ?
- How important is reputation? Do I possess the faith and love that would inspire others?
- Do I love all the saints, regardless of their status, maturity, and personality?

Points to Ponder (verse 5):

- The hope of heaven! What a motivating factor. It colors so many of my decisions. It is the ground of my faith and love. I am on my way to the celestial city. I am a stranger and sojourner here. I must influence others to join me someday. What will heaven be like?
- The gospel—good news for all—for every generation. In a sense we are writing our own gospel, our own story of how Jesus Christ

came to deliver us from sin, from ourselves, from Satan, from spiritual death. Oh, the glorious Gospel of God! It is meant to be treasured in our hearts and transmitted to the whole world. How can I best do it?

Points to Ponder (verse 6):

- How did this gospel come to me? Through what means? What is my responsibility to see that others also hear it?
- Praise God for the power of the gospel. The church is springing up in every corner of the globe. God's kingdom is so vast—both here and in heaven—visible and invisible.
- Oh, Lord, please bear fruit through me to my generation. What will it take for me to become a conduit through which the love and mercy of God flows?
- Oh, the fullness of God's grace! Can we really comprehend the grace of God? Every day, in many amazing ways, God's grace is at work in my life. Lord, please help me to recognize Your undeserved favor as You protect, nourish, and sustain me.

In just four verses, the mind explodes with thoughts relating to our spiritual life. It is as if we are engaging in a mental diary of sorts. The result is that our concept of God is heightened and our level of humility is revealed. And here is the amazing thing about the Word of God: Every person who takes time to contemplate its message will experience different insights. That is the mystery and genius of the Bible. And little wonder, since it contains the mind of God. But to plumb its depths requires a commitment of time in order to weight its essence. We must again hear the Lord's word to Joshua: "This book of the law shall not depart out of thy mouth; but thou shalt meditate therein day and night, that thou mayest observe to do according to all that is written therein: for then thou shalt make thy way prosperous, and then thou shalt have good success" (Joshua 1:8, KJV).

THE "WARM-HEARTED" FOLLOWER

But when I was silent and still, not even saying anything good, my anguish increased. My heart grew hot within me, and as I meditated, the fire burned; then I spoke with my tongue (Psalm 39:2,3).

But if I say, "I will not mention him or speak any more in his name," his word is in my heart like a fire, a fire shut up in my bones. I am weary of holding it in; indeed, I cannot (Jeremiah 20:9).

WHAT DO YOU THINK OF when someone is described as being "warm hearted?" If you are anything like me I suspect you would say something like, "loving, tender, affectionate, caring, and friendly." But the psalmist and Jeremiah seem to give it another twist. They speak of having their hearts set ablaze by the Word of God. They try to keep silent, but there is something within them—a conviction, an excitement, that must be expressed. They have been "musing," as the King James Version puts it. And the result is that a fire burns within. They have taken time to think about the mighty acts and words of God. They are moved and cannot hold it in!

Perhaps you have had moments like that. I know I have. How many times, for example, have worshipers entered into the house of the Lord with heads and hearts bowed in discouragement. The race has become almost too hard to run; there seems to be too many hills and little level ground. The way is dark and the birds have stopped their singing. Then suddenly it comes—a warm feeling, a fire of conviction burning within. It comes by way of a hymn or gospel song, a scripture, a testimony, a sermon. And there, in that moment, a feeling of God's presence overwhelms them. And when they leave the service, it is with a vow to share with someone soon the glory and goodness of God.

It is utterly amazing how the Spirit of God will invade our thought processes (if we give Him entrance and time) to reinvigorate our faith. Do you remember the two disciples who were on the road to Emmaus after the Resurrection? Jesus walked with them and quoted passages from the Old Testament, explaining what they meant and what they said about Him. Later, after He left them, "they began telling each other how their hearts felt strangely warm as he talked with them and explained the Scriptures during the walk down the road" (Luke 22:32, TLB).

They were on fire! Within the hour they were on their way back to Jerusalem, back to tell the other disciples all that had happened. One cannot spend very much time with Jesus and walk away unaffected by His presence or words. He changes everything. In Mark's gospel, chapter seven, there is recorded one of our Lord's many miracles, the healing of a deaf and mute man. After his healing, Jesus told his friends not to tell anyone. Verse 36 says, "But the more he did so, the more they kept talking about it." They just could not keep silent. They had been with Jesus; they saw His mighty power at work. They were eyewitnesses of it. Surely their hearts must have burned within them and they could not contain it. As the hymn writer put it, they sang for they could not keep silent; His love was the theme of their song!

As a boy he worked long hours in a factory in Naples, Italy. He longed to be a singer, but his family was very poor. When ten years old, he took his first lesson in voice. "You cannot sing. You haven't any voice at all. In fact, your voice sounds like the wind in the shutters," said his teacher. The boy's mother, however, had visions of greatness for her son. She believed in him. She believed that God had given him a talent to sing. Putting her arms around him, she whispered, "My boy, I am going to make every sacrifice to pay for your voice lessons." And she did! Her confidence in him and constant encouragement paid off. That boy became one of the world's greatest singers. His name? Enrico Caruso! And every time the great tenor became discouraged he thought about his mother's words. And the fire burned.

That sounds a great deal like what happened in Jeremiah's situation. Here he was, weary of the gloom and doom he was forecasting. He had the reputation every man of God fears—the "hell-fire and brimstone" preacher. So he had determined to just keep silent. Then God came to him and put His enormous arms about him, just as the Psalmist testified to in 125:2: "As the mountains surround Jerusalem, so the Lord surrounds his people both now and forever more." He drew this discouraged prophet close and reminded him of His greatness and glory. And the more Jeremiah thought about God, the more the fire burned within. It started with just a spark, then it grew to a flame; soon it was like a blow-torch, consuming the bones. Now, more than ever, he was determined to be God's spokesman, regardless of the cost. And cost him, it did! But it did not matter because God had spoken and Jeremiah was tune in to His frequency!

Lord, ignite within me a burning desire to glow for you. Rekindle my passion for You and Your work. When I feel like my flame has almost disappeared, help me to take the time to think deeply about Your promises and presence. Then I know that my faith will once again come alive and I will speak of it often and with a burning conviction.

THINKSGIVING

He gave you manna to eat in the desert, something your fathers had never known, to humble and to test you so that in the end it might go well with you. You may say to yourself, "My power and the strength of my hands have produced this wealth for me." But remember the LORD your God, for it is he who gave you the ability to produce wealth, and so confirms his covenant, which he swore to your forefathers, as it is today (Deuteronomy 8:18).

IN THE EARLY 1900s, a policeman was walking his beat in the city of Chicago when he observed a man standing before a little mission. His hat was in his hand, and the officer thought he was acting strange because he was mumbling. Thinking he might be drunk or ill, the policeman approached him. He noticed the man's eyes were closed so he nudged him and said, "What's the matter, Mac, are you sick?" The man looked up and smiled. "No, sir, my name is Billy Sunday. I was converted right here in this mission. I never pass this way without stopping. I stand quietly for a moment and whisper a prayer of thanksgiving." The officer grinned understandingly. And giving the famed evangelist a hearty grip, he said warmly, "Put 'er there, Billy! I've heard a lot about you. Keep right on praying and I'll see to it that no one bothers you."

So there you have it then—a clear cut case of "thinking," which led to thanking. That may not always be the case, but for the child of God, it is a given. As a matter of fact, in the old Anglo-Saxon, *think* and *thank* were the same. Some scholars even suggest that *thank* may be the past tense of *think*. For example, Robert, a deaf mute, used sign language to say grace at mealtime. Although he could not speak, he could think, and his thinking led to an expression of gratitude.

In the New Testament, the principal word for "thanks" occurs some 55 times in various forms and has for its main base the word *favor*. If you think, you will thank. On the other hand, if one is thoughtless, he will probably be thankless.

Somewhere in our thinking there should be thoughts of God.

Perhaps we should start there. God! What a train of thoughts should be started when we think of Him! Power, wisdom, goodness, grace, love, care—these are just some of the thoughts that cluster around the word, God. The truth is, however, most of our memories are short and need constant jogging. That is why God had to constantly remind Israel of His constant goodness to her. He instituted national feasts such as Passover and Pentecost in an effort to help them to remember. The entire eighth chapter of Deuteronomy exhorts the Israelites not to forget their deliverance from Egypt. Then follows a recitation of blessings: manna, clothing that did not wear out, long-lasting health, and water.

How easy in our blessed nation with its abundance, to somehow conclude that all these things—our bank account, our furniture, our car, our appliances, our home, our good position—we earned by our own ingenuity, our own industry.

An atheist asked why he should thank God for his food when he had earned it by working with his own hands. But where did the strength and health and brains come from to enable him to work with his hands? And what of his body which is capable of controlling physical coordination? And besides all this, he needed proper oxygen content in the air, temperature to sustain life, and the sun to give healthful rays. Had the atheist really thought about it, perhaps he would have been thankful, if not to God, at least to nature.

Those who saw the miracles of Jesus did some serious thinking and then glorified God. The woman who washed Jesus' feet with her tears and wiped them with her hair had a thoughtful appreciation for His forgiveness.

Every year, several days before May 30, candles are distributed to every home in the foothill community of Ford City, Pennsylvania. Then exactly at 10 p.m., the day before Memorial Day, the bells in every church begin to toll. Gradually the lights in every home, store, and automobile are turned off. All traffic ceases; even the night freight train stops. Stillness and darkness envelop the town. Then the people step out to their front porches and lawns and light their candles. By loud speaker comes a prayer, than a rifle salute followed by the playing of taps, and, finally, the singing of the Lord's Prayer. The candles are then extinguished. Cars begin to move. But for ten minutes everyone has remembered the boys who died for their country. Thinking leads to thanking.

The Lord's Supper was given as a memorial: "This do in remembrance of me (I Corinthians 11:24). Meditation on the crucified body and shed blood should provoke hatred for sin in our lives and renewal of vows to live unto Him who loved us and gave Himself for us. If you think, truly think, you will thank.

The chief requisite for an ungrateful heart is a poor memory. The Bible is replete with the sad tales of those who forgot about God's goodness. Many New England villages have attractive public greens or commons, but one green which should be posted with warning signs, according to Bunyan in Pilgrim's Progress, is "Forgetful Green." Here Christian had his battle with Satan. Today's pilgrims tread dangerous ground when they walk forgetful of divine mercies.

In early New England it was a Thanksgiving custom to place five grains of corn at every plate. This served as a reminder of those stern days of the Pilgrim's first winter at Plymouth when food supplies ran so low that a ration of only five grains was given each individual at a time. They remembered, and were thankful.

O, the value of taking time to think! Who can measure its effectiveness adequately? It will help us to be grateful instead of grumbling. A man bought several Christmas cards from a local printer. Several envelopes were spoiled while he was addressing them, so he threw away the cards that went with them. An idea struck him. The printer should include extra envelopes with each box of cards. That would create goodwill and enhance his sales, so he called him and suggested it. The printer replied, "Oh, I thought of that some years back. I packed two extra envelopes in each box of fifty cards, but I soon stopped." "Why?" replied the man. "Didn't the customers appreciate the extra envelopes?" "No," answered the printer. "Many folks just complained that their boxes were short two cards!"

If these customers had done some thinking, they might have counted their cards, then done some thanking!

The memories of days past and their attending blessings can temper the difficulties of the present. Here is a little poem that expresses this quite well:

There was a dachshund once, so long
he hadn't any notion
how long it took to notify
his tail of his emotion;
And so it happened, while his eyes
were filled with woe and sadness,
his little tail went wagging on
Because of previous gladness.

Someone has said, "God gave us memories so we might have roses in January." Every time we return from a trip we should thank God for safety. Every time the fire whistle blows or the ambulance goes by with siren blaring, we should be grateful for protection. Every time we leave the hospital after a visit we should be thankful for our health. I agree with whoever said, "Gratitude is a lively sense of favors yet to come." That is why we say grace at mealtime. We must constantly stir up our minds to remember. Just as a great artist mixes his colors with brains, so a man of God carefully mixes his thoughts with thanks. If you put on your thinking cap, you will soon fill your thanking cup!

IT'S ALL IN YOUR HEAD!

The man without the Spirit does not accept the things that come from the Spirit of God, for they are foolishness to him, and he cannot understand them, because they are spiritually discerned. The spiritual man makes judgments about all things, but he himself is not subject to any man's judgment: "For who has known the mind of the Lord that he may instruct him?" But we have the mind of Christ (I Corinthians 2:14-16).

WHEN I WAS IN HIGH SCHOOL we had a gym teacher who was really hard-nosed. Whenever someone would complain about being hurt or tired, he would say, "It's all in your head!" What he really meant was, "It doesn't hurt that bad, so be tough and run it off." When someone made a mistake, he would bellow out one of two remarks: "Use your head!" or "There you go again, thinking when you should be executing!" He was trying to teach young men that their minds could impede or add to their success.

In the majority of cases the difference between success and failure is found between the ears. I like what Solomon wrote centuries ago, "As a man thinks within himself, so he is" (Proverbs 23:7). The mind is a powerful tool, for good or evil. How we use our minds determines not only attitude, but physical health as well.

The brain has tremendous power. Although it weighs a bit more than three pounds on average, it has twelve billion cells and 120 trillion connections. If the mind were a computer, it would be the size of the Empire State Building. It supervises everything from the heartbeat to the most studied decisions. While the heart, hands, legs, and feet wear out, 90% of the brain is unused.

Psychologists have studied it, pathologists have dissected it, and surgeons have rearranged it, and still it remains a mystery. Modern technology is trying to simulate it, but it cannot be duplicated or understood. Only one person fully understands the mind of men, and that is its Creator.

If we want to use our minds to their maximum, then we had better listen to the mind's Creator, don't you think? The mind absent the help of God is a dangerous thing. It often draws the wrong conclusions. We cannot possess a perfect mind in this life, but we can achieve what the Bible calls "the mind of Christ" (I Corinthians 2:16).

What exactly is the mind of Christ? Let me suggest first of all that it is a *spiritual* mind—a product of the Holy Spirit. The only way to acquire it is by transplant; surgery is required. We make the incision by the act of our will. God, the Master Designer, then begins to reprogram us. He takes divine thoughts and puts them into our minds. Another way to describe this spiritual transformation is to say that He re-educates the conscience, confirming or denying biblical truth that resides therein. That is what happened to Al Johnson. At age nineteen he joined two other men in robbing a Kansas bank. The case was closed by police after two other convicts were killed in an auto crash and mistakenly identified by bank officials as the robbers. Al felt sure he would never be caught. He married a Christian girl and pretended to be a Christian before her. She knew nothing of his past crime. Then someone sent him a gospel tract in the mail entitled, "God's Plan of Salvation." The Holy Spirit used that tract to convict Al of his sin and he knelt in prayer to receive Christ. His life changed dramatically. The Spirit continued His work on Al's mind and heart. He stopped a life-long habit of lying. And after much thought and prayer, he confessed his crime, first to his wife and then to the authorities. Under a Kansas statue of limitations, he was set free, although he chose to repay his share of the stolen funds to the bank. Al Johnson went on to become the manager of a service station, the father of three admiring children, and an outstanding Christian layman—all because he received the mind of Christ.

In the second place, the mind of Christ is a *discerning* one, a biblical defense system composed of God's thoughts about life through the study of the Scriptures. The reason so many people are destroyed by anxiety is that they are defenseless in the war of ideas. They are un-walled cities, open to any and all ideological assaults. A discerning mind is able to sort out values, philosophies, and opinions which are in opposition to God's truth. The media has taught Americans, in particular, that we deserve only the best, and has redefined "need" to be "greed." This kind of thinking is a hothouse for worry. When 95% of what people hear is this seductive and anti-Christian philosophy, without a biblical defense system they are in a helpless state. Anxiety will attack in great waves fueled by the ideology of the flesh. We must be resolute in our efforts to learn the Bible so as to distinguish between truth and error.

Thirdly, the mind of Christ is *disciplined,* i.e., trained to think a certain way. All minds are trained. It is just a question of who does the training. Parents lead the way; peers follow close after. Teachers are probably next, followed by the media. But behind all of these are two overriding influences—God and Satan. Both are at work, one to brainwash and the other to cleanse and bless.

Some minds are trained for failure, some for success. Bill was a rookie traveling salesman on a trip when he had a flat tire while driving through the rural south. He walked to the nearest farmhouse and knocked on the door, but his mind was full of negative thoughts:

- No one will open the door.
- They'll shoot me for trespassing.
- They'll sick their dog on me.
- They won't even have a jack.
- If they do, it won't fit my car.
- People don't help like they used to; they are afraid to get involved.
- They won't let me use their phone either.

When the farmer opened the door, the salesman was so worked up mentally that he blurted out, "I didn't want your stupid jack anyway!" He stomped off into the darkness leaving a confused farmer standing in the doorway.

God wants positive minds that are realistic without being pessimistic. What does a positive mind see? The good in life without ignoring the bad; the stars instead of the bars, the fingerprints of God everywhere! Its motto is: THE FUTURE BELONGS TO THOSE WHO BELONG TO GOD.

Paul says that the only way out of an anxiety-ridden life is to train your mind to focus on the positive and the good (Philippians 4:8). This training of the mind is accomplished when the student cooperates with his teacher. He accepts the facts as truth, does his homework, and puts into practice what he has learned.

The mind of Christ: How do I get it? We get the mind of Christ through the Spirit of Christ (I Corinthians 2). He dwells in us if we have embraced Christ as personal Savior. Then by yielding to His controlling influence, our minds are renewed, reprogrammed, and we apply the truth we have received.

IS YOUR HEART SITTING DOWN?

Be still before the LORD and wait patiently for him; do not fret when men succeed in their ways, when they carry out their wicked schemes (Psalm 37:7).

Thou wilt keep him in perfect peace, whose mind is stayed on thee, because he trusteth in thee (Isaiah 26:3, KJV).

Let the peace of Christ rule in your hearts, since as members of one body you were called to peace (Colossians 3:15).

PEACE, AH SWEET PEACE! If ever a generation needed it, it is ours. Matthew Henry, the great Bible commentator, once said, "When Christ died He left a will in which He gave His soul to His Father, His body to Joseph of Arimathea, His clothes to the soldiers, and His mother to John. But to His disciples, who had left all for Him, He left not silver or gold, but something far better—His peace!"

And what a peace it is! Peace of mind, of heart. Peace in the midst of life's storms. He modeled it and He promised it for all who would trust His Word. One of the last things He said to His disciples dealt with the issue of peace: "Do not let your hearts be troubled. Trust in God; trust also in me…Peace I leave with you; my peace I give you. I do not give to you as the world gives. Do not let your heart be troubled and do not be afraid" (John 14:1,27).

Some time ago in Latin America, some missionary translators were working diligently to find a word or phrase for the concept of peace among a primitive people. At last, a native, who was assisting them, found a combination of words that had the concept: "Jesus will make your heart sit down." Is your heart sitting down today? Do you possess a level of peace that sustains you in the hour of trouble? Is it the kind that says, "I don't understand everything, but I'll just rest in God and He will bring me out." It is this kind of tranquility of soul that causes one to say, "Though a host should encamp against me, my heart shall not fear." It is the peace that says, "If God be for me, who can be against me?"

Out of the depth of our heart comes a sense of well-being and we say to ourselves, "I know whom I have believed and am persuaded that He is able to keep that which I have committed unto Him against that day."

Is your heart sitting down? If it is not, it may be because you have not taken time to be still. Be still, that you may hear the voice of God. Be still in order to concentrate. Be still that you might call to remembrance His promises and mighty acts. Be still that you might properly worship His majesty. Be still—cease from activity and anxiety. Rest for a while under His wings.

You can obtain and sustain the peace that only God offers. It is there for the taking. How? First of all, it can never be obtained by one who claims he has no need of it. We must be willing to admit to God, that is, agree with Him and ourselves, that we do not have it apart from Him. Many there be who strive with unresolved guilt, or fear issuing from some circumstance. They long for inner peace, but to no avail. The first step to peace is admitting that it is missing in our lives.

In the second place, before one can have the peace of God, he must have the God of peace. Jesus is our peace. In fact, He is peace personified. All other attempts at securing genuine and lasting peace are as hopeless as those who chase after the wind. Since inner tranquility begins with a personal relationship with Jesus, it makes perfect sense that the more we open ourselves up to His presence, the greater degree of peace we will experience.

Here is another important element to be considered. We have to get the poisons out of our minds so that peace can flow unhindered. Take the example of a man writhing in pain due to an appendix which has burst. A surgical procedure brings some relief, but then the wound is left open for a while to allow the poison to drain out. At last, the discomfort subsides until it is only a fading memory. That is the way it is with a person's soul. We must rid ourselves of the poisons that have invaded our minds, poisons such as unforgiven sins, bitterness, resentment, jealousy, and anger gone amuck. How do we rid ourselves of these destructive forces? God alone can do it, but first we have to ask Him. He alone can reach into our minds and hearts with His divine scalpel and remove them. Fanny Crosby was right on target when she penned these words:

> Oh what peace we often forfeit,
> Oh what needless pain we bear,
> All because we do not carry
> Everything to God in prayer.

And that is not the end of the matter because once we rid ourselves of certain mental poisons we must begin to fill our minds with right things, else other negative forces will invade the vacuum created. Remember the words of our Savior as recorded in Luke 11:24-28: "When an evil spirit comes out of a man, it goes through arid places seeking rest and does not find it. Then it says, I will return to the house I left. When it arrives it finds the house swept clean and put in order. Then it goes and takes seven other spirits more wicked than itself, and they go in and live there. And the final condition of that man is worse than the first."

We must fill our minds with right things, with the Word of God. Psalm 119:165 says it best: "Great peace have they who love your law and nothing causes them to stumble."

The prophet Isaiah lived in troublesome times, yet he understood the importance of focusing our thoughts on God: "Thou wilt keep him in perfect peace who mind is stayed on Thee because he trusteth in thee" (26:3, KJV). In other words, when we focus our thoughts upon God, a certain and complete sense of serenity floods our soul.

In a large city in Sri Lanka there is a huge statue of Buddha in a reclining position. The chiseled face is calm, the eyes are closed, and the head rests upon one hand. A full fifty feet long, the image is impressive except for one thing—Buddha is sleeping while the world passes by. He is paying no attention to his worshippers. How unlike that our God is. He cares for us. He watches over us and protects and blesses us. Shame on us when we are filled with fear and uncertainty. The One who watches over Israel is the same One who watches over all His children. He neither slumbers nor sleeps.

Finally, if our hearts are going to be sitting down, we must pray believingly. A psychiatrist was quoted in the newspapers as saying that he could not improve upon the Apostle Paul's prescription for human worry: "Be anxious for nothing; but in everything by prayer and supplication with thanksgiving let your requests be made known to God. And the peace of God which passes all understanding, shall keep your hearts and minds through Christ Jesus" (Philippians 4:6,7, KJV).

So if it is peace you need, ask for it and do not doubt. In fact, as Paul says, the evidence that you believe that God is going to provide it is found in your willingness to thank Him for it in advance. Archbishop Trench's words are worth memorizing at this point: "Prayer is not overcoming God's reluctance; it is laying hold of His highest willingness."

Is your heart sitting down? If not, it can, as soon as you invite the God of peace in and get the poisons out. Then fill your mind with right things and pray believingly. When the boat on which you sail suddenly finds itself being tossed to and fro by the winds of adversity, remember, Jesus is asleep below.

ACHIEVING MAXIMUM POTENTIAL

My soul finds rest in God alone; my salvation comes from him. Find rest, O my soul, in God alone; my hope comes from him (Psalm 62:1,5).

THE TELEPHONE KEEPS RINGING; other workers keep asking a myriad of questions; the boss schedules another meeting. It is hard to work or think efficiently surrounded by such normal, but distracting interruptions, so a "quiet hour" has been set aside for accounting workers at Contel Service Corporation, Western region headquarters for Continental Telephone Company. They reserve 8 to 9 a.m. to work on long-term projects, research, reports or other creative work that requires concentration.

The quiet hour, officially called "Achieving Maximum Potential," was started because the accounting department staff works in a large open area, making it hard to sneak into a quiet corner to concentrate.

"It's like an invisible force field we can create to allow us one hour of quiet time," said Ted Carrier, Contel's staff manager for general accounting. "The mangers can close their doors to get a quiet moment," added Carrier, chief architect of the project. "The rest of us don't have offices and don't have doors we can close."

The Bakersfield office is Contel's headquarters for ten western states, and employees throughout the region are accepting the idea that they cannot telephone the accounting department between 8 and 9 a.m., Carrier said. The employees are not involved in meetings, errands, running printers or other distractive activity.

If we applied that same discipline to our spiritual lives, we, too, as followers of Christ, could expect to "achieve maximum potential." Just a few moments alone with God at the beginning of each day would reap tremendous dividends in terms of spiritual productivity. Jesus said, "Come to me, all you who are weary and burdened, and I will give you rest" (Matthew 11:28). Most of us are weary and burdened at the start of the day as we begin to think about the day's activities. If we start the day by going to the Lord and committing each moment to Him, what a difference it could make!

Several years ago I had the high privilege of working for the Billy

Graham Evangelistic Association as a field representative in the development department. As part of my training, I spent two weeks at the headquarter offices, familiarizing myself with their computer programs. Each morning when I reported to the office, I was encouraged to use the first thirty minutes as a "quiet time." It was really wonderful to observe the other employees using this time to read the Bible, meditate, and pray for strength for the tasks ahead. Perhaps this is one of the secrets of this ministry's success. Could it be that God smiles on such commitment? I choose to think so.

I met God in the morning
When my day was at its best
And His presence came like sunrise,
Like a glory in my breast.

All day long the Presence lingered;
All day long He stayed with me;
And we sailed in perfect calmness
O'er a very troubled sea.

Other ships were blown and battered,
Other ships were sore distressed,
But the winds that seemed to drive them
Brought to us a peace and rest.

Then I thought of other mornings,
With a keen remorse of mind,
When I too had loosed the moorings
With the Presence left behind.

So, I think I know the secret,
Learned from many a troubled way;
You must seek Him in the morning
If you want Him through the day.

—Author Unknown

SUMMARY

In the British Navy, whenever any sudden disaster, such as an explosion, occurs, it is the bugler's duty to play what is called, *The Still.* And when the sailors hear it, each is to cease their activity and remain perfectly quiet for a moment and recollect their senses, thus to be better prepared for intelligent action in the crisis.

Emergencies invade our peaceful lives from time to time. Perhaps we should adopt a similar response. Taking a few moments to take a mental breath has its benefits, especially if we take time to dwell on the real presence of God. Wise is that person who takes time to lift a prayer for strength and wisdom before leaping into some action that he may later regret.

That is what this book has been all about—the need at various times to "Be still and know,"—to linger for a while at the Well and let our souls drink deeply from its refreshing, living, sustaining, and limitless supply. Come to think of it, perhaps it is in order to apply this strategy for the mundane as well as the emergency. When we hear in our minds that little voice that screams, "Break Time!" we would do well to sit for a while and gather energy from above. Grab an occasional iced tea, stretch out on the hammock and enjoy the refreshing breeze, not only of nature, but of the Spirit. No time to do it? Take time. When you arise, new strength will course through your veins! The button is near. The choice is yours. Go ahead, push "Pause."

Breinigsville, PA USA
11 October 2010
247094BV00003B/3/P

9 781609 200046